Shifting Allegiances

Australian College of Theology Monograph Series

SERIES EDITOR GRAEME R. CHATFIELD

The ACT Monograph Series, generously supported by the Board of Directors of the Australian College of Theology, provides a forum for publishing quality research theses and studies by its graduates and affiliated college staff in the broad fields of Biblical Studies, Christian Thought and History, and Practical Theology with Wipf and Stock Publishers of Eugene, Oregon. The ACT selects the best of its doctoral and research masters theses as well as monographs that offer the academic community, scholars, church leaders and the wider community uniquely Australian and New Zealand perspectives on significant research topics and topics of current debate. The ACT also provides opportunity for contributors beyond its graduates and affiliated college staff to publish monographs which support the mission and values of the ACT.

Rev Dr Graeme Chatfield
Series Editor and Associate Dean

Shifting Allegiances: Networks of Kinship and of Faith

The Women's Program in a Syrian Mosque

MOYRA DALE

Foreword by
PETER G. RIDDELL

WIPF & STOCK · Eugene, Oregon

SHIFTING ALLEGIANCES: NETWORKS OF KINSHIP AND OF FAITH
The Women's Program in a Syrian Mosque

Copyright © 2016 Moyra Dale. All rights reserved. Except for brief quotations in critical publications or reviews, no part of this book may be reproduced in any manner without prior written permission from the publisher. Write: Permissions, Wipf and Stock Publishers, 199 W. 8th Ave., Suite 3, Eugene, OR 97401.

Wipf & Stock
An Imprint of Wipf and Stock Publishers
199 W. 8th Ave., Suite 3
Eugene, OR 97401

www.wipfandstock.com

PAPERBACK ISBN: 978-1-4982-3718-5
HARDCOVER ISBN: 978-1-4982-3720-8
EBOOK ISBN: 978-1-4982-3719-2

Manufactured in the U.S.A.

Contents

List of Figures | xi
Foreword by Peter G. Riddell | xiii
Acknowledgements | xvii
Conventions | xix
   Transliteration
   References
   Dates
   Glossary

1 Introduction | 1
   Women in Mosques
   Shifting Communities of Allegiance
   Mapping the Story

2 Women and Text in Islam | 6
   Women and the Coming of Islam
   Muhaddathat (Spoken to by Angels) and *Muhaddithat* (Transmitters of Traditions)
   Muslim Women in Modern Discourse
   In Public and in Print
   Texts and *Tafsir*
   In Which Space?
   From Feminism to *Daʿwa*
   Piety Examined

3 Research in Context | 21
　Research Worldview
　Ethnography
　Collecting Data
　　Participant Observation
　　　Joining the Program
　Reflexivity
　　Standpoint
　　Interviews
　　Document Analysis
　　Permission and Oversight
　　　Multiple Authorship of Field Notes
　　Researcher Responsibility
　Rigor
　　Credibility
　　Transferability
　　Dependability
　　Confirmability
　Conclusion

4 Setting the Scene: Women's Mosque Program | 35
　Visiting the Mosque
　Women's Program in the Mosque
　　Tuesday Lecture
　　Thursday Lecture
　　Dhikr
　　Memorization of the Qur'an and *Tajwid*
　　Other Classes
　　Library
　　Special Occasions
　　Ramadan
　The Women Who Came
　A Form of Faith:
　　Embodied Encounter
　　Time
　　　Hours and Seasons

Geographic and Communal Space
Wider Influences
Conclusion

5 Alternate Community | 53
Communities of Kinship
Imagined Communities
Grid–Group and Communal Response
Grid and Group
Membership of the Wider Community
Local Mosque Group
The Place of the Mosque
Including Dress
Communities in Tension: Negotiating Another Allegiance
Communities in Contact: The Place of *da'wa*
Conclusion

6 Ideal Leader | 83
Introduction: Leadership, Authority, and Mimesis
Mimetic Paradigm
Community and Leader, Ideal and Actual
Muhammad—Ideal Leader
Practices of Life and Faith
Imitation
Contact or Contagion
Copy and Contiguity
Connecting With the Source of Power
Model Muslim Women
Women's Vocation
Precedents or Paradigms?
The *da'iya*—Embodied Model
Becoming a *da'iya*: The Making of a Missionary
Authority and Representation
Conclusion

7 Performative Practices | 111

Introduction
Individual Body in Social Formation
Family: Embodied Honor, Shaping Behavior
Mosque Community: Behavior and *ikhlaq*
Being and Behaving in Everyday/Everynight Life
Performative Practices in the Mosque Community
    Clothes and Covering
        Form
        Meaning
'awrah—Concealing Shape and Sound
Salah
Feasts and Fasting
    Eids
    Ramadan
Piety and Purity
    Purity and Defilement in the Mosque Community
    Leadership
Conclusion

8 Texts, Practices, and Meanings | 142

Introduction
Physical Presence
Qur'an in Homes
Qur'an in Hearts
Right Recitation—*tajwid*
Beyond Recitation to Interpretation
    Contemporary Commentators
    Tafsir Modeled—Mimesis
    The Importance of *'ilm*
        Tafsir 'ilmi
        Learning and Life in Religion
The Qur'an and the Community
Meaning and Application
    On Troubling Texts
Conclusion

9 *Dhikr* | 173
   Introduction
   Development of Sufism
      Women in Sufism
   Dhikr in the Garden Mosque
   Dhikr Content
      Taking Refuge
         In salah
         Danger Without and Within
      The Compassionate, the Merciful
      Forgiveness
         In salah
      Qur'an
         In salah
      Invocatory Phrases
      Praiseworthy
       In Praise of Muhammad
      Du`a'
         Emotions
      Silence
      Songs
         Tarnim
         Anashid
   Conclusion

10 Conclusion | 206
    Growth in the Women's Mosque Movement
    Shifting Allegiances
    Caught in Time

Appendix 1: Grid and Group | 215
   Hierarchical—High Grid, High Group
   Egalitarian—Low Grid, High Group
   Individualistic—Low Grid, Low Group
   Authoritarian—High Grid, Low Group
   Cultural Theory Implications

Appendix 2: Tajwid—Instruction and Practice Observed | 223

Bibliography | 227

Figures

Figure 1 | 62

Figure 2 | 63

Figure 3 | 216

Figure 4 | 217

Figure 5 | 218

Figure 6 | 220

Figure 7 | 221

Foreword

SOME DOCTORAL THESES ARE highly esoteric and are destined to remain on the shelves of university libraries after completion, attracting little attention and having little impact. This is certainly not the case with this new work by Dr Moyra Dale, which represents the published version of a very interesting and important doctoral thesis completed in 2014.

The focus that this book places upon a particular mosque community in Syria is of great current importance and interest. Syria has captured much of the world's attention since the civil war erupted in 2011. Anyone interested in the prelude to those events would do well to read this work.

This volume is important for a number of reasons. First, it benefits from being the result of various research methodologies. The author is a gifted ethnographer, and this comes through clearly in the ground-breaking material that she has gathered from different forms of interaction. At the same time, Dr Dale has demonstrated gifts as a text-based scholar, engaging with the primary texts of Islam—Qur'an and Hadith—to consider those key textual elements that contribute to the shaping of women's existence in the communities under examination.

Furthermore, the book casts the spotlight on the lived experiences of a particular group of Syrian Muslim women. The topic of women in Islam is fraught, subject to diverse stereotypes ranging from utopian presentations by eloquent Islamist women to terrifying monochrome presentations that portray every Muslim woman as living under the jackboot of Muslim men. In that context, this study scores very highly because it is appropriately nuanced. It focuses on real women, in real families, preoccupied by the daily concerns of women the world over, but carving out some time and space to explore new expressions of what it means to be Muslim and female.

Many Islamic women living in highly traditionalist surroundings, shaped by family and community, have played narrow roles in their communities down the centuries, with their functions restricted to procreation and home duties. However, this important contemporary study describes a process which has enabled Muslim women to establish alternate communities, centered on the mosque. It provides a fresh angle on the whole question of Islamic revival, which has been much studied in recent decades. Many studies of Islamic revival treat it as uniformly threatening and full of foreboding. This present study suggests that greater Islamic awareness has enabled the women described in these pages to breathe more freely and to have more options and opportunities for self-expression as modern Muslim women.

Islam is a missionary faith. Islamic mission is usually expressed as *da'wa*, signifying a call to Islam, with the *da'iya* being the missionary caller who summons others, both Muslims and non-Muslims, to follow Islam more closely and more faithfully. This present study provides as close to an insider's view of the work of a *da'iya* as an outsider is likely to get. The gifts and the skills of the central female *da'iya* in the mosque in question are fascinating to observe, and provide a starkly different and refreshing perspective on Islamic mission from that which is often seen being modeled by more assertive, at times militant, Islamist groups.

There is a further reason why this work is vitally important and it is a reason that the author could not have possibly foreseen at the time of carrying out the research that led to this volume. The book captures a series of snapshots of life in Syria not many years before the outbreak of the Syrian civil war. It was a country that was steeped in rich traditions and was characterized by diverse ethnicities and expressions of religious faith. The city of Damascus, which forms the focus of this study, was a significant site in Christian history. Paul's conversion to become an apostle, walking in the steps of Jesus Christ, took place on the road to Damascus. When the city fell to Muslim armies within two years of the death of Muhammad, it gradually assumed diverse features of the Islamic faith which co-mingled with leftovers of its Christian past. For the last 1350 years, Damascus in particular and Syria in general have been the site of a rich melting pot of cultures, faiths, and communities. Such was the environment that provided the context to this present book.

As I write this, however, millions of Syrians have been displaced by the civil war since 2011. Hundreds of thousands are sheltering in refugee camps in neighboring countries or indeed find themselves among the vast numbers of refugees streaming into Western Europe. No doubt some of the women who were consulted by the author for this present study are presently found among Syrian refugee communities somewhere. Perhaps some others number among the hundreds of thousands of people killed in the civil war.

In short, the Syria of 2015 barely resembles the Syria described in this book. This study captures a precious moment in time, now lost, and one which will tragically not return for a very long time, if at all. For that reason, readers should savor every word presented in the following pages as they read, because it provides a window into the near but radically different past.

Dr Dale has produced a work of great importance. It is well written, subtly reflective, and very nuanced. It represents a valuable contribution to a range of disciplines: ethnography, Islamic studies, women's studies, and other related fields. Teachers and students involved in those disciplines should read and recommend this excellent study.

Professor Peter G. Riddell

Melbourne
November 2015

Acknowledgements

THE PROCESS OF WRITING this book has kept me deeply engaged with happier hours spent in Syria, only to emerge daily to face the news of the unfolding tragedy of civil war in that country. So I start by acknowledging my debt to our friends there—co-teachers, neighbors, students—people with whom we spent many pleasurable hours, with no foreboding of the cataclysm to come. I have lost touch with many people now, and all those with whom I am in contact carry news of some family members dead or disappeared, and others widely dispersed in different countries. These thanks are difficult to write in such an atmosphere of uncertainty and grief.

Anisah Huda al-Habash stands out in her willingness to welcome me, as well as many other foreigners, to attend her program over a prolonged period, and to see Islam lived out in her daily and family life as well as in the mosque. I appreciated her deep commitment to, and articulation of Islam, as well as her hospitality not just in teaching, but also in making times for our husbands and also our daughters to meet. Enas, her daughter, was also always helpful. Ebtisam was the person who introduced me to the program and to Anisah Huda. She spent hours checking my notes, and greeted me always with a smiling face, welcoming me amid her busy days, patiently answering questions. I don't know where she is now, or what has happened to her and the other members of her family in the current disturbance. And there were many other women with whom I talked, or sat, who helped me write down notes or explained the program or other aspects of life and faith to me, and invited me to their homes. I remember you all constantly.

Elisabeth Buergener was a companion on the research journey and I enjoyed our discussions of meanings, life, and faith. I am always indebted to Audrey Grant, my first mentor in ethnography, who has continued to offer insightful suggestions and questions for this research. Shirley Brice Heath is a constant example in her ethnographic work; it was her suggestion that

I look again at Taussig to see what insights he contributed. And Ziya Meral took my understanding of mimesis further in introducing me to the work of Girard.

David Williams and Mary Lewis were colleagues who took time to read and comment on earlier drafts of some of these materials: I always gain from their wisdom. Carol Bartlett took on the task of proof-reading my doctoral thesis, and I am thankful for her persistence and eye for detail. My thanks to Adrian Gully for his early insights and suggestions as beginning supervisor. And I have benefited from the constant encouragement and guidance of Peter Riddell from start to completion of writing up this study.

My family have been invaluable encouragers and critics in this task. I am so thankful for Tarek and Miriam Dale. And Lauren, dear companion, my gratitude for your patience and challenge throughout this, making it possible and bringing joy to the journey.

Conventions

Transliteration

ARABIC HAS BEEN TRANSLITERATED into Latin script for greater accessibility. As this is an ethnographic study, transcription reflects the spoken Arabic language used by the women; I have used the literary form only when it was employed by the women, or for written sources. Arabic words are introduced with their meaning in the body of the text. Words that are used more than once are included in the glossary. *Ahadith* that have been referenced in the mosque program are translated from Arabic, and all *ahadith* (unless otherwise noted) have been sourced and checked through the Islamic English website, www.searchtruth.com. Hence, I have followed that site's standard citation format, where the *hadith* commences with "Narrated ..." and the name of the person to whom the *hadith* is attributed. The content or body (*matn*) of the *hadith* then follows.

References

Qur'anic references are usually denoted by the name of the chapter followed by its number and verse. I have sought to keep the narrative integrity of ethnographic description of the women and the mosque program. For that reason I have chosen at times to make wider use of footnotes to reference the broader debate. I have also sometimes italicized key sentences to enable focus on the central argument within the descriptive detail of the wider account.

Dates

When two dates are separated by a slash the first is AH (dated from the year of the Hijra in the Muslim calendar), the second AD. For example: "480/1087" or "d. 230/ninth century." In cases of ambiguity AH and AD are indicated, for example: "d. AH 840" or "d. AD 1426."

Glossary

aʿbaya: woman's outer covering cloak, usually black.

ahadith (pl.): traditions.

ʿahkam: religious rulings.

ahl al-kitab: people of the Book (Jews, Christians).

anashid (pl.): religious choruses, accompanied only by a frame-drum.

anisah: Miss, or Teacher.

ʿaql: the mind.

aʿsar: mid-afternoon (time of prayer).

ʿawrah: deficiency, imperfection; shameful.

barakah: blessing/power.

bidaʿ: innovation/heresy.

b'ism Allah al-Rahman al-Rahim: In the name of God, the Compassionate, the Merciful.

dar al harb: literally, "house of war," where Islam is not in control.

dar al salam: literally, "house of peace," where Islam is in control.

darwish: dervish.

daʿiyah (pl. *daʿiyat*): Islamic teacher/preacher/missionary.

daʿwa: mission, or call to (true) Islam.

dhanb (pl. *dhunub*): sin.

dhikr: recollection of God through reciting the names of God or other religious invocations.

dhuhr: midday (time of prayer).

din: religion.

du'a': petitionary prayer.

eid: feast.

Eid al-Adha: feast of the sacrifice, at the conclusion of the annual pilgrimage to Mecca.

Eid al-Fitr: feast of breaking fast, at the conclusion of Ramadan.

Eid al-Hub: literally, "feast of love," Valentine's Day.

fajr: dawn (time of prayer).

fard: duty, command.

Fatihah: first chapter of the Qur'an: recited in each *raka'ah* of prayer.

fatwa: religious ruling.

fiqh: Islamic jurisprudence.

hadirah: civilized.

hadith (pl. *ahadith*): traditions relating what was said or done by Muhammad or his Companions, authenticated by a chain of oral transmitters.

hadith (pl. *hidath*): modern, contemporary.

hajj: annual pilgrimage to Mecca, culminating in the feast of sacrifice.

halal: permitted.

haram: forbidden.

hasad: envy (linked with the evil eye).

hasanah (pl. *hasanat*): merit.

hijab: head covering for Muslim women.

hub: love.

'ibadat: acts of worship.

ijazah: license (to teach Qur'anic recitation).

ijtihad: independent reasoning.

ikhlaq: morals.

'ilm: knowledge.

'isha': evening (prayers).

isnad: chain of transmitters of *hadith*.

istaghfir: asking forgiveness from Allah.

jahiliyyah: time of ignorance (before Islam).

jamal: camel.

jamilah: beauty.

janabah: major impurity.

jihad: religious war/struggle.

jinn: spirit, often mischievous.

juz': section or division of the Qur'an.

ka'bah: cuboid building in Mecca, around which pilgrims circumambulate.

khalifat: literally "successors." Most often used to refer to the succession of leadership of the Muslim community after Muhammad's death.

khalwah: retreat, seclusion.

khatayyah (pl. *khatayyat*): errors, mistakes.

khitmah: sealing/complete recitation of the Qur'an.

khushu': submissiveness.

khutbah: Friday sermon to the Muslim community.

kuffar: (pl.) unbelievers.

kursi: chair/stand for the Qur'an.

kuttab: (pl.) Qur'anic schools.

layl: night.

laylat al-qadr: night of power/vigil.

maghrib: sunset (time of prayer).

mahram: forbidden; being in a degree of consanguinity precluding marriage.

mandil: handkerchief, a black cloth covering part or all of a woman's face.

mawlid (pl. *mawalid*): celebrations of the birth of Muhammad or local saints.

mu'adhdhin: announcer of the call to prayer.

mu'amalat: literally "actions" of daily life.

mudhahib: (pl.) schools of teaching within Islam.

muhaddathat: spoken to by angels.

muhaddithat: female transmitters of traditions (*ahadith*).

mujtahid: someone qualified to use independent reasoning in interpreting the Qur'an.

mu'minah: female believer.

munshidin: singers.

murshidah: female guide or teacher.

murtadd: apostate.

mushrikin: those who commit *shirk*: polytheists, idolaters.

mutadayyinat: religious women.

najasah: impurity.

nafilah: supererogatory.

nisa'i: feminism.

niyyah: intent.

qiblah: direction of prayer (towards Mecca).

qiyam: rising up.

qiyam al-layl: literally, "rising at night," night prayer.

quwwam: protector or authority.

rabb: Lord.

rak'a (pl. *raka'at*): one round of standing, bowing, kneeling, and prostrating with head to the ground, then rising again; the basic unit of *salah* prayer.

radiy Allah 'anha: may God be pleased with her.

risalah: mission, vocation.

sahur: prayers in the early morning hours before the pre-dawn meal in Ramadan.

salah (*salat* in conjoined form): formal prayer.

saum: fast.

shahadah: creed.

shari'ah: Islamic law.

shaykh, shaykhah (f): elder, religious leader.

shirk: polytheism, associating another with God.

shuruq: sunrise (time of prayer).

sirat al-nabi: stories of the life of Muhammad.

siwak: stick used to clean the teeth.

sufi: mystic.

sunnah: required, from the example of Muhammad.

surah: chapter of the Qur'an.

tafsir: interpretation of/commentary on the Qur'an.

tahajud: stay awake at night to pray.

taharah: purity.

tajawwad: active verb for Qur'anic recitation according to prescribed rules.

tajwid: correct recitation of the Qur'an according to prescribed rules.

takbir: Allahu akbar (God is greatest).

tamhid: exalting God.

tarawih: communal evening prayers in the mosque after breaking fast in Ramadan.

tariqa: Sufi order.

tarnim: religious songs.

tasbih: praising God.

thawab: recompense, merits.

'ulama': Muslim scholars.

umm: mother.

ummah: world-wide community of Islam.

'umrah: lesser pilgrimage to Mecca (not at the prescribed time of pilgrimage).

wadha'if: duties.

wa'i: aware.

wird: litany for private worship.

wudu': ritual washing before *salah*.

ya: vocative particle.

1

Introduction

FOR THE CASUAL INHABITANT of the Middle East, the Islamic revival developing in the last few decades of the twentieth century found visible form in the increasing numbers of women wearing *hijab*, along with growth in Islamic groups. The 1990s witnessed the developing movement of women into mosque space. Crowds of women gathering around or emerging from mosques became a common sight, along with women taking up the role of religious exhortation in public female space, such as the women's metro carriage on bustling Cairo subways.

As a teacher in the Arab world seeing these trends, talking with colleagues and students, neighbors and friends, I was curious about the shift that was happening. There was the growth in Islamic practice, and also a move in women's perception of themselves and their faith, that was leading to a women's movement into mosques and textual teaching—spaces that had previously been occupied largely by men. Most of the women I had known personally were based primarily in their homes and sometimes work places, and the gatherings they attended were family ones. While they performed *salah* (formal prayer) at appropriate times and fasted during Ramadan with public devotion and more or less private diligence, domestic responsibilities and fashions engaged them more than faith issues. Heath and Street urge the ethnographer "to know yourself as a constant learner," remembering that "we study something because we already know something."[1] As I met more devout Muslim women, my own commitment to faith and practice of the life and teaching of the Messiah found both correspondence and contrast with their devotion in faith practice and perspective. We shared allegiance to God (according to our perceptions of Deity), and adherence to the significance of our respective sacred texts and their implications for all of life. Friendship required a deeper appreciation of their position. Commonality called for a greater understanding of differences. Within a

---

1. Heath and Street, *Ethnography*, 30.

communal conservative reading of texts, Christian women can find that gender restricts access to some spaces or roles, as much as ability. And so I was curious about how these Muslim women were negotiating the boundaries of pious practice in more public space.

Then some years ago I was invited with my daughter to a party in a Syrian suburb for women who had memorized the Qur'an. Chapters 3 and 4 tell of how I moved from that invitation to a growing involvement in the women's program in a mosque, meeting and talking with the other women who attended, and learning from the teachers in the program and particularly Anisah Huda, its founder and leader.

For these women in Damascus who were part of the growing mosque piety movement, I wanted to ask how they viewed their community (of family and of faith) and themselves within it. What practices shaped their participation? How did they read the Qur'an and other texts as women, and read themselves in the texts? How did they relate to God in and through their community? What did these faith practices look like in the lives of the women, and what place did they occupy in the wider context of discussions and movements within Islam? In this book I discuss the women's program in that mosque.

Women in Mosques

The presence of women in mosques is not new in Islam. *Ahadith* (traditions) attributed to Muhammad, Prophet of Islam, which refuse to ban women from mosques[2] support accounts of their attendance during the time of Muhammad, including the Friday sermon and feasts. However, in subsequent centuries, as Islam expanded, the practice of women attending mosques became more unusual.

Today the presence of women in large numbers, who are attending mosques in order to learn, marks a new development within Islam. The women's mosque movement emerges within the worldwide growth in

---

2. Narrated Ibn 'Umar: The Prophet said, "If your women ask permission to go to the mosque at night, allow them." (Book #12, Hadith #824) Narrated Ibn 'Umar: The Prophet (PBUH) said, "Allow women to go to the mosques at night." (Book #13, Hadith #22) Narrated Ibn 'Umar: One of the wives of 'Umar (bin Al-Khattab) used to offer the Fajr and the "Isha" prayer in congregation in the Mosque. She was asked why she had come out for the prayer as she knew that 'Umar disliked it, and he has great ghaira [self-respect]. She replied, "What prevents him from stopping me from this act?" The other replied, "The statement of Allah's Apostle (PBUH): 'Do not stop Allah's women-slave from going to Allah's Mosques' prevents him." (Sahih Al-Bukhari Book #12, Hadith #824, Book #13, Hadith #22 and #23)

women's education, together with women's wider access to religious materials through pamphlets, audiovisual materials, radio, TV, satellite programs, and internet, both feeding and fed by the increasing influence of radical Islam with its emphasis on religious education.

Shifting Communities of Allegiance

Women's actions and behavior, and how they position themselves in relationship to other people and to religious texts, are guided by their choice of investment in community membership. The movement of women into mosques signals not just increasing personal piety, but also a change for the women in their community of primary allegiance. The majority of women in the Middle East have built their lives around extended family networks. Family, rather than friends, are the principal arbitrators of behavior and values. Women who work outside the home include social interaction with colleagues in their professional lives, but their primary allegiance is to family. Kinship networks tend to be the basis of loyalties, in political or daily life decision-making. The understanding and practice of religion for women is similarly based around extended family expectations and practices.

As they become part of the contemporary piety movement, Muslim women negotiate the tensions between family expectations and mosque attendance. In conforming to new norms of dress and religious practice, they are choosing networks of faith beyond family as alternate communities of allegiance and identity.

These different communities of allegiance can be seen in terms of the community itself, of the mimetic ideal that embodies community values, and of how allegiance is lived out in actual practices and ways of being, in word (ways of engaging with authoritative texts) and in communal worship.

Mapping the Story

Chapter 2 offers a brief examination of the place of Muslim women in relation to (sacred) text. This is not a study of what the Qur'an and *hadith* say about women, but rather the place of women as transmitters, students, and teachers of text, within the Middle East. An overview of the history of women and women scholars within Islam since its inception, through colonial movements of resistance and emancipation, takes us up to recent movements of secular and Islamist feminism, the context in which the women's mosque movement finds its place.

Chapter 3 discusses the context and process of the research. How did my quest for understanding lead to an ethnographic case study? Rigor in research demands that the researcher's presuppositions be made explicit. And I look at how the process developed, how I started attending the mosque program, and the negotiated accountability for the notes I took in my time as guest of the women there.

Chapter 4 takes us to the mosque, to the place, the program, and the women who attend it. In this chapter I consider how faith finds embodied form in time and space, and survey the wider political and cultural context of the women's program.

Chapter 5 explores the mosque as a place of alternate community to kinship networks for the women. The mosque female congregation is the local realization of the wider imaginary sorority of pious Muslim women and the *ummah* of Islam is realized in the local mosque community. The women negotiate the tensions between the primary kin community and the new community of allegiance around the place and priority of their domestic roles.

Chapter 6 asks about leadership in terms of the mimetic ideal. Communities find embodied definition in their mimetic ideal or model leader. Within Islam, Muhammad has always been the ideal model upon whom daily practices of faith and life are based in minute detail. In the context of the local mosque community, there is a shift from women within the immediate and extended family as primary models. Leaders within the mosque group provide an alternative model of behavior and devotion, enlarging the possibilities for women within the community of faith.

In chapter 7 I ask, if community allegiance is embodied in the ideal model, what does that look like in particular practices, in ways of being and doing in space and time? This chapter addresses how allegiance takes gendered form in performative practices of dress, patterning of time around daily and annual *salah*, feasts and fasts, issues of purity and piety, and questions of leadership.

Chapter 8 is concerned with sacred word: texts, and how they are read and interpreted. Allegiance to a community of faith is demonstrated in particular ways of relating to the sacred texts that define it. In the mosque community, the women go beyond a focus on the physical form of the Qur'an and its function in healing and protection, to take up the Qur'an through memorizing and reciting it. The chapter reviews how the community shapes patterns of interpretation and application, including how they address gendered texts in Qur'an and *hadith*.

Chapter 9 looks at community worship through the use of *dhikr* in the women's mosque program. Analysis of the *dhikr* words and elements is used to explore how God is defined within this community, and how its members perceive themselves and their faith practices in relation to God.

Chapter 10 draws the book to a close, looking both at its conclusions and at the troubled times which have overtaken Damascus and the women of that suburb. In the last few years issues of communal allegiance have come to take on life and death import. How does that communal allegiance find form? And what might be the implications for the future?

2

Women and Text in Islam

A female religious scholar of fifteenth-century Hadramawt, Yemen, al-Shaykha Sultana bint 'Ali al-Zubaydy was well-known for her piety, knowledge, and teachings. One of her male counterparts, expressing the conventional opinion that religious scholarship and teaching were the domain of men, challenged her in verse: "But can a female camel compete with a male camel?" She completed the couplet, responding: "A female camel can carry the same load as a male, and produce offspring and milk as well."[1]

Women and the Coming of Islam

THE PLACE OF WOMEN within Islam has been much debated.[2] While a number of writers agree that women had some freedom in the time of Muhammad,[3] Jawad considers that it was because Muhammad elevated women's status from their pre-Islamic state.[4] In contrast Ahmed suggests that women's active role in society was progressively curtailed by the establishment of Islam and the privileging of patrilineal, patriarchal marriage.[5] Hekmat and Mernissi[6] agree that polygamy was not widespread at the time of Muhammad, and Ahmed and Engineer[7] indicate that women

---

1. Boxberger, *Two States*, 119. See Malti-Douglas, *Women's Body*, ch. 2 for further examples of male-female verbal wit exchanges in Muslim history.
2. Glaser and John, *Partners*.
3. Mernissi, *Women's Rebellion*, 82, 99.
4. Jawad, *Rights*, 5–6, 14; Stowasser, *Early Islam*, 15; Gerner; *Roles*, Kung, *Islam*, 157.
5. Ahmed, *Women and Gender*, 42. Cf. Mernissi, *Beyond the Veil*, 34–37; Engineer, *Rights*, 34–35.
6. Hekmat, *Women and the Koran*; Mernissi, *Beyond the Veil*, 140–41.
7. Ahmed, *Women and Gender*, 44; Engineer, *Rights*, 27.

as well as men had been able to initiate divorce in the time of the *jahiliyyah*. Ahmed proposes that the lives of Khadija and 'Aisha embody the change brought by Islam: "[Khadija's] economic independence; her marriage overture, apparently without a male guardian to act as intermediary; her marriage to a man many years younger than herself; and her monogamous marriage all reflect Jahilia rather than Islamic practice." 'Aisha, in contrast "was born to Muslim parents, married Muhammad when she was nine or ten, and soon thereafter, along with her co-wives, began to observe the new customs of veiling and seclusion." Ahmed concludes that through selectively sanctioning some practices and prohibiting others, "Islam fundamentally reformulated the nexus of sexuality and power between men and women."[8]

Muhaddathat (Spoken to by Angels) and *Muhaddithat* (Transmitters of Traditions)

In pre-Islamic times there were diviner-prophetesses. The role of women religious leaders within Islam is more controversial. Clarke summarizes the debate among Muslim scholars about whether women can be prophetesses. Historically, discussion has focused in particular on whether Mary (the only woman named in the Qur'an, and whose name is also the title of a *surah* [19]) has prophetic rank.[9] Although Mary and some other women are granted a high status and named *muhaddathat* (spoken to by angels), the tradition "is reluctant to grant them religious authority over others."[10]

However, women have always been recognized as among the *muhaddithat* (women transmitters of *hadith*). Of Muhammad's wives, 'Aishah is most commonly cited for her role in transmission of *hadith*; sometimes also Umm Salamah.[11] Hafsa's role as keeper of the transcribed Qur'an suggests that she may have been able to read and write.[12] Among Muhammad's female companions, Naseebah and Umm Sulaym are described as narrators of *hadith*. Abdel-Halim adds the names of Al-Khansa' and 'Umara bint Abdel-Rahman in the first century AH, 'Aisha 'Abd-al-Hadi in the

---

8. Ahmed, *Women and Gender*, 43–45.

9. Smith and Haddad, *Virgin Mary*; Stowasser, *Women in the Quran*; Clarke, *Religious Practices*.

10. Clarke, *Religious Practices*, 353.

11. Deeb, *Religious Practices*, 335; Nadwi, *al-Muhaddithat*, 248; Roded, *Women in Islam*, 49.

12. Zeidan, *Novelists*, 12.

seventh, and Nafissah (great-granddaughter of Muhammad) and Rabiaʿa al-Adawiyya in the eighth century AH, as early women scholars. In Syria Umm al-Darda' was a famous female *muhaddithah* and jurist in the early years after Muhammad. In the seventh century women were part of a revival in *hadith* scholarship in Syria, learning and teaching *hadith* in some of the main mosques in Damascus, in gardens, and in private houses.[13]

Nadwi's introductory book on the *muhaddithat* examines the role of women narrating *hadith* from the centuries since the time of Muhammad until the present. He suggests that the first and second centuries AH (the early emergence of Islam), followed by the sixth to ninth centuries AH (which included defeats from the Crusaders and the Mongols) were the most significant times for women scholars within Islam. It seems that times of disruption allow more space for women to flourish: at times of consolidation they are found again in traditional confines.[14] It could be argued that the role of *muhaddithat* is as transmitters of authoritative material, rather than having authority themselves. However, Nadwi also notes examples of women involved in *fiqh*, including *tafsir* and giving *fatwa*s, and insists that "women scholars acquired and exercised the same authority as men scholars."[15]

Contemporary writers can draw on historical records of women within Islam. Al-Khatib al-Baghdadi (392–463/tenth century) in his *Ta'rikh Baghdad* included 29 women in his list of 7831 scholars over a 300-year period.[16] Mernissi lists a number of biographies and religious histories which mention prominent women. They include:

1. Ibn Saʿad (d. 230/ninth century) *Al-Tabaqat al-kubra*. Volume 8 is devoted to the subject of women.
2. Abi Abdallah Ibn Musʿab Al-Zubeiri (ninth century) *Kitab Nassab Goraich*.

---

13. ʿAli Qutb, *Women,* 189, 212; Abdel-Halim, *Did You Know,* 19; Nadwi, *al-Muhaddithat,* 266–67.

14. Nadwi, *al-Muhaddithat,* 246, 255. See the ebullient publicity given to women protesting publicly during the "Arab Spring," which did not refer back to their role in historical protests: nor has it kept pace with consequent restrictions. Mernissi, viewing the social disruptions of the Gulf War, asked: "Traditionally women were the designated victims of the rituals for reestablishing equilibrium. As soon as the city showed signs of disorder, the caliph ordered women to stay at home. Will it be we, the women living in the Muslim city, who will pay the price . . . ?" (*Veil,* 9).

15. Nadwi, *al-Muhaddithat,* xviii, ch.10; also Roded, *Women in Islam,* 96.

16. Fernea, "Women in Muslim History."

3. Al-Tabari, Abu Jafar Muhammad Ibn Jarir (d. 310/tenth century) *Tarikh al-uman wa al-muluk*. He discusses the role of women in a text inserted at the end of the thirteenth and final volume.

4. Ibn Hazm al-Andaloussi (d. 456 /eleventh century) *Jamharat ansab al-'Arab*.

5. Ibn Amir Yusuf-al-Namri al-Qurtubi (Ibn 'Abd al-Barr) (d. 463 /eleventh century) *Kitab al-Isti'ab*. His book ends with women's biographies.

6. Ibn al-Athir (d. 631/thirteenth century) *Usd al-ghaba fi ma'rifat al-sahaba*. Volume 5, *Kitab al-nisa*, is on women.

7. Al-Dahbi (d. 748/1370) *Siyar a'lam al-nubula*.

8. Ibn Hisham (d. AD 833) *Al-Sira al-Nabawiya*, which describes the active involvement of women around Muhammad.

9. Sakina Shihabi's editing of the comments of Imam Ibn 'Asakir's (d. 571/1175) special volume on women, *Tarikh Dimashq*, which contains 196 biographies of famous Muslim women who either lived in or visited Damascus, where she notes "it gave Ibn 'Asakir an opportunity to summarize all existing data until his time (twelfth century AD) on some of the most active and forceful women of our civilisation."

10. Ibn Hajar, al 'Asqalani, (d. 852/1449) *Al-Isaba fi tamyiz al-sahaba*. Volume 7 acknowledges 1552 women as disciples.[17]

Lindsay also refers to Ibn Asakir's description of women in the twelfth century being able to study, earn *ijazah*s, and qualify as scholars and teachers (particularly in families of scholars), and notes that Ibn Asakir himself had studied under eighty different female teachers. And Roded comments on al-Sakhawi (d. 902/1497) following al-Asqalani in devoting the final section of his biographical dictionary to female scholars, including over one thousand, of whom: "38% of these women studied, received licences (*ijazah*s) to transmit their learning and/or taught others."[18]

Ahmed also records a number of women scholars in medieval Islam (ninth–twelfth centuries/fifteenth–eighteenth centuries). Traditionally female religious scholars were often relatives of male clerics, from the 'ulama class.[19] These women were often taught by a male relative such as their father and sometimes also had access to private tutors.[20] In the

17. *Women's Rebellion*, 82–100
18. Lindsay, *Daily Life*, 196–98; Roded, *Women in Islam*, 132.
19. Ahmed, *Women and Gender*, 113–14; Nadwi, *al-Muhaddithat*, xii.
20. Lane, *Manners*, 64; Gerner, *Roles*, 77; Baron, "Women's Press"; Hatem, *A'isha Taymur's Tears*, 74.

eighteenth–nineteenth centuries a few girls, mostly of middle-class families, attended the small local Qur'anic schools (*kuttab*) present throughout the Muslim world.[21] Generally female literacy was low and even when taught, Shaarawi and Mernissi both record being discouraged in their desire to learn more of the Qur'an because of their gender.[22]

If scholarship for women was controversial, women's leadership was more so.[23] However, Mernissi records a number of prominent women leaders in the history of Islam. She asserts that there were fifteen queens in the non-Arab Muslim world, including four princesses who succeeded each other in Aceh in Indonesia in the second half of the seventeenth century (1641–1699). Asma (d. 480/1087) and Arwa (ruled 485/1091–532/1138) were Shi'ite (Ismaili) queens in Yemen.[24] Thurlkill notes that Arwa, like the queens of the Safavid dynasty in sixteenth-century Iran, assumed many of Fatima's characteristics.[25] Other Muslim countries which have had female heads of state and prime ministers include Pakistan (Benazir Bhutto), Senegal (Mame Madior Boye), Turkey (Tansu Çiller), Kosovo (Kaqusha Jashari), Indonesia (Megawati Sukarnoputri), and Bangladesh (Khaleda Zia and Sheikh Hasina successively). And women have always played a part as charismatic leaders in Sufi orders: this is discussed in chapter 9.

Muslim Women in Modern Discourse

> The battle of modernity and cultural authenticity has been fought over women's bodies and souls.[26]

Early pleas for educating women, such as that of Qasim Amin in Egypt, were based on nationalism and the role of women in cultural reform of Muslim societies.

> Egyptians . . . must believe that there is no hope that they will become a vibrant community, one that can play an important role alongside the developed countries, with a place in the world of human civilization, until their homes and their families become a proper environment for providing men with the

---

21. Wilks, *Islamic Learning*, 165; Eickelman, *Art of Memory*, 493; Wagner, *Becoming Literate*, 44.
22. Shaarawi, *Harem Years*, 40; Mernissi, *Harem Within*, 102–3.
23. See note 55 for the *hadith* against female leaders.
24. Mernissi, *Forgotten Queens*, 110.
25. Thurlkill, *Mary and Fatima*, 4–5.
26. Gerami and Safiri, *Qur'an*, 255.

characteristics upon which success in the world depends. And there is no hope that Egyptian homes and families will become that proper environment unless women are educated and unless they participate alongside men in their thoughts, hopes and pains, even if they do not participate in all of their activities.[27]

Amin collaborated with al-Sayyid Jamal al-Din al-Afghani and Muhammad 'Abduh; and Ahmed also cites the writing of Rifa'ah Rafi' al-Tahtawi (1869). All of these were influenced by their studies in France, and their concern for the reform of Muslim countries and liberation from Western domination. They based their arguments for reform on an appeal to return to the true Islam that had been corrupted over centuries. Mubarak and Fahmi also published books supporting education for women in 1875 and 1894.[28] Women's development was promoted, not for the women's own sake, but because of Muslim children's need for a good mother (this linked into trends in the global discussion of the role of women at the time). Discussions about Muslim women and scholarship were located in ideological discussions of modernization. Cromer (British consul general of Egypt) argued that veiling and segregation of Muslim women exemplified their degraded position in Islam and need for Western civilization .[29]

In Public and in Print

The nineteenth century saw the increasing emergence of Middle Eastern women into public space. This began in print, as women were writing in and publishing magazines for women at the end of the seventeenth century and beginning of the eighteenth. Baron suggests that the movement from women's anonymous writing or use of pen names to signing their own name was the textual equivalent of unveiling, appearing personally in the public sphere.[30] As women joined public protests in the Middle East against

27. Amin, *Liberation of Women,* 66 (first published in Arabic 1899 as *Tahrir al-mar'a*).

28. Ahmed, *Women and Gender,* 133–68; Badran, *Feminism,* 19–21.

29. Ahmed notes that while Cromer advocated liberation for Middle Eastern women, he was at the same time in England a "founding member and sometime president of the Men's League for Opposing Women's Suffrage" (*Women and Gender,* 152–54). Early Egyptian feminists Shaarawi, Musa, and Hifni Nassef espoused a more gradual approach to unveiling than that advocated by Qasim Amin and Cromer (and also by Attaturk in Turkey and Rezah Shah in Iran) (*Women and Gender,* ch.8; Abu Lughod, *Remaking,* 8–9; Badran *Feminism,* 23, 73–76; Baron, "Women's Press"; Shakry, *Schooled Mothers,* 149).

30. Baron, "Women's Press"; Ahmed, *Women and Gender,* 140–41.

colonial occupying forces, public unveiling by upper class women occurred in the context of demonstrations for independence.³¹ While working closely with Huda Shaarawi (1879–1947: founder of the Egyptian Feminist Union), women like Nabawiyya Musa (1890–1951) and Malak Hifni Nassef³² (1886–1918) promoted education and public involvement for women in the context of an Islamic framework.

Nazira Zayn al-Din was encouraged by her father (a Druze Sheikh and judge in Lebanon) to study. At the age of twenty she published a book in Beirut in 1928 called *al-Sufur wa al-Hijab* (*Unveiling and Veiling*), noting in the introduction to her book that the events in Damascus in 1927, where Muslim women were harassed and prevented from appearing on the streets unveiled, had stimulated her writing. In arguing against the *hijab* and seclusion of women, Zayn al-Din contended for women being able to interpret religious texts. The book aroused a storm of criticism, and after publishing another book the following year called *al-Fatah wa al-Shuyukh* (*The Young Woman and the Shayks*), Zayn al-Din retired from public view.³³ When rioting broke out in Damascus in 1945 against the French occupation, women went onto the streets to join the protests against occupation. However, again there was a conservative Sunni backlash against their presence.³⁴

Zaynab al-Ghazali (1917–2005) also chose to locate her activism within Islam, abandoning her initial involvement in Shaarawi's organization to found the Muslim Women's Association. In 1939 Hasan al-Banna proposed a merger of her association with the Muslim Brotherhood. Al-Ghazali declined, but worked closely with al-Banna and the Brotherhood, and herself spent six years in prison until released in 1971 by Anwar Sadat.³⁵ Al-Ghazali argued for women's primary place in domestic space and obligations to husband and family, at the same time she encouraged women to play an active role in public life, providing this did not interfere with their central familial duties. Al-Ghazali's divorce from her first husband (because the marriage held her back from her involvement in *da'wa*) was controversial: commentators are divided on whether her own example contradicted her teaching

---

31. Ahmed, *Feminist Movements*, Shaarawi, *Harem*; Ali Atassi, *Veiling*.

32. More widely known by her pen-name, Bahithat al-Badiya ("Seeker in the Desert »).

33. Shaaban, *Contradictions*, 61–77; Mojab, *Islamic Feminism*; Keddie, *Women*, 96; Badran, *Feminism*, 313; excerpts in Kurzman, *Liberal Islam*, 101–6.

34. Syrian author Idilbi (*Sabriya*, 132–42) describes the protest and reaction through the eyes of her principal character.

35. Ten years later, Sadat interned another famous woman activist, Nawal El-Saadawi in the same prison, Qanatir Women's Prison; she was soon released following Sadat's assassination in October 1981 (El Saadawi, *Women's Prison*).

on the place of women.³⁶ Al-Ghazali taught through her writings and also instructed large groups of women. Mahmood³⁷ discusses Zaynab al-Ghazali's move outside family roles to leadership of Muslim women alongside the Brotherhood in Egypt. She suggests the possibility of this move finds its basis in the increased opportunities available to women of her socioeconomic background and developing acceptance of women in the public domain in the 1930s and 1940s.

With growing access to education and to public space, women began to be appointed to positions in the civic realm. El-Saadawi was Director General of Public Health Education in Egypt's Ministry of Health from 1958–1972. In Syria President Hafez al-Asad appointed a woman as Minister of Culture in 1976. Whether secular or religious, women taking up places of public leadership do so on a foundation of well-developed (if still debated) discussion of women's rights and public participation.

Yamani's volume looks at how women's issues have played out in legal and literary space, with also Marsot's discussion of women's involvement in economic transactions in the Ottoman era.³⁸ The contemporary place of Muslim women in Middle Eastern society has been explored in a number of studies.³⁹ Some of these studies have focused on particular social groups.⁴⁰ Other women have used autobiography of their own experience as a lens to look at wider issues of gender and society.⁴¹ Sociological studies of Middle Eastern women, using an economic or development paradigm, can include women of both Muslim and Christian backgrounds.⁴² Joseph offers reflections from a number of Lebanese women on identity in the context of family and social relationships. Mir-Hosseini and Moghadam focus on Iran. Doumato's study contributes the perspective of women's practices of folk religion interacting with Wahhabism in the Arab peninsula. Saliba, Allen and Howard, and Badran examine the shifting trends in women's movements in the Middle East.⁴³

---

36. Ahmed, *Women and Gender*, 197–202; Shehadeh, *Women*, 121–140; Mahmood, *Politics*, 67–72; Badran *Feminism*,

37. Mahmood, *Politics*, 182–3.

38. Yamani, *Feminism*; Marsot, *Entrepreneurial Women*.

39. E.g., Hussain, *Muslim Women*; Brooks, *Nine Parts*; Moghadam, *Gender*; Kandiyoti, *Gendering*; Abu Lughod, *Remaking*.

40. Abu Lughod, *Bedouin, Women's Worlds*; Watson, *City*; Early, *Baladi*.

41. El Saadawi, *Women's Prison, Woman Doctor, Isis*; Mernissi, *Harem*; Shaarawi, *Harem*.

42. Hoodfar, *Marriage*; Bibars, *Victims*; Atiya, *Khul-Khaal*.

43. Joseph, *Brother-Sister*; Mir-Hosseini, *Islam and Gender*; Moghadam, *Islamic Feminism*; Doumato, *God's Ear*; Saliba et.al., *Gender*; Badran, *Feminism*.

Texts and *Tafsir*

> If one says, "A Muslim woman ought to wear the *hijab* (cover her whole body except her face and hands)," or if one says it is immodest for a woman to reveal her hair, this assertion ... relies on a reference to a set of Qur'anic verses, Prophetic traditions, reports about the Companions and most importantly, the cumulative juristic efforts in selecting, preserving and giving meaning to these textual sources.[44]

In a religion centered upon a sacred Book, texts are foundational in determining or justifying doctrinal positions. Stowasser has explored how women mentioned in the Qur'an are understood within historical traditions of interpretation, and John discusses a number of texts on women in the Qur'an and *hadith*. The same tradition may of course evoke different interpretations, thus a quoted speech of Ibn 'Umar about the behavior of Muhammad's Companions with their wives during Muhammad's lifetime[45] finds opposite meaning for El Fadl, and Glaser and John, in interpreting the tension between Islamic reforms and social attitudes.[46]

Muhammad Abduh (1849–1905) and his disciple Rahid Rida (1865–1930) called for a return to the original sources (Qur'an and *hadith*) and advocated use of *ijtihad*. They gave more attention to the literal meaning of the verses as well as their place within the *surah* and the whole Qur'an. Mahmood traces literalist Salafi readings back to Abduh and Rida; Stowasser sees them as the inspiration of the Modernists. She posits three contemporary approaches to interpretation: Traditionalists, Modernists, and Fundamentalists. Riddell similarly identifies Traditionalist, Radical, and Modernizing views. Duderija discusses the different methods of interpretation between the "Neo-traditional Salafi and Progressive Muslim."[47]

The Fundamentalist or Radical view (see the writings of Sayyid Qutb [1906–1966] and Maududi [1903–1979]—particularly his *Purdah and the Status of Woman in Islam* [1981]), is summarized by Stowasser as: "In her traditional role as loving wife and nurturing mother, the woman fights a holy war for the sake of Islamic values where her conduct, domesticity, and

---

44. El Fadl, *Speaking*, 98.

45. Narrated Ibn 'Umar: During the lifetime of the Prophet we used to avoid chatting leisurely and freely with our wives lest some Divine inspiration might be revealed concerning us. But when the Prophet had died, we started chatting leisurely and freely [with them]. (Sahih Bukhari Book #62, Hadith #115)

46. Stowasser, *Women*; Glaser and John, *Partners*, 77–113; El Fadl, *Speaking*, 223.

47. Mahmood, *Politics*; Stowasser, *Qur'an*, 5–6; *Gender*; Riddell, *Poles*; Riddell and Cotterell, *Islam in Context*, chs. 11 and 12; Duderija, *Constructing*.

dress are vital for the survival of the Islamic way of life. Religion, morality, and culture stand and fall with her."[48] Shehadeh identifies the common elements as "domesticity as women's primary role; gender differences as universal and immutable . . . and the element of danger inherent in women's nature." Hekmat, by contrast, insists that the Qur'an is a dangerously controlling text for women.[49]

In the Modernist school, Engineer[50] maintains that Islam and the Qur'an offer women full rights. More recently Wadud and Barlas have argued for a new (woman's or non-patriarchal) reading of the Qur'an, drawing on Rahman.[51] However, Wadud invokes El Fadl's "conscientious pause" for *Al-Nisa'* 4:34.[52] Mernissi disputes the *hadith* against women's political leadership,[53] by challenging its transmitter. Glaser mentions some of the contemporary re-readings by Ahmed, Engineer, Mernissi, and others, of troublesome texts on women.[54]

In Which Space?

Badran describes secular feminism in the Middle East as drawing on nationalism, Islamic modernism, human rights, and democracy. Muslim women writers have recorded variant responses to the relationship between "feminism" or "*nisa'i*" and Islam. Ahmed poignantly described "the plight of the Middle Eastern feminist," seeking to remain loyal to her own society and culture, "forced almost to choose between betrayal and betrayal."[55] More recently Mahmood relates her discomfort with Islamic revival movements, locating herself in a secular-liberal epistemology, where "the slightest eruption of religion into the public domain is frequently experienced as a dangerous

---

48. Stowasser, *Qur'an*, 7; see also Sikand, *Women*, on the Tablighi Jama'at's attention to women.

49. Shehadeh, *Women*, 219; Hekmat, *Women and the Koran*.

50. Engineer, *Rights*.

51. Wadud, *Qur'an, Rereading*; Barlas, *Believing Women*; Rahman, *Themes*.

52. Wadud, *Gender Jihad*, 199–200; El Fadl, *Speaking*, 33; Scott, *Contextual Approach*.

53. Narrated Abu Bakra: During the days (of the battle) of Al-Jamal, Allah benefited me with a word I had heard from Allah's Apostle after I had been about to join the Companions of Al-Jamal (i.e. the camel) and fight along with them. When Allah's Apostle was informed that the Persians had crowned the daughter of Khosrau as their ruler, he said, "Such people as ruled by a lady will never be successful." (Sahih Bukhari Book #59, Hadith #709)

54. Mernissi, *Women's Rights*, Glaser and John, *Partners*, 113–42.

55. Badran, *Feminism*, 4; Ahmed, *Early*, 122.

affront, one that threatens to subject us to a normative morality dictated by mullahs and priests."[56] Moghadam quotes both Shahidian, who insists that Islam is characterized by "political repression, cultural conservatism and the control of women" so "Islamic feminism is an oxymoron," which "fails to offer a liberating alternative to the dominant Islamic discourse and practice of gender and sexuality;" and Afkhami, who asserts, "The epistemology of Islam is contrary to women's rights. But you can use what you need to. I call myself a Muslim and a feminist. I'm not an Islamic feminist—that's a contradiction in terms."[57]

Mernissi, while she could describe the "Muslim system" as "opposed to ... the growth of the involvement between a man and a woman into an all-encompassing love, satisfying the sexual, emotional and intellectual needs of both partners," contends that:

> Nisa'i is for me an adjective that designates any idea, project, program, or hope that supports women's rights to full-fledged participation in and contribution to remaking, changing and transforming society, as well as full realization of one's own talents, needs, potentials, dreams and virtualities. And it is in this sense that I have always lived and defined women's liberation, whatever the language—"feminism" or "*nisa'ism.*"[58]

Inevitably the different movements and schools of interpretation do not operate in isolation from one another. Mir-Hosseini notes how Sa'idzadeh from Qom, Iran "uses Islamic scholarship to argue for gender equality," leading to some conclusions similar to Wadud's and Mernissi's readings. She comments, "I have assimilated some of his views, but at the same time I believe my questions and way of thinking have affected his."[59]

From Feminism to *Da'wa*

In recent decades, the secular nationalism with its promise of modernity (often identified with westernization) pursued by emerging independent nations, has given way to the "reassertion of Islam into everyday life."[60] The defeat of Egypt by Israel contributed to the Islamic revival that has grown through the Muslim world since the 1970s. This has been more visible

56. Mahmood, *Politics*, xi.
57. In Moghadam *Islamic Feminism*, 30, 32; Parvaz, *Islamists*.
58. Mernissi, *Beyond the Veil*, viii; *Rebellion*, 106–7.
59. Mir-Hosseini, *Islam and Gender*, 247.
60. Shehadeh, *Women*, 1.

through the increasing number of women wearing *hijab*, as well as the neologism "*mutadayyinat*" (religious women) that was coined in the 1980s and 1990s, signaling a new space being taken up by women.⁶¹ While it has roots in the history of women scholars within Islam, this is a contemporary development, with unprecedented numbers of women involved in the Islamic revival, or *daʿwa* movement.

The word *daʿiya* comes from the root *daʿwa* meaning, "to call" or "to invite." In religious terms *daʿwa* is "the invitation, addressed to men [*sic*] by God and the prophets, to believe in the true religion, Islam (Qur'an 14:46)." It determined the Muslim community's relationship to non-Muslims: "Those to whom the *daʿwa* had not yet penetrated had to be invited to embrace Islam before fighting could take place." The term *daʿiy* was originally used by Shiʿa sects to describe missionaries or religious teachers. However, it is now increasingly used in the Sunni community for religious teachers, and Gaffney suggests that it has "somewhat the sense of a 'missionary.'"⁶²

The contemporary piety movement relates *daʿwa* not only to non-Muslims, but also to the duty of every practicing Muslim to urge fellow Muslims to observe correct Islamic practice. The development of *daʿwa* links with the principle of "enjoining (others) in doing good or right and forbidding the evil."⁶³ *Al-Imran* 3:104, 110 specifically links *daʿwa* and enjoining/forbidding: "and let there be from you people **inviting** to the good, **enjoining** what is right and **forbidding** what is wrong" (*waltakun minkumu ʿummatun yadaʿuna ʿila al-khayr wa-yaʾamuruna bilʾmaʿruf wa-yanhawna ʿan al-munkar*).

However, *al-Taubah* 9:71 addresses men and women equally, "the **believing men and believing women**" to be engaged in **enjoining** and **forbidding**, along with prayer and alms-giving and godly obedience (**wal-muʾminuna wal-muʾminatu** baʿduhum ʾawliyaʾu baʿd **yaʾmuruna** bilʾmaʿruf wa-**yanhawna** ʿan al-munkar wa-yuqiymuna al-salah wa-yuʿtuna al-zakah wa-yutiyʿuna Allah wa rasulahu). Hence Emerick puts *daʿwa* alongside enjoining/forbidding and *jihad* as the three fundamental duties for all Muslims.⁶⁴

The endorsement of *daʿwa* as a duty for all Muslims (including men and women) comes together with the shift in the traditionalist understanding,

---

61. Ahmed, *Women and Gender*, 216–22; Badran, *Feminism*, 8.

62. Canard, *Daʾwa*, 168–70; Gibb and Kramers, *Islam*, 68; Gaffney, *Prophet's Pulpit*, 33.

63. Mahmood, *Politics*, 58–62.

64. Emerick, *Islam*, 50–51. He lists the seven beliefs, five faith practices and three duties: *daʿwa* (calling others to Islam), *jihad* (striving in God's cause), and encouraging good while forbidding wrong.

which, while viewing Islam as a complete system based on scripture and interpretation, has left behind the "deficiency" view of women[65] to move towards an emphasis on "women's equality with men in the spiritual and cultural sense," with "woman's emotionality (prime quality of the good mother) against man's rationality (prime quality of the head of household and its provider)."[66]

Just as the increased availability of written material through the printing press, and growth in literacy among upper and middle class women helped fuel feminist movements in the Middle East in the 1800s and 1900s, so the general growth in women's literacy, together with accessibility of Islamic teaching through pamphlets, cassettes, radio, TV, and satellite, have given recent impetus to the Islamic revival movement and to women's part in it. Guessoum proposes the increased literacy among the general populations in modern times as a possible causal factor in the increasing popularity of literal interpretations. Haddad also notes the increased leisure time in the middle classes, which the Islamist movement seeks to channel "into public religious and charitable activity directed towards the common good."[67] Some women preachers are self-educated but religious institutions are increasingly offering training to women. Al-Azhar University in Cairo began training women preachers in 1999.[68]

Piety Examined

Women's pious activism has attracted attention in a number of recent studies. Mahmood's influential ethnographic study among women in the mosque movement in Egypt demonstrates their conscious use of ritual practices such as *salah* towards the formation of the pious self. She challenges Western/feminist definitions of agency and freedom that are tied to individual autonomy, arguing that they need to be understood within specific contextual assumptions about self and authority. In the mosque movement, ethical living is enacted not through political struggle or resistance, but through ritual performative behavior, incorporating volition, emotion,

---

65. For example, Muhammad Atiya Khamis: "Woman was created crooked, lacking in intelligence and religion." (In Haddad, *Social Change*, 9, from Khamis's *al-Shari'ah al-Islamiyah wa al-Harakah al-Nisa'iya*, Cairo: Dar al-I'tisam, 1987:56.) See chapter 8 for a discussion on the re-reading of that *hadith*.

66. Haddad, *Social Change*, 6; Stowasser, *Gender Issues*, 37.

67. Guessoum, *Religious Literalism*, 819; Haddad, *Social Change*, 19; Krause, *Women*.

68. See Rausch discussing Egypt; Deeb, the Arab States; Huq, South Asia; Ali, Sudan; Demirer, Turkey; and Kalinock on Iran, in Joseph, *Encyclopedia*, 335–54.

experience, and bodily expression. Hafez asks how desire and subjectivity are formed in her discussion of how the social activism of an Egyptian women's organization imbricates both Islamic discourse and secularism. Following Mahmood, she notes how practices of personal faith formation include actions of social reform, challenging secular notions of private and public spheres, and of secular-religious binaries. Similarly Krause examines the activities of women's Islamic-oriented associations in the United Arab Emirates, in promoting growth in individual knowledge of Islam, particularly Qur'anic memorization, as a vehicle of societal reform. Networking through these associations allowed women's collaborative effort, including the establishment of a women's shelter and community centers.[69] Ahmad's study focuses on the al-Huda center and other groups offering religious studies among middle and upper-class women in Pakistan. These studies encouraged women to take on formative disciplines of becoming pious or ethical subjects, framed in Islamic rather than Pakistani terms. Van Doorn's[70] study discusses the reformist 'Aisyiyah (founded 1917) and more traditional Muslimat (founded 1946) women's groups, embedded respectively within the Muhammadiya and Nahdlatul Ulama groups. Islamic boarding schools in Indonesia have equipped women and men with years of study of Islamic sources. Within the interpretive methodologies of the NU or Muhamadiya, the women apply their readings of Islamic discourse to their daily lives. Like Mahmood, Van Doorn notes that Western liberal feminist ideas of individual agency are not apt for Indonesian religious and ideological frameworks. Unlike the Middle East where women cannot do public Qur'anic recitation, Rasmussen has studied the widespread performance of public women Qur'anic reciters in Indonesia. In the light of the rich tradition she describes, she suggests that the dissonant voices of urban reformism will not prevail. Jaschok and Shui have described women's mosques among the Hui in China, some subordinate to and some independent of men's mosques. These provide a place of worship (including washing) where women leaders offer Islamic education. Bano and Kalmbach's conference publication on *Women, Leadership and Mosques* has brought together a range of writers offering diverse examples of women in mosques from many parts of the Muslim and Western world. They focus on the emergence, exercise, and impact of female Islamic authority within the context of gendered interpretations and practices. Rinaldo gives a more summary discussion of Muslim women's piety movements. Sarah Islam has a chapter in Bano and Kalmbach where she discusses the elusive Qubaysiyyat movement among middle and

---

69. Mahmood, *Politics*; Hafez, *Islam*; Krause, *Women*.
70. Ahmad, *Al-Huda*; Van-Doorn, *Reading Qur'an*.

upper-class women in Syria and beyond. Kalmbach's article discusses the conservative shape of Anisah Huda's leadership, from her research during the same period that I was attending the women's program. Maher, and Meltzer and Nix have done video documentaries of Anisah Huda's mosque program (Maher also includes other women preachers in Egypt, Lebanon, and Syria), from which I have also drawn.[71]

Among the foregoing, this ethnographic case-study offers a more detailed look at one particular women's mosque program, integrating together the discussion of community, leadership, pious practices and textual interpretation. An in-depth understanding of one situation with all its complexities offers the possibility of a more nuanced awareness of possible issues and interactions in other contexts. A fine-grained scrutiny of the different aspects of this women's mosque program locates them in relation to other movements and trends occurring within Islam world-wide. In this study, I move away from Mahmood's emphasis on the women's individual self-faith-formation, to explore in particular the communal aspect in terms of women's community allegiance. Bano, looking at the Red Mosque siege in Pakistan in 2007, notes that, "Not only did these girls risk their lives, they also risked social stigmatization and exclusion from their own families and extended kinship networks."[72] What is the nature and strength of a shift of allegiance that is stronger than traditional loyalty to family and kin, traditional female values of "docility and piety," and obedience to government? This study asks what that shift in allegiance might look like, expressed in the dimensions of alternate community, ideal leader, (gendered) ways of being and doing in the faith community, ways of reading and understanding religious texts, and ways of worship and understanding God in *dhikr*.

Little has been said or written about the last area, *dhikr*, in relation to women in the mosque movement. Where some might suggest that *dhikr* stands in opposition to the Islamic piety movement,[73] this study explores how it is practically integrated within the mosque program as part of the women's lives and faith, and asks what the *dhikr* prayers tell us about their understanding of God and their position in relation to him.

The next chapter takes us to consider how the research was done—the methodology best suited to this context, and some of the issues that arose.

---

71. Nelson, *Reciting*; Rasmussen, *Women*; Jaschok and Shui, *Women's Mosques*; Bano and Kalmbach, *Women*; Rinaldo, *Women*; Islam, *Qubaysiyyat*; Kalmbach, *Change*; Maher, *Veiled Voices*; Meltzer and Nix, *Light*.

72. Bano, *Female Leadership*, 513–14.

73. Retsikas also challenges the assumption that categorizes reformist Islam in terms of modernity and Sufism under "tradition" (*Becoming Sacred*, 121).

3

Research in Context

3:10 p.m. and all is fairly quiet upstairs in the mosque, though as always there's an undercurrent of activity. I see four women just sitting, another one praying, and a few having their *tajwid* of the Qur'an heard. Three groups of young women, each eight to twelve people, are on the inner balcony sitting in circles, and there's a computer class in the library. Children pass through rapidly. People stand upstairs in the ablution area, talking. A woman puts her bag at the end of the mattress I'm sitting on, steps back and begins praying. I've greeted a couple of women, sat with one for a little while while she practiced reciting. Anisah Huda sits in the front middle of the room, and others behind her. A young woman kneels in front of Anisah Huda, speaks to her. A woman is fixing up a microphone, a long one attached with wire to a wall socket, which she places on the ground in front of Anisah Huda. Piercing whines and screeches from the microphone, which continue for a few minutes.

3:30 p.m. Anisah Huda begins *duʿaʾ* prayers. A girl squats beside her to ask something—she nods, without stopping in the invocation, continues with another one. She asks "the sisters" to close the doors and windows and continues to whisper quietly. A woman is reading the Qur'an. Others are sitting with their palms open, or with prayer beads. A few young girls run through the room. Women are walking through the room. A woman locks the door onto the inner balcony. I'm feeling sleepy. The woman who was reading earlier has noticed, and thoughtfully brings me a coffee-flavored sweet. There is silence, broken only by the noise of children upstairs, and Anisah Huda murmuring "*Allah*" about ten times. A couple of older women are in pantsuits. More young women are arriving, taking their place in the center or round the edge.

Research Worldview

Observing the increasing numbers of women becoming involved in mosque programs, I wanted to learn why women were becoming involved, and how they understood their involvement. Qualitative research seeks to understand and explain social phenomena, considering people in their own context. Ontologically, this research recognizes multiple realities, with a commitment to using people's actual words, diverse forms of evidence, drawing on different perspectives. Epistemologically, the research is based as close as possible to the participants, in the context where they live, learn, and pray. Methodologically, it is inductive. Hence, the research looks for particulars before generalizations, using detailed description of the context: and research questions are developed or revised in response to field data. And it is interpretive, seeking to understand how people make meaning of their worlds, the social reality of individuals, groups, and cultures.

Researching in a Middle Eastern Muslim context is gender-shaped: men cannot research women's lives, and the converse is little easier. Does research by a woman about women make it feminist? Feminist research focuses on women's experiences, but goes beyond gender to examine how power imbalances shape both daily interactions and the production of knowledge, drawing on a range of methodologies.[1] However, Mahmood joins other non-western feminists to critique a framework based only on liberal-feminist understandings of agency and autonomy.[2]

Feminist research emphasizes reflexivity and attention to standpoint. It gives particular attention to the relationship between researcher and participants. Spickard et al. note the challenge of the relationship between researcher and participants, which is highlighted in religious contexts.[3] Altorki and El-Solh, and Alcalde describe the complexities of doing research as "insiders" in the community.[4] Davidman tells poignantly of the need to go beyond personal resistance to a particular tradition within a religion in order to understand and "make sensible to others, the meaning of this choice for the women who embraced it."[5] Ingersoll suggests ethnography

---

1. Gelling, *Feminist*, 6; Lather, *Feminist*; Ackerly and True, *Reflexivity*; Loftsdottir, *Feminist*, 199–200.

2. Mahmood, *Politics*; Abu-Lughod, *Debate*.

3. Spickard, *Personal Knowledge*, 6–7; Ganiel and Mitchell, *Religious Ethnography*; Clarke, *Anthropology*, 11.

4. Altorki, *At Home*; Alcalde, *Going Home*.

5. Davidman, *Truth*, 24; also Mahmood, *Politics*, x-xi; Jamal, *Between Us*.

as a "key tool" in researching the experiences of women, which are "often neglected in documentary and textual sources," particularly "in conservative religious traditions."[6]

Ethnography

Ethnography is the detailed inquiry into a cultural context, where the ethnographer spends a prolonged period of time involved in the lives of the participants, to understand characteristic cultural forms, behavior, and beliefs—or as Agar puts it more simply, it is "one human trying to figure out what some other humans are up to."[7] It looks at the practices of everyday life and the shared knowledge out of which those practices are built, with an emphasis on thick or rich data.[8] While the researcher has an idea of where and at what they want to look, and the methods they will use, doing ethnography takes place with people in their natural context and unfolds with situations which occur and new possibilities that arise, moving "back and forth between the different components of the design, assessing the implications of purposes, theory, research questions, methods, and validity threats for one another."[9] So the research (and questions) evolve over time, in interaction with the participants. Heath and Street suggest that it is this recursive nature of ethnography that distinguishes it from other forms of qualitative research. The iterative movement between field observations and literature is paralleled by the ethnographic commitment to both "emic" (insider) and "etic" (outsider) perspectives, to being able to appreciate the details of the local view, at the same time as locating it within the wider panorama. This finds geographic realization in the ethnographer movement of immersion in the local context and then distancing and return to the home culture, in what can become a repeated "cycle of proximity and distance."[10]

Case study research seeks to understand the complexity of a particular case or bounded situation, retaining the "holistic and meaningful characteristics of real-life events," by direct observation, and interviews with people involved, rather than manipulating or intervening in behavior. An instrumental case study seeks insight into a general question by studying a

---

6. Ingersoll, *Against Univocality*, 162.
7. Agar, *Professional Stranger*, 2.
8. Geertz, *Interpretation*.
9. Maxwell, *Qualitative Research*, 4.
10. Heath and Street, *Ethnography*, 33–34, 50, 65.

particular case. Asking "how?" and "why?" questions, the results are generalizable to theories (analytical) rather than frequencies or populations (statistical).[11]

Collecting Data

In ethnographic research the researcher is the primary instrument of data collection, typically relying on intense and/or prolonged contact with the field situation. The researcher seeks to collect "thick" detailed data, which is used to generate "empathetic and experiential understanding."[12] This enables an intuitive response to each situation, with some form of analysis and categorizing happening constantly and concurrently with data collection. Researcher discomfort or uncertainty, the "culture shock" of when the unexpected or inexplicable happens, is not only part of the data, but becomes a means of developing theory. Agar describes these as "rich points," which are "the raw material of ethnography,"[13] because they force the ethnographer to re-examine their framework in order to bring it into more conceptual coherence with what is happening, to make sense of it in terms of the participants' meanings and actions. The researcher gathers information from a variety of sources,[14] using multiple methods to triangulate the data.

Participant Observation

The principal method in ethnography is participant observation, with use, also, of interviews and document analysis. Participant observation "demands near total absorption" from the researcher; "personal commitment, trust, and time are the key to rich data and useful interpretations."[15] Participant observation can be anywhere on the spectrum from observer to full participation.

---

11. Yin, *Case Study*, 4–12.
12. Holloway, *Basic Concepts*, 9.
13. Agar, *Professional Stranger*, 32.
14. Cohen et al. describe the ethnographer as "a methodological omnivore" (*Research Methods*, 235).
15. Glesne and Peshkin, *Becoming*, 174, 175.

Joining the Program

From 2005–2007, while I was living in Syria, I attended events that were part of a women's program in a Sunni mosque. Access was initially through my daughter, who had become friends with Ebtisam, a young female teacher in one of my husband's classes. Ebtisam invited my daughter to a graduation party for young women who had memorized the Qur'an (the party itself was unusual in that it was held in a [closed] room of a public restaurant, not in the mosque). I asked to accompany my daughter, and there was introduced to Anisah Huda who had set up and led the women's program of this particular mosque. She invited me to her house to join in the weekly talks on Islam she was giving to a few expatriate women. I was then invited to attend the opening of a library for women set up at the mosque. From there I was given permission to attend the mosque sessions for women. There were two teaching sessions a week, one in the morning that was mostly for older women and housewives. The other, after the mid-afternoon prayers, was more for younger women, university graduates, teachers, and others. I attended the lectures and also sat in on *dhikr* sessions and *tajwid* lessons, and on celebrations of religious feasts and other special occasions, and visited some of the women in their homes. All participant research and discussion was conducted in Arabic. My involvement in the program was mostly limited to observation, being in the various sessions and taking notes.[16] At a few of the feast celebrations when some of the women shared their experience of the mosque program, I was asked to the microphone also for my perspective. At times of significant religious feasts I usually visited or rang Anisah Huda and some of the other women to give them greetings for the feast. The mosque was situated in another suburb but a number of the women attending it had extended family roots in the area in which I was living.

Relationships of trust are built over time; the women became more used to my presence and I got to know individuals in the mosque or in the context of their homes. There was some family contact with Anisah Huda: she invited me to visit with my husband to meet her husband. Her daughter was the same age as mine, and when my daughter joined us on school holidays Anisah Huda would make time for us all to meet over a meal, or encourage our daughters to meet up.

> A woman comes and sits heavily on the seat beside me, and asks me about where I'm from, my husband, where he's from, my religion, what I do here—she takes my face in her hands and

---

16. See Clarke's description of the challenge of different degrees of participation in Muslim gatherings in Lebanon, and how it was understood by both other participants and onlookers (*Integrity*).

kisses my forehead, then stands again for the next segment of prayers.... The women greet each other, rest, and talk. Another woman greets me. The woman who sat beside me earlier rejoins me. We chat, and she kisses me again, and tells her neighbor briefly who I am.

In the mosque people regularly kept me company, especially when I was new—coming to sit with me, make me welcome, introduce me to other women. If I was attending something for the first time, or if I had questions, people readily showed me round or explained the significance of what was happening. They told me what satellite channels to watch that offered Islamic instruction, in Arabic or in English, helped me to write down *dhikr* prayer chants, offered me the chance to try reciting the Qur'an correctly, or prayer beads to use during the *dhikr*, helped me find my place in the Qur'an, and encouraged me to join in offering prayers of supplication, particularly at times of especial efficacy like the Night of Vigil in Ramadan.

The researcher into religious communities encounters heightened issues of insider-outsider status, and not infrequently the pressure to cross the boundary and join the community.[17] Mahmood, Ahmad, and Jamal describe the experience of being "partial insiders," from the same faith and, for both Ahmad and Jamal,[18] the same nationality; but with more liberal views than their research communities. As a "believer,"[19] I shared with the women in the mosque a common worldview of faith as pervading every part of life, expressed in practices such as regular prayer, study of sacred texts, and fasting. However, some were uncertain about my attendance over a prolonged time without involvement in the shared *salah* ritual (thereby highlighting my different Christian allegiance).[20] Anisah Huda stated that she believed in talking to people to explain about Islam—not to convert them, but to explain it and leave their response to their understanding.[21]

17. Famously, Harding, *Invited*; also Davidman, *Truth*; Tweed, *Between*.

18. Mahmood, *Politics*, Jamal's interlocutor tells her, "Please think carefully when you write about Islam and Muslims. After all you are one of us. We might be targeted first [the woman pointed to the scarf covering her head and face to indicate that she was talking about veiled Muslim women] but you will not be spared either" (Jamal, *Between Us*, 22; Ahmad, *Transforming Faith*, 202).

19. In Arabic, "believer" (*mu'minah*) is used to describe someone of either Muslim or Christian background who is committed to practicing the tenets of her faith.

20. My identity as a Westerner was also part of the "multiple social identities" of researcher and participants to be navigated in the research context (Plankey-Videla, *Informed Consent*, 5; Jamal, *Between Us*, 203). See chapter 4 for discussion of attitudes to the West, in the context of the cartoons of Muhammad.

21. See Landres, *Being*, 102, for a remarkably similar exchange between researcher and the pastor at an evangelical church in California.

Other women in the program were more direct, asking me if I had become convinced of Islam or Islamized yet. A young woman inviting me to visit her told me about another Western woman who used to visit her and had become a Muslim—the implicit suggestion was clear. Anisah Huda and some other women were able to interact on a basis of partial faith reciprocity: sometimes they would say to me, "Intercede for me, and I intercede for you."

Reflexivity

Heath and Street suggest that contemporary ethnography is characterized by reflexivity rather than innocence. Finlay describes reflexivity as "thoughtful, conscious self-awareness, so that the lived experience between researcher and participant, and the process of exploring and interpreting it, can be made public."[22]

There were times I went to the mosque, attended the sessions, and returned, with limited interaction with women there; at other times they warmly welcomed me. In my journal I recorded feelings ranging from being moved by the beauty of the *dhikr*, of enjoying being with the women, getting to know them, their welcome and acceptance of me sitting there, writing notes, and the freedom to exist there on the boundary, to feeling buffeted by women trying to Islamize me, by teaching that assailed my own beliefs, feelings of variance and uncertainty. Generally I find mosques welcoming spaces. I enjoy the uncluttered space to sit, the variety of occupations going on around me, from people praying, sleeping, talking, picnicking as families in the courtyard—the sense of space set apart for worship, and welcome of people into that space.

However, learning to negotiate rules of behavior as a participant observer took time. My notes record a woman I knew coming to greet me at the end of prayers. I wrote: "Looking at my headscarf she quickly averts her eyes as though she has seen something indecent: then greets me courteously. Later I see from a reflection that some of my hair is showing." On another occasion in the early hours of the Night of Vigil (about 1:30 a.m.) I noticed a phone text message to say that my husband had come to collect me—it had been sent about twenty minutes earlier but I hadn't heard it. I made my way out with difficulty between the packed rows of women standing shoulder to shoulder in prayer. It became increasingly apparent from their expressions that I was doing the wrong thing in walking over their prayer space. Halfway through, one woman put her hands on my chest and thrust me back. I should have waited another ten or twenty minutes for the

---

22. Heath and Street, *Ethnography*, 34; Finlay, "'Outing,'" 532–33; Bowie, *Belief*, 17.

next break in the cycle. Later I found the *hadith* relating to walking in front of someone's prayer space.[23]

Standpoint

Plankey-Videla describes finding herself associated at different times in her research with the workers or with management.[24] I found myself positioned differently in relation to the women I sat amongst, in various situations. When the government was restricting mosque opening hours, I was situated with the women, as a participant in their meetings. At other times, I was positioned (implicitly, not explicitly) over against those sitting around me, as a Western Christian,[25] when Anisah Huda instructed the women how to deal with non-Muslims, or rejected Christian teachings. Sometimes she encouraged the women to emulate what was good in the West; at other times it was described as the enemy of Islam (in response to attacks on Muhammad).

Interviews

Interviews can vary between formal structured exchanges, to informal conversations that grow out of situated participant observation. Qualitative interviews are generally more unstructured and informal. In the context of participant involvement, they are used to explore further, and to confirm material collected through participant observation. Borg and Gall suggest

---

23. Narrated Abu Salih As-Samman: I saw Abu Said Al-Khudri praying on a Friday, behind something which acted as a Sutra. A young man from Bani Abi Mu'ait, wanted to pass in front of him, but Abu Said repulsed him with a push on his chest. Finding no alternative he again tried to pass but Abu Said pushed him with a greater force. The young man abused Abu Said and went to Marwan and lodged a complaint against Abu Said and Abu Said followed the young man to Marwan who asked him, "O Abu Said! What has happened between you and the son of your brother?" Abu Said said to him, "I heard the Prophet saying, 'If anybody amongst you is praying behind something as a Sutra and somebody tries to pass in front of him, then he should repulse him and if he refuses, he should use force against him for he is a satan.'" (Sahih Bukhari Book #9, Hadith #488)

Narrated Busr bin Said: that Zaid bin Khalid sent him to Abi Juhaim to ask him what he had heard from Allah's Apostle about a person passing in front of another person who was praying. Abu Juhaim replied, "Allah's Apostle said, 'If the person who passes in front of another person in prayer knew the magnitude of his sin he would prefer to wait for 40 (days, months or years) rather than to pass in front of him.'" Abu An-Nadr said, "I do not remember exactly whether he said 40 days, months or years." (Sahih Bukhari Book #9, Hadith #489)

24. Plankey-Videla, *Informed Consent*; Ganiel and Mitchell, *Inside Out*.

25. The two were generally conflated in the women's thinking.

that they provide method triangulation, which "helps to demonstrate validity and open up new perspectives about the topic under investigation."[26] My initial involvement with Anisah Huda was attending the sessions she was giving to a few expatriate women in her home, where she would talk about an aspect of Islam, and we could ask questions. Sitting in the different mosque meetings included conversations with the women about what was happening. Over time I drew up a set of questions that emerged from my participation there. When I asked some of the women with whom I regularly sat during the teaching sessions, they preferred to defer to Anisah Huda for the expert response, although they were willing to comment on some questions. I had a lengthy interview with Anisah Huda, going through the questions, which was recorded. She agreed that I could also ask some of the other young women at the program whom she would select, and asked to listen to the interviews before I used them. I wasn't able to check the interviews with her, so have not drawn on them.[27]

Document Analysis

Document analysis has the wider sense of "'documentation,' which . . . signifies any process of proof based upon any kind of source whether written, oral, pictorial or archeological."[28] In this research it includes religious texts (Qur'an, *hadith* collections), lecture notes given out at the mosque, notices around the mosque, wall decorations (usually textual), and the physical lay-out of the mosque, including the main and smaller meeting rooms and the library with its contents. The process of taking field notes also involved different layers of intertextuality, discussed below. I have also drawn on recordings of meetings, events, and interviews from the mosque program recorded by Maher, and Meltzer and Nix.

---

26. Hitchcock, *Research*, 153–171; Borg, *Research*, 397.

27. There was also an issue with transcription. My husband organized an acquaintance of his to transcribe them for me. The young man was eager to help, and offered to answer the interview questions himself, as he felt he understood Islam better than the women (although there was little evidence of practice of prayer and mosque attendance in his daily routine). I found his transcriptions to be an approximation of what was actually recorded, perhaps influenced also by his belief about what they should have said. In itself, a statement about gender and religion in that context.

28. Caulley, *Document Analysis*, 19.

Permission and Oversight

When I was negotiating my involvement with Anisah Huda, she agreed that I could attend the mosque program, but declined a written agreement. Gilbert and Mostert note that in some cultures people distrust any signing process, particularly where they have lived under oppressive regimes, where signed documents could expose them to risk. Schrag argues for the accountability concept of "morally wrong": "We morally wrong people when we violate fundamental moral principles in our dealings with them, for example, when we fail to respect them as persons, treat them unjustly, invade their privacy, or gratuitously harm them physically or psychologically."[29] Anisah Huda agreed with my suggestion that they check my field notes to ensure I hadn't misunderstood anything.[30] This ensured a higher level of accountability and feedback than could have been gained through signing a form.

MULTIPLE AUTHORSHIP OF FIELD NOTES

Ebtisam took on the role of checking. She had introduced me to Anisah Huda, and was one of her trusted disciples (she regularly translated in Anisah Huda's meetings with foreigners), and had good English for the task. Ebtisam herself felt that she knew Anisah Huda's teaching enough to scrutinize my notes even if she wasn't at the lecture. In checking, filling in details, noting when something I took down wasn't clear enough to be corrected (and was therefore discarded) she became an interpreter of my observations. I would type up my handwritten notes (in English with some Arabic); and then give a number of them to her. She would write any corrections and sometimes write her response to questions I had noted down, or she would verbally clarify a point as she returned them. She would add a note if she felt I had not understood an idea well enough. So she wrote comments on issues ranging from points about girls' education, group prayer, the nature of *jihad*, to the pre-existent Word of God, Muhammad and other Prophets, and *jinn*.

On a couple of occasions Ebtisam asked me to remove details from my notes. When I first visited Anisah Huda in her home, there were only women present and she wasn't wearing the usual *hijab* and manteau. I described her appearance, but Ebtisam wrote on my notes: "Muslims prefer

---

29. Gilbert, *Consent*, 4; also Fluehr-Lobban, *Ethics*; Fitzgerald, *Comprehension*, on the inadequacy of the standard informed consent process in non-Western contexts. Schrag, *Ethical*, 140.

30. She had previously checked the notes of another visitor, and found that the battle of 'Aisha's camel (*jamal*) had been described as 'Aisha's beauty (*jamaal*).

not to describe a woman without the head cover." So I deleted those details. In some other notes I described a woman as "being in a condition of not being able to pray" and Ebtisam wrote: "Muslim women don't prefer to talk about their period." The question of what was permitted to a woman during her menstruation could be discussed in detail, but not with reference to an identifiable woman.

Other women in the mosque also had input. In conversation outside a teaching session, they might quote a *hadith* and get someone to write it in my notebook. Others from outside the mosque would also add comments or clarification of common practices. Sometimes this became multiple layers of authorship: I would write down my notes, along with my neighbor's summary of what we were listening to, and Ebtisam later added her comments. For example I wrote:

> The woman beside me gives me her summary in English of Anisah Huda's words: "All the Muslims [Ebtisam later added: 'most, but not all'] don't behave as Muhammad said. They're not as good as he was, they don't do what Islam said, they're not as good as he wants them. So those killing each other in Iraq, those kidnapping journalists—they're not Muslims [Ebtisam: 'not real Muslims'), Islam doesn't say that."

On other occasions, the women would see me transcribing a *dhikr*, and take my notebook to write it out for me, and then Ebtisam might later correct their version that I had typed out. I wasn't sure if the discrepancy was because the women were still learning the *dhikr* or if there was more than one version of it in currency.

Lassiter's discussion of collaborative ethnography shows it as an old (if not always told) practice that is moving now into more central space in ethnography. It reflects the concerns of feminist research for dialogic research, which breaks down power imbalances between researcher and participants. Lassiter notes that "feminist ethnography's central focus on voice, power and representation is converging with the central focus of ethnography in postmodern anthropology," with its understanding of multifaceted realities. The involvement of Ebtisam in a role of "principal consultant as reader and editor"[31] and of the other women, means that this research is more likely to represent their practice and understanding, rather than solely an external view.

---

31. Lassiter, *Collaborative*, 91, 94.

Researcher Responsibility

Jamal comments that although her interlocutors viewed her with suspicion, they were willing to participate in the research both to change her misapprehensions about them, and for her to communicate with a wider public to whom they had limited access.[32] Similarly the women at the mosque felt that Western images generalized all Muslims and Arabs as terrorists, and all Muslim women as oppressed, and they sought a better representation through me and other visiting Westerners. We explicitly discussed this at times and one of my interview questions reflected it: "If you could say anything to women in the West, what would you like to say?" I was also very aware of the need to not be voyeuristic in presenting the words and lives of Muslim women. This was reflected in their care that I not discuss personal details. When the women asked me to pray for them, I took that seriously as I did when they told me they would pray for me. At times it was a general request, at other times for success in studies. The researcher is responsible to protect the identity of the participants. Anisah Huda was happy to have her name known, as she has a high profile from her appearance in other presentations, I have not concealed her name or her daughter's.[33] All other people in the research are identified only by pseudonyms.

Rigor

Good research is rigorous research. Tobin and Begley suggest "goodness" as "the means by which we show integrity and competence," or rigor, in qualitative inquiry. Haye and Severinsson make use of Burns and Grove's standards to evaluate eight studies, on the basis of the following criteria: Descriptive vividness or validity; Methodological congruence (rigor in documentation, procedural rigor, ethical rigor, and auditability); Analytical preciseness; Theoretical connectedness; and Heuristic relevance.[34] The criteria suggested by Lincoln and Guba to evaluate qualitative research continue to be widely used: Credibility (truth value), Transferability (applicability), Dependability (consistency), and Confirmability (neutrality).[35]

---

32. Jamal, *Between Us*, 206; Wilcox, *Dancing*, 54; Clarke, *Integrity*, 213.

33. See Jamal, *Between Us*, 207, for a similar context and response.

34. Tobin, *Rigour*, 390–91; Haye, *Rigor*, 61-68; Burns, *Practice*, 675–9.

35. Lincoln, *Inquiry*, ch. 8; Miles, *Analysis*, 277–80; Edge, *Justifying*, 345; Houghton, *Rigor*, Koch, *Rigor*.

Credibility

How credible are the research findings to the participants and the readers? Do they see them as intrinsically true to the context? Ebtisam's checking of field notes and the contribution of other women gave a high level of participant review of data notes. Prolonged engagement also gives depth to the researcher's interpretation. The emerging theory is strengthened by triangulating observations from a variety of different sources and types of data, and searching for "negative cases" to disconfirm or modify it. I have combined sitting in classes for teaching, reciting, and memorizing the Qur'an, prayer times, celebrations of religious feasts, with visiting people in their homes, asking questions of teacher and students, and drawing on written and recorded material. I have included some of the detailed "thick description" which should enable others to see the basis for interpretations, or enable them to make their own alternative interpretations.

Transferability

Thick description is also an important part of enabling transference to be made from this material to other situations, together with description of the methods and their theoretical grounding. Detailed reference to field notes and other sources enables auditability, which has been enhanced through peer presentations and the supervisory process.

Dependability

Dependability asks how consistent the research questions are with the study design and the underlying paradigms; how explicit the researcher's role is; and emphasizes the importance of peer review. The research should show dependable conclusions from the data over a full range of contexts. Triangulation of data strengthened conclusions, as well as peer debriefing with other researchers involved in similar areas, and in conference presentations and discussions.

Confirmability

Qualitative research doesn't seek freedom from researcher bias. It is rather about using bias as a central part of the hermeneutic method. Bateson describes reflexivity as "observing the observer—observing yourself—as well, and bringing the personal issues into consciousness."[36] Jootun, McGhee, and Marland describe its role in adding rigor to the research process.[37] Conflict arising from bias becomes a challenge to the researcher, which leads to further reflection and exploration in order to reach an understanding which is closer to that of the participants. Confirmability, then, is rather about transparency. Reflexivity was enabled by keeping a journal of my own emotions and responses, on which I have drawn in my description of the research.

Conclusion

Research is about understanding: feminist research reminds us that rigor also involves relationships. I have sought to honor the women who were my hosts: that includes at times choosing not to use material that they asked me not to include or had not reviewed, or that could misrepresent them. The research process was based principally on participant observation in the program, and included a high level of member reading and review of my field notes. This chapter has discussed the methodology I chose, my reasons for doing so, and something of my relationships with the women involved.

The next chapter takes us to the mosque program.

---

36. Bateson, *Daughter's Eye*, in Taylor, *Growing Up*, xiii; Michrina, *Person to Person*, 3–21.

37. Jootun, *Reflexivity*; also Heath and Street, *Ethnography*, 122–25.

4

Setting the Scene: Women's Mosque Program

It is *Eid al-Adhah*, and the upstairs hall is filling up rapidly. About seven women singers sit at the front facing rows of chairs which are soon taken, with more people standing at the back. Anisah Huda welcomes everyone, and talks about the importance of attending the mosque as an expression of love for each other, showing God's love—the need to come, to ask after one another, even to visit—but at least to telephone. Different women get up and talk about coming to the mosque, with much praise for Anisah Huda's leadership. Some have struggled with illness; others with life circumstances or resistant family; a woman describes her path from a non-devout background to regular involvement; another from a Sufi background had enjoyed Sufi *dhikr*s but the feeling never lasted, so she came to this mosque, happened to arrive at a *dhikr* the first time, and then also found the lectures meeting the gap she felt.

THIS CHAPTER INTRODUCES THE mosque, the women's program, and those who attended it. I go on to discuss how faith finds particular form in the body and how it occupies time and space. This scene-setting chapter concludes with a brief discussion of the wider cultural and political context of this women's program.

Visiting the Mosque

The spacious autostrade is lined with wealthy high-rise apartment buildings and spaced trees. Young people dressed in international fashions talk over delectable fruit drinks or bubble-pipes in the chic cafes, places where the visitor can while away a few hours waiting for an appointment, and know they will be deliciously air-conditioned in the broiling summer and warmed when winter gets more snow-tinged cold. In this upper-middle-class suburb, many of the families in the flats have *"srilankans"*—maids, often from the Philippines or Indonesia as well as Sri Lanka—around whom have grown up the myths about their deceitfulness, use of magic, and untrustworthy ways, through the language and cultural barriers that employer, and more painfully, employee, have to negotiate. The through-farer, heading out of town to the mountains and border beyond, catches only a glimpse of the mosque minaret above adjacent buildings from its position on a side-street.

But people don't have to go far off this boulevard-style road to enter more traditional realms just behind it: narrow ways that twist and wind, with small doors in high walls hiding the traditional courtyard-centered houses behind them, vestiges of local villages now overtaken by the spreading city intent on replacing older housing with modern "planned housing" of neat rectangular blocks on straight-line streets. For now this area remains, people whose families have lived here for generations, supporting a rich variety of shops selling every kind of household appliance, fruit and vegetables spilling onto pavements, bakeries whose enticing smells waft past the queues of customers into the surrounding streets, butchers marked by hanging carcasses, estate agents keeping note of all the different shapes and sizes of rooms or flats to rent, small shops selling mobile phones and accessories, or artfully displaying a selection of pens, pencils, and exercise books of different colors and prices, or household gifts such as cultured lamps and glass jugs and vases, and a myriad of other buyers, sellers and business men.[1]

The front entrance to the mosque is via a street leading off the autostrade. Clearly visible as soon as you enter the street, the mosque has high walls, a sprawling complex, stretching minaret and regal dome, behind a high fence with entrance gates at different points. The street itself is straight, well-bitumened, with neat pavements giving access to the gates opening into the mosque courtyard. There is a back entrance to the mosque, from the labyrinth of streets and low-built traditional houses that lie behind. Most of the women who attend the mosque classes come from this area; but there are some other visitors who come from more far-flung suburbs, who encountered Anisah Huda in their school days or through someone else, and have kept coming, albeit more sporadically.

As I approach, all-covering full-length coat and headscarf absorb me with the anonymity of the dozens of other women entering through the

---

1. The wider area housed a notorious political prison until 2000, whose inmates once included Hafez al-Asad, the previous president, for a few days. As the current civil unrest developed, it was one of the earlier areas where anti-regime protest and fighting occurred.

gates, across the yard, past the places for men to wash, avoiding the spacious main door of the mosque to enter behind the curtain hung between the corner of the building and the perimeter wall. It conceals the side entrance, where one of a small set of double iron doors is open to permit access to a set of carpeted stairs, leading to the upper area. Wooden racks are at the bottom of the stairs and the landing, and we remove our shoes and leave them there, making our way up the stairs in socks or stockinged feet.

The upper landing houses a couple of water dispensers, and five steps leading up to the large meeting hall. The hall is minimally furnished apart from the carpet: some shelves for books at the back, a few plastic chairs, sponge mattresses around the side, and a desk-and-seat which is pulled into position for the speaker. As I enter, seven of the eight ceiling fans are whirring, and three double strips of fluorescents across the width of the room give light. The four chandeliers are unlit. An embossed framed picture of a large bunch of grapes, bearing the names of God, hangs on the wall, along with another framed picture of Arabic text within the shape of a doorway. Here people come and go for the different meetings and activities, perform the ritual *salah* or greet acquaintances or friends, softly recite over pages of the Qur'an or just sit quietly on the floor or one of the narrow covered sponge mattresses around the side walls. A few smile a welcome to me as I take my seat among them. Off this hall are the office and other smaller areas. The area above includes the ablution area for women—a trough inset on three walls and raised wooden slats on the floor to keep people's feet dry. Inside the door to the toilet area are a motley collection of wooden bath clogs for people to don as they come in. Another door leads through an elongated room space to the newly-opened women's library. Both library steps and main hall give onto the balcony overlooking the main mosque area where the men pray. Theirs is the high roof, sense of space; here there is more limited space, a lower roof, looking through balustrade or windows onto the main part—behind, seeing, and unseen.

Women's Program in the Mosque

> The woman in the mosque learns the Qur'an; she learns about *shari'ah*; she learns if someone dies, how inheritance is distributed; she learns the Arabic language; we have a day to learn about the role of *shari'ah* teachings; on another day, like Tuesday, for interpretation of verses of the Qur'an; Thursday on contemporary rulings and I discuss what is required of attentive (female) Muslims and young women. (Anisah Huda)

Learning the Qur'an involved both memorization and recitation (*tajwid*), and there were competitions to memorize *tafsir* (interpretation/commentary) of the Qur'an. There was *dhikr* before the Tuesday morning and Thursday afternoon lectures and other regular *dhikr* sessions. *Salah* was performed together by the women around these activities and by individuals at any time. The mosque became a place for pious pursuits to intensify at significant religious times. Anisah Huda told the women, "For the ten days before the *hajj*, there will be worship in the mosque, three hours a day, like in Ramadan, from twelve till three. Small groups doing different things—some will read the Qur'an, some will be praying."

Tuesday Lecture

The Tuesday lecture was usually on the Qur'an (and at some special seasons, like the month in which Muhammad's birthday fell and Ramadan, the lectures diverged to focus on the current theme). Anisah Huda taught with a book of *tafsir* in front of her, but with a focus on contemporary application to women's daily lives.

Thursday Lecture

The Thursday lecture, by contrast, was on topical themes. Sometimes Anisah Huda would just speak from prepared notes; at other times she would give the women a photocopied handout of notes. These lectures covered a range of topics. Some related to daily life, such as how women should care for their children and bring them up in the faith; or how to give appropriate words encouraging people in Islam at special occasions like funerals or weddings. Other themes were subjects like *shari'ah*, historical Islamic teachers from among the *'ulama*, and Ramadan. The place of Islam and Muslims in the world today was a recurrent theme. At these lectures Anisah Huda would sometimes ask one of the young women to summarize to the women a book they had been reading, such as about scientific history and the Qur'an. These studies are discussed further in chapter 8.

Dhikr

There was a time of *dhikr* before the main lectures. Ebtisam wrote on my notes:

There is always *dhikr* before a lecture in our mosque. Why? Because first, we make *istaghfir* (asking for forgiveness) to feel the mercy of Allah. Second, we pray for blessing on our Messenger and we remember *(dhikr)* Allah who is our creator and who can help the teacher to teach and the audience to learn.

There were other times put aside specifically for *dhikr*. In a narrow room over the entrance to the mosque or sometimes in the library, a few dozen women would sit in silent concentration, only the muted sound of voices whispering to themselves, lips moving: sometimes a few phrases of adoration or supplication heard aloud quietly from the leader. These were often on a Saturday (weekend), and sometimes another day.

This focus on *dhikr* reflected the mosque's association with the *Abu-Nur* mosque and associated Islamic foundation under the leadership of Sheikh Ahmed Kuftaro, Grand Mufti of Syria from 1964 to 2004, as well as the sheikh of a main branch of the Naqshabandi order, the most prominent Sufi group in Syria. Both Anisah Huda and her brother Muhammad al-Habash (Imam of the Garden Mosque) had studied at the *Abu-Nur* mosque, and al-Habash was married to a daughter of Kuftaro, and has written two books about him.[2]

Although Anisah Huda advocated this time of spiritual focus and separation from the issues of home or work, in her lectures she dealt with the everyday concerns of the women's lives. And while she emphasized the importance of *dhikr* in preparing for the lesson, she also told the women, "If you need knowledge, take the time you spend in *dhikr* to learn." While *dhikr* was an important part of her public performance and private practice, she positioned herself clearly as a teacher within Sunni Islam, not as a Sufi leader.[3] Chapter 9 explores the use of *dhikr* in the program.

Memorization of the Qur'an and Tajwid

There were groups on how to memorize and correctly pronounce (*tajawwad*) the Qur'an.

Attended by between five to fifteen women, the leaders sometimes had a whiteboard, but more often instruction was oral, with reference primarily to the Qur'an, and sometimes to a book on *tajwid*[4] written by Muhammad al-Habash, which was available from an Islamic bookshop nearby. These

---

2. Kalmbach, "Social and Religious Change," 38.
3. Personal conversation; also ibid., 48.
4. Al-Habash, *Qu'ran*.

sessions often preceded a *dhikr* time (on Saturdays) or one of the two main lectures.

More important than the group lessons on *tajwid* was when instructors sat with individual learners hearing them recite the verses. I frequently observed women sitting alone as they quietly practiced reciting a passage of the Qur'an in preparation for being heard by an instructor, or women sitting in twos, with one reciting and the other listening and correcting as appropriate. Ebtisam was one of those qualified to hear and correct the learners. She had herself completely memorized the Qur'an and *tajwid*, and received a certificate of *tajwid* (the latter had to come through a certified chain of instructors, which could include women).[5] Chapter 8, and appendix 2 deal with the process of memorization and learning *tajwid*.

Other Classes

A number of smaller classes also took place. Some, described as literacy classes, focused on reading/reciting the Qur'an. These were often attended by older women. Young women came for computer classes. I was shown a book that a group of young women were about to study in a Saturday class, which covered "all the scientific discoveries made within Islam, who discovered what, a scientific history, and also how the discoveries related to the Qur'an." And a mother, telling me how she came before the Thursday lecture to bring her secondary school-age daughter to the *fiqh* class from 2:00–3:00 p.m., explained: "There are different classes for the different ages, and also one for adults. The *fiqh* class is on the rulings (*il-'ahkam*) for different areas—purity, fasting, *jihad*, *salah*, the schools (*mudhahib*) and the difference between them, stories—and also on the rules of *tajwid*."

Like the *tajwid*, these classes were led by other women than Anisah Huda, usually women who had come through her program of teaching.

Library

My first visit to the mosque was for the opening of the women's library. This was a large room in the upper area of the mosque used by the women, with bookshelves on the wall on either side of the entrance door from the balcony, and round both corners. The bookshelves included sections on the *hadith*, the teachings on the pillars of Islam, books on the way of the Prophet and his life, a section on Shi'ite faith and general reading, with

---

5. See also the description in Kunkler, *Two Mujtahidahs*.

some children's books. There were also a couple of sections devoted to *tafsir* of the Qur'an. Desks along either side of the hall (which could be pushed aside when more floor space was needed at times like the *tarawih* prayers in Ramadan) included three with computers. Open on Tuesday and Saturdays (9:00 a.m.–5:00 p.m.) and Thursdays (1:00 p.m.–5:00 p.m.), the room could also be used at times for *salah, dhikr* sessions, or other classes as well as private study. It was a new move to have a library set up for women, and this one had been founded on private donations, with the books chosen by Anisah Huda or donated. Saturday was when most women came to borrow books. When I asked Anisah Huda why she felt the need for a library especially for women, she told me first about the 200 verses in the Qur'an on knowledge, and then explained:

> There were a few libraries here in Damascus, but they weren't particularly close, and the need to travel, negotiate the paperwork for enrolling, meant that women didn't make the effort. So this would be available to all the ones who came to the mosque. If men were interested they could arrange a couple of days for them to come. But it needs to be only men or women (and this is in contrast with the days of the Prophet when men and women prayed in the same mosque), as, if it was mixed, women wouldn't be relaxed and able to think well.

She concluded, "An hour's thought is better than a year's worship."[6]

Special Occasions

On special feast days, like *Eid al-Fitr* (at the end of Ramadan), *Eid al-Adhah* or the New Year (*Hijrah* calendar), there was a celebration at the mosque. This most often happened during the time of the Thursday afternoon lecture, between the '*asr* (mid-afternoon) and *maghrib* (sunset) *salah*. The program would begin with about an hour of *anashid* (religious chants) led by a chorus of usually five to nine young women sitting on chairs facing the rest of the group, accompanied by one or two on drums. Sometimes Anisah Huda would speak (a well-known female author was invited as visiting speaker for the opening of the women's library) and usually women in the group would be invited to speak about their involvement in the mosque program. Some of the women mentioned family problems in attending. Anisah Huda, while encouraging women's involvement in the program, also

---

6. This saying is popularly attributed to Muhammad, however, its status is described as "weak" (Auda, "Reflection") or "fabricated" (Syed, "52 Weak Ahadith").

suggested that doing one's duty at home was worship in its own right. And the time often concluded with cakes and lemonade served to the women.

Ramadan

During Ramadan the regular lecture themes were sometimes abandoned to focus on the theme of fasting. But the main addition to the program was the evening meetings for *tarawih* prayers, when both men and women came to the mosque for the prayers following the sunset break-fast. This was a couple of hours of *rakaʿ*[7] interspersed with readings from the Qur'an[8] and teaching from the sheikh. These prayers drew far more women than those who usually attended the program, with consequent increased variation in dress beyond the usual full-length overcoat and headscarf that characterized the regular participants—here I saw more use of the prayer over-skirt and head-torso shawl to cover tight-fitting trousers and over-shirts that were barely hip-length. The climax of the month was the Night of Vigil, when the mosque was packed with people, men below and women in the upper rooms, until 3:30 or 4:00 a.m. Ramadan is further discussed within chapter 7.

The Women Who Came

Most of the women I talked to who now attended classes at the mosque, or sent their daughters there to memorize the Qur'an and Islamic teaching, had not attended the mosque in their own childhood.[9] Those attending the program, from primary and secondary school girls attending group lessons given by the young women leaders on Islamic rules and conduct, to those in their sixties or above memorizing the Qur'an, were generally middle class, drawn from the local area. Tuesday morning lectures were for older women, often housewives who were free to come then, while the Thursday afternoon lectures focused more on university students and young graduates, with some overlap in attendance between the two groups. The lectures commonly attracted around between eighty and a hundred women. Younger women sat on the carpet in the center of the room to listen to the lecture, while those who were older preferred a place on one of the mattresses around the

---

7. The round of standing, bowing, kneeling, and prostrating with head to the ground, then rising again, the basic unit of *salah* prayer.

8. Following the division of the Qur'an into 30 sections, the Qur'an was read through completely in sections over the month of Ramadan in the evening *tarawih* prayers.

9. Also in Minesaki, "Gender Strategy," 399.

perimeter, where they could lean against the wall. A few elder women chose plastic chairs to sit in. It was harder for women who lived at a distance to attend regularly, given the challenges of public transport (usually one or more buses), and the need to negotiate household responsibilities and permission from the husband's family. But there were some, often ex-students of Anisah Huda, who made the effort to come when they could.

While proximity is an important consideration in choice of mosque, especially for women, it is not the only one. Many of the women mentioned how Anisah Huda's mode of teaching appealed to them. Other factors may include how effective the voice of the leader is in inducing emotional response (particularly in attending times of worship like the *tarawih* or *suhur* prayers).[10] The growing availability of women's meetings interacts with the range of religious perspectives taught that are accessible in any local area (or through family networks) to determine the scope of choice which shapes the direction of growth in women's religious awareness and daily practice. Geographic, family, and other factors help define the potential communities to which the women could belong, with their attendant understandings of women's roles and responsibilities.

The women attending the mosque are part of that community as well as of their own immediate families. Beyond concrete relationships of family and faith, workplace and education, they also see themselves as part of the wider community of Muslim women and of Islam; and the struggles of the wider community are personally felt.[11] Norton reminds us that identity is often "multiple and contradictory," the site of struggle. Identity deals with how a person understands and constructs her relationship to the world over time and space, and imagines possibilities for the future.[12] It is shaped by competing personal, social, and global narratives.[13] Chapter 5 takes us further into these dimensions of community and identity.

---

10. Similarly Mahmood finds that her participants assess a preacher "not only by her command of doctrinal knowledge, but also by the passional conditions of her rhetorical performance" (*Politics*, 86).

11. Afshar, *Feminisms*; Cooke, *Muslimwoman*; see also Kanno, *Imagined*, 241.

12. Norton, *Imagined*, 5, 10–11, 124–29; *Identity*.

13. Dale and Grant, *Women's*; White, *Narratives*, 73; Dale, *Women*, 38–48.

A Form of Faith:

Embodied Encounter

Encounter with God takes place in manifest form. We look to texts to describe or define faith, and the texts themselves are a material embodiment of the interaction between God's Word and world. The response of world to Word is tangible: faith takes shape and becomes real in historical time, geographical space, in a culturally specific context, doing particular activities—where people are, in their bodies. This is where the response to God's initiative (however it is perceived) becomes actual, concrete, real. One way of encountering (another) faith is to ask about the ideal context within that faith for the best response to God. What activities, and what sort of body, incorporate the ideal response to God?

According to Islam, God's initiative has happened supremely through the Qur'an and the life of Muhammad, Prophet of Islam. Within Islam, what is the appropriate response to this initiative? What activities take place at what time in what sort of space, in what body, to properly respond to, or worship, or submit to God? Chapter 6 discusses the role of Muhammad as exemplifying the ideal response and how right response is modeled by a local female leader.

Islam as gendered faith defines the space of my questions, so the locus of this research is the female body. The account of the female worshipper offers a different and necessary perspective into what has until recently been defined primarily in male terms. In communities of faith the female is usually the effective transmitter of faith to the next generation, as the keeper of domestic space, the nurturer, the one who can daily exemplify to children the response of worship and submission by observance of formal daily *salah*, right dress, and through guidance at times of rites of passage.

Anthropology has noted the relationship between the physical and corporate, or community, body. Societies treat the physical body as a map of the corporate body. Hierarchy in parts of the body and a concern for body margins, reflects ranking in divisions and the significance of boundaries in society.[14] The physical body is the site of interaction between individual, social and political body. Social borderlines are translated into anxiety over body perimeters. Bowie notes,

> the relationship between body symbolism, pollution beliefs, and the nature of a particular society. Concern over the body's

---

14. Douglas, *Natural Symbols,* 78; Van Wolputte, *Hang On*; Semerdjian, *Naked Anxiety.*

physical boundaries indicates anxiety over social boundaries.
... any group concerned to protect its ethnic/group identity is
likely to place limits on commensality with outsiders.[15]

In Islam this is reflected in the prohibition of marriage between Muslim women and non-Muslim men, and dietary restrictions which limit eating with non-Muslims. Where borders are emphasized, the world is viewed through binary categories: all people are either in a state of purity or impurity at any given time; for women, men consist of those by whom they may be freely seen (close family) and those with whom they must remain covered (all others); food and activities are either *halal* (permitted) or *haram* (prohibited). Religion is realized in the body, which both symbolizes and demarcates the state of the body social and politic.

Chapter 7 will explore how faith, or submission, is ideally located in the (female) body—in rules of purity and proper dress, in behavior, in boundaries of space and time, where the body is allowed to go, by whom it is allowed to be seen. In exploring faith response we also ask about preferred hours and places. How does faith interpret and divide time and space?

Time

> Time in Islam is holy. ... We are taught that you can't pray a given *salah* ten minutes before its time. So nine o'clock means nine, ten means ten, eleven eleven, and so on. (Anisah Huda)

Hours and Seasons

Muslim women face the challenge of integrating time across three dimensions: personal body cycles, the hours and lunar months of faith observance, and the twenty-four hour solar calendar that determines patterns of business and educational life.

---

15. Bowie, *Religion*, 65, 73; see Douglas, especially *Purity*, 122.

Marking the hours: a sundial on a mosque wall

The times of *salah* mark the daylight hours, stretching and contracting with the seasons, marking the passage of day with the *muʿadhdhan* call in Muslim countries.

Creation rather than clock defines times of *salah*. Anisah Huda described them:

> Dawn prayer (*al-fajr*)—begins when the sun begins to rise, about an hour and a half before the sun is risen, when the time of dawn prayer finishes.
>
> Midday prayer (*al-dhuhr*)—takes place at midday.
>
> Mid-afternoon prayer (*al-ʿasr*)—is about two and a half hours after midday prayers, when a shadow is about twice the length of the object,[16] and it lasts until sunset.
>
> Sunset prayer (*al-maghrib*)—extends from the going down of the sun, and lasts as long as there is still a red glow or red line in the sky.
>
> Evening prayer (*al-ʿashaʾ*)—is when the sun has completely gone.

A few women told me of rising for the early prayer and reading the Qurʾan in that quiet space before daily routines began. But these hours were not just for personal observance: the mosque program was based on diurnal rather than clock-determined rhythms, with the start of the Tuesday and

---

16. Saqib (*Guide*, 15–16) argues for the end of *dhuhr* prayer and start of *ʿasr* at the time when the shadow of everything is equal to itself, based on a *hadith* affirmed by Ahmad, Nasai, Tirmidhi, and Bukhari; also Mujahid, *Prayer,* 6.

Thursday lectures set according to the prayer times, shifting with the seasons. For ease of urban dwellers, poetic descriptions of nature have turned into electronic devices which can show *salah* times for different cities in the world, according to season. A board in the main body of the mosque showed the date, time, and prayer, which changed daily, in red electronic writing. On a mid-December (winter) day it recorded the times as:

- *al-fajr*: 4:56 a.m.
- *al-shuruq*: 6:30 a.m.[17]
- *al-dhuhr*: 11:31 a.m.
- *al-'asr*: 2:11 p.m.
- *al-maghrib*: 4:32 p.m.
- *al-'asha'*: 5:35 p.m.

There were preventive factors (such as menstruation or post-natal bleeding), and also ameliorating circumstances: for the person pressured by work or other obligations, the midday and mid-afternoon prayers could be combined, and similarly the sunset and evening prayers.[18] As well as the compulsory five times, the worshipper is offered two optional extra times: mid-morning (*salat al-duha*) and at night (*salat al-layl*). So the basic five times could be reduced to three or expanded to seven. Anisah Huda not infrequently referred in her lectures to staying up to pray at night (*qiyam al-layl*)[19] as a mark of devotion. But there are other special times in the daily round, from first dawn until sunrise, and before sunset. These times are particularly mentioned in the Qur'an as propitious times for prayers (such as Ghafir 40:55, Sad 38:18)—times at the blurring of the boundaries between day and night, when "intercessions are answered, a time of nearness to God" (Anisah Huda).

Islamic lunar months rotate through the seasons and solar calendar months. Special times in the Muslim year were marked by public holidays

---

17. *Al-shuruq* is not another prayer, but gives the time of sunrise, which ends the period for *al-fajr* prayer.

18. Saqib allows the combination of prayers for someone on a journey (which then requires the distance and duration to be specified which would make the combination valid) (*Guide*, 62, 63). However, some of our colleagues in time-pressured jobs combine prayers in this way. Philips also suggests this combination of prayers for a woman who has prolonged bleeding which prevents her praying, quoting a *hadith* from *Sunan Abud Dawud*, Book #1, Hadith #294 and authenticated in *Saheeh Sunan Abee Daawood*, Book #1, Hadith #281, and Hadith #282 (*Rules*, 41).

19. Or "*tahajjud*," performed during the midnight hours, up to *fajr* (Emerick, *Islam*, 138).

and extended family observance. The women were also encouraged to observe them within the mosque program. Each of the lunar-marked Islamic occasions carries its own activities (extra hours in the mosque for prayer and reading the Qur'an in Ramadan and before the *hajj*): its obligations (reciting the Qur'an each night during the *tarawih* prayers in Ramadan, with three portions the first night so they could complete the Qur'an by the 27th), and its opportunities (the Night of Vigil, *laylat al-qadr*, was especially effective in praying for others and seeking forgiveness for sins).

Special celebrations were held at the mosque for the women at *Eid al-Fitr*, *Eid al-Adhah* and the Islamic New Year. Other days celebrated in popular commercial culture were assessed according to their values. Mother's Day always caused some questions and was discussed each year as it approached. It fits aptly into the high place mothers have in Middle Eastern society,[20] but many questioned the widespread adoption of a Western non-Islamic custom. Anisah Huda assessed it on how Islamic the underlying values were: "Enter into joy, honor your mother ... these things are close to our religion." And the following year, "There are traditions that affect our religion. *Eid al-Hub* (Valentine's Day)—what's that to do with us? But *Eid al-Umm* (Mother's Day) is good." While mosque attendance in the women's program decreased during exam times,[21] it increased for the feasts. Ramadan attracted the greatest attendance and participation, as a time when people could bank up religious observance through the regular daily program and in the *tarawih* evening prayers. These women manage to interweave times of religious observance and faith response amid their home and professional responsibilities and the cycles of body life.

Geographic and Communal Space

Mecca is the center of Muslim prayer, the place that sets the orientation for everyone's direction of *salah*. Millions of Muslims converge in the *hajj*, the annual pilgrimage to Mecca (*Al-'Imran* 3:97), to carry out the prescribed rites. At this heart of time, space and activity are both exclusion and inclusion. Both men and women are included, participating almost equally in this ritual:[22] but non-Muslims are excluded, forbidden to enter Mecca.

---

20. See chapter 6, Women's Vocation.

21. Anisah Huda commented at a lecture during exam time, "some people haven't come because they are facing exams—it's their right to not come, but we won't stop the program." It affected not only students and teachers, but also mothers, responsible to ensure their children studied well and succeeded.

22. A woman may not have her face or hands covered on *hajj*, even if she normally

Anisah Huda saw it as a sign of both unity and universality: "There are no geographical limits or nationality—Mecca is for everyone."

Syria was traditionally a major place for pilgrims setting out on the *hajj*.[23] However, since the numbers have increased so much with ease and affordability of travel, so that each country is now subject to a quota of how many it is allowed to send, it is harder for those under sixty years of age and without connections to gain a place. A few of the women had made the pilgrimage: some more had done the *'umrah* (lesser pilgrimage).[24]

The direction of Mecca gives spatial order to the Garden Mosque, as women line up in rows for *salah*, and mark the space with handbag or miniature prayer mat. But unlike Mecca, here worship space is gendered; women and men meet in their different sections. The women here have joined many others in this country and around the world in making space for themselves in the mosque.[25] Anisah Huda describes the entry of women into this space:

> When we came into the mosque, there were no rooms [for women], we worked together and did these rooms and extended the space. We are responsible, having created and opened the place, for opening and closing the rooms and for whom we open and shut them to. . . . We hope to always use the same rooms which the women are using. The place the women use, when the mosque doesn't have enough room and there's the pressure of Friday *salah*, they [men] use the whole mosque for all those attending and they use this place. . . . For the rest of the days it's all for women; this part is specially for women.

Undoubtedly Anisah Huda's relationship to the Imam of the mosque facilitated the women's access to space. The women's own donations had funded room furnishings and program activities (collections were taken among the women in the mosque towards projects like a carpet, an

---

does in her own country. The menstruating woman is still allowed to participate in the *hajj*, "with the exception of the formal prayers and the rite of walking around the *ka'abah* seven times" (Philips, *Menstruation*, 18).

23. See Idlibi's lyrical description of the annual caravan departure for Mecca in *Grandfather's Tale*, 13–15.

24. Pilgrimage to Mecca which can be performed at any time of the year, and involves fewer ceremonies than the *hajj*.

25. Jamila Hussein (*Subversive*) has written about restricted availability of women's space in Australian mosques: and Spielhaus discusses it in the context of mosques in Germany (*Female*, 446). American activist Asra Nomani derives her struggle for men and women to share prayer space in North American mosques from her experience of standing at the *ka'abah* in Mecca with her family, with no gender segregation (Hammer, *Activism*, 470).

air-conditioner, prizes for girls in the program, or for setting up an income-generating project with the revenue to go to the mosque); and, most notably, the women's library in the mosque, in a way that is reminiscent of Jaschok and Shui's description of the development of places for women in mosques in China.[26] However, for Friday prayers the women ceded their space to the men.

Wider Influences

Traditional cultural understandings of the place and role of women are also part of the context within which women must negotiate their mosque attendance and faith observance. Syrian society is a multi-faceted amalgam of different socio-economic, ethnic, and faith communities.[27] Even in this middle-class urban Sunni community, the women had to manage mosque attendance around social beliefs that women's worship and duties were primarily located in the home, and that women should seek agreement from their husbands before they go out. Kalmbach suggests that leaders like Anisah Huda are able to maximize their authority by keeping within the conservative boundaries of socially accepted behavior and teaching about women.[28]

Muhammad al-Habash, Anisah Huda's brother, as an internationally known Sunni scholar, Imam of the mosque, and also government MP for some years, had a position of significant influence. However, like other mosques, the Garden Mosque also had to negotiate its place within the uneasy relationship between the ruling party and more mainstream and popular movements within Islam. Restrictive regimes had dominated countries in the region, supported by the repressive apparatus of secret police and internal security. While it was never openly discussed, many people had experience of a family member who had been (or was still) imprisoned and tortured for some form of opposition or criticism of the ruling oligarchy. This affected people's openness with others beyond known family circles.

In such a context, internal opposition that was forbidden in the political context could only find expression within Islam (which notionally gives legitimacy to the rulers). Even though Syria has been led by a declared secular group (the Baath party), the President is constitutionally required to be a Muslim,[29] and the government needed the support of an alliance with

26. Jaschok, *Women's Mosques*, 154.
27. Shaaban, *Contradictions*, 102.
28. Kalmbach, *Change*.
29. Article 3:1, Constitution of Syria. Alawites have traditionally been regarded by

the majority Sunni population. This had led to an edgy dance of restriction and appeasement between the government and conservative Islamic groups. Aside from religious debate about women's place and presence, both family and country-wide politics can curb women's entry to mosque space.

The women were aware of the portrayal of Muslim women as "other" (terrorists, oppressed, backwards) in some Western discourses, and sought ways to challenge it. Anisah Huda exhorted the women, if they read an attack on Islam on the internet, to respond to it. Anisah Huda herself set up an internet site for Muslim youths to interact with Westerners: but later she told me that the government had closed it down, claiming that it included Jews among its participants. And Anisah Huda's choice of "women" and "violence within Islam" as themes to teach expatriates demonstrates how global discourses shape discussion and response within Muslim countries and communities.

Regional and global trends contributing to the social awareness of women in non-domestic, or public space,[30] linked with the worldwide growth in popular media and in women's education, have facilitated the movement of women into mosque space. The rise of women's movements, even on a secular basis, have contributed to a redefining of the place of women within Islam, in what Ahmed describes as "the emergence of women themselves as a central subject for national debate."[31] Women's attendance in mosques constitutes a spatial challenge to the traditional view of women within the home. However, it does not do so on the basis of secular feminist understandings of women's rights, but rather is legitimated from within Islamic history and religious texts (while building on contemporary global discourses of women in public space). Existing gatherings of women, which usually occurred along family lines but with a religious focus (such as Sufi *dhikr*s or Qur'anic recitations), have been extended through links of neighborhoods and friendships, to being located within women's teaching movements and within a shift from homes into mosques. This in turn reinforces women's awareness of being part of a wider movement.

Sunnis as *kuffar* (disbelievers) and even by Twelver Shi'ites as *gulat* "exceeding" all bounds in their deification of Ali. However, in 1973 Musa al-Sadr, Lebanese chair of the Supreme Islamic Shi'ite Council (SISC), issued a *fatwa* that the Alawites were indeed Muslims, giving them a place within Twelver Shi'ism and securing Hafez al-Asad's legitimation as president (Kramer, *Syria's*; Seale, *Asad*, 173).

30. See Thompson's (*Public*) discussion of gender boundaries in the Middle East and the use of the terms "public" and "private" space.

31. Ahmed, *Women and Gender,* 128.

Conclusion

This chapter has taken us into the mosque and the women's program. Females of a range of ages participated each week in a variety of activities, including lectures, classes on reciting the Qur'an, *dhikr*, and teaching on aspects of *fiqh* and the practice of Islam in daily life. A discussion of the body as the site of experience and expression of Islam led into a brief exploration of how religion marks the inhabitation of space and time for these women. Body rhythms interact with daily and annual markers of religion, cycling through seasons and solar time. Space is shaped by religion and also gendered access to place. This women's mosque program finds its place within wider cultural, national, and international trends.

The next chapter looks at the mosque program as an alternate community of allegiance for the women who attend it.

5

Alternate Community

> It doesn't take too much time to telephone to ask after [other women in the mosque program]—it's a responsibility of love to the other. We're frightened if someone asks for our phone number, that they'll give it to the secret police—but it's just to ask after them. We love the mosque, the sisters of the mosque. ... If some days I've got a difficult situation, [they are] sisters in God. On the resurrection day, who will know you or testify to you more than sisters, spouse, parents? [It will be] the women who say that you asked after them. (Anisah Huda to the women in the mosque.)

THE PREVIOUS CHAPTER INTRODUCED us to the women and the women's program in the mosque. In this chapter I discuss the mosque sorority as an alternate network to the women's original primary community of family and kin. The imagined community of Muslim women within the Muslim *ummah* worldwide finds concrete realization in the local mosque group. Activities and teaching within the mosque shape ways of gathering and public dress, and address the intimate details of the women's worlds. The tensions elicited by competing loyalties are regularly discussed by the women, while the meeting of different communities becomes a place to practice *daʿwa*.

Communities of Kinship

Arab researchers testify to the compelling power of community norms in setting behavior, as they seek to reconcile ethnographic principles with doing research in their own communities. Altorki found her involvement required, "observing all the taboos and attending to all the obligations my culture prescribed for me." For Joseph, allegiance to a specific ethnic religious family group was required. She was "expected to act categorically. Other behavior was suspect," and she noted "the ways in which people enjoyed and felt comforted by prescriptive identities."[1]

Women in the Middle East are intricately embedded in family relations and family networks. Family, rather than the individual, is defined as the most basic unit of society, and family claims have primacy over separate members. Joseph suggests a definition of the self in Arab societies as characterized by relationship or connectivity[2] (rather than as individualist or corporatist, terms which can be value-laden). She describes "persons in Arab societies as embedded in relational matrices that shape their sense of self but do not deny them their distinctive initiative and agency." Middle Eastern society is also animated by patriarchy, which allocates power along lines of gender and age, so that women and men are differentially affected by patriarchal connections. Joseph suggests that this "patriarchal organization of familial culture meant the privileging of the assertions of desire by males and elders and a sense of responsibility by females and juniors to assimilate and act upon the assertions of desire by males and elders," so that "excavating and acting upon the desires of others was disproportionately female labor."[3]

Women have commonly had their principal social interaction with women in their extended family, or the family into which they married. Abudi comments that "marriage marks a girl's transfer from the authority of her father to that of her husband." At times women at the mosque made reference to traditional norms. Anisah Huda told the women, "There have been times when women haven't been educated, only left the house three times in their lives: from her mother's womb to her parent's house, from her parents' house to her husband's house, from her husband's house to the grave." Meltzer and Nix record teenage girls from Anisah Huda's mosque classes quoting the same saying, and on another occasion talking of their desire for a husband from whom they didn't have to ask permission every time they wanted to leave the house. However, as Joseph notes, not just gender but also seniority confers authority. In adult literacy classes in Egypt, I found that the influence of mothers- and sisters-in-law was often a more

---

1. Altorki, *Arab*, 56; Joseph, *Feminization*, 30.

2. "Connectivity as a notion of self in which a person's boundaries are relatively fluid so that persons feel they are a part of significant others. Connective persons do not experience boundary, autonomy, separateness, as their primary defining features. Rather, they focus on relatedness. Maturity is signified in part by the successful enactment of a myriad of relationships" (Joseph, *Gender*, 16–17, 24, 117; *Desire*, xxvii. See also Kraus, *Women*, 30, on tribal allegiance).

3. Joseph, *Relationships*, 11–12; *Gender*, 17; *Desire*.

significant determiner of whether a woman could attend literacy classes or not, than her husband's expectations or her own motivation.[4] Kraus describes the major role played by some women, mothers or grandmothers of the ruling sheikhs, in running tribal affairs in the Emirates. Women and men in the extended family, rather than peers or other groupings, have been the principal influence on a woman's choices about dress, behavior, and activities.[5]

Family and domestic space has also traditionally provided the major context for women within which religious activities take place.[6] So the women in a household may pause their activities to perform *salah* together, or meet together in a home as women of the extended family to seal/recite the Qur'an. External attendance at mosques (particularly for the *tarawih* night prayers during Ramadan) or in homes for Sufi *dhikr*s has also been along family or neighborhood lines. (Family and neighborhood were traditionally coterminous before work or housing requirements gave rise to the migration of nuclear families into new areas. It is still common today for extended family members to live in the same apartment building or district.)

Home is seen as the primary domain for women's roles. While some voices within the Islamist movement argue against women working outside the home,[7] economic pressures and changing attitudes have made it more commonplace. Anisah Huda does not oppose women working in non-domestic space, whether in her teaching or in her own example as a busy *daʿiya*, and many of the leaders in her progamme are university graduates

---

4. "A woman's life cycle in the patrilocally extended family is such that the deprivation and hardship she may experience as a young bride are eventually superseded by the control and authority she will have over her own daughters-in-law. The powerful post-menopausal matriarch is thus the other side of the coin of this form of patriarchy" (Abudi, *Mothers*, 44 citing Kandiyoti, *Islam*, 32).

The *hadith* of ʿAisha quoted in Schleifer neatly defines the power gradient: "'Narrated ʿA'ishah: The person who has the greatest right over the woman is her husband, and the person who has the greatest right over the man is his mother.' (Al-Hakim in *al-Mustadrak*; Al-Bazar)" (*Motherhood*, 85–86).

5. Abudi, *Mothers*, 23; Meltzer and Nix, *Light*; Krause, *Women*, 30.

6. An exception to this is women visiting shrines to seek supernatural help or to make vows.

7. *Al-Ahzab* 33:33 "Remain in your houses," is quoted as well as the hadith: Narrated ʿAbdullah bin ʿUmar: The Prophet said, "Everyone of you is a guardian and everyone of you is responsible [for his wards]. A ruler is a guardian and is responsible [for his subjects]; a man is a guardian of his family and responsible [for them]; a wife is a guardian of her husband's house and she is responsible [for it], a slave is a guardian of his master's property and is responsible [for that]. Beware! All of you are guardians and are responsible [for your wards]." (Book #62, Hadith #116). Also: "Take care of the home. That is your jihad," ascribed to Musnad Ahmad (Abudi, *Mothers*, 52; Baig, "Home").

and teachers. However, all are agreed that it cannot be at the expense of woman's primary role in the home and sphere of family.[8]

Imagined Communities

Benedict Anderson introduced his concept of the nation as an "imagined community," in alignment with the preceding systems of religious community and dynastic realm. However, where the dividing lines between nations have been relatively recently defined (often crossing lines of creed and ethnicity), then extended kin and ethnic fealties have continued to supersede national loyalties. Joseph describes how "kin groups create imagined communities upheld by the power of 'nature,'—usually sanctified by the authority of God." In Lebanon, analogous to Syria and other countries in the region, "the kin group has been seen as the primary identity and loyalty for any Lebanese—superseding national identity and loyalty to the state and competing only with religion."[9] The resurgence in religious (Islamist) identity in the region can be linked to the failed promises of nationalism, particularly following Egypt's defeat in the 1967 Arab-Israeli war.[10]

Anderson's defining characteristics of the imagined community suggest how links of faith rather than kin (or nation) are functioning as imagined community within the women's program in the mosque in invoking the allegiance of its adherents. He describes it as:

> *imagined* because the members of even the smallest (nation) will never know most of their fellow-members, meet them, or even hear of them, yet in the minds of each lives the image of their communion.

> *limited* because even the largest of them . . . has finite, if elastic, boundaries, beyond which lie other (nations).

and

> *community* because, regardless of the actual inequality and exploitation that may prevail in each, the nation is always

---

8. Metzer and Nix, *Light*; see also Schleifer, *Motherhood*, 58, 63; Shoup, *Customs*, 125, 134.

9. Joseph, *Gender*, 108–9, 117.

10. The events of and following the Arab Spring may be read as these three concepts of community in conflict: the Arab Spring revolts born out of resurgent desires for equity within the nation, and subsequent struggles for power that often re-fall along extended kinship-tribe and/or religious borders of allegiance (Ahmed, *Women and Gender*, 216; Bunton, *Arab*, 19).

conceived as a deep, horizontal comradeship. Ultimately it is this fraternity that makes it possible, over the past two centuries, for so many millions of people, not so much to kill as willingly to die for such limited imaginings.[11]

Anderson looks back to the effect of vernacular printing presses at the time of the Reformation and nation-conflicts of the 1600s, when print languages "created unified fields of exchange and communication" between people who may have been divided by dialect differences. As they became more able to comprehend one another "via print and paper . . . they gradually became aware of the hundreds of thousands, even millions of people in their particular language-field, and at the same time that *only those* hundreds of thousands, or millions, so belonged."[12] In the last decades, the Islamist revival has similarly grown out of, and given further impetus to, the exponential growth of affordable print, audiovisual, electronic, and satellite media. Kanno and Norton, in their article on imagined community and educational possibilities, note that "technological advances in the last two decades have had a significant impact on what is possible to imagine." Muslim women have benefited from growing access to education and multimedia, and Islam becomes an increasingly important identity marker for many Muslims.[13]

The women in the mosque were both aware of, and consumers of, local TV and international satellite channels that promoted Islam and particular forms of Muslim identity. One woman, showing me an Islamic book on women that she was reading, told me that the author was a sheikh who taught at the local *shari'ah* college, and the day and time of his program on Syrian TV. Some of the young women talked to me enthusiastically about 'Amr Khalid[14] and the influence of his teaching on them. A teacher in a

---

11. Anderson suggests a fourth characteristic, "sovereign," because the concept of nation was born at the time of the delegitimization of "the divinely-ordained, hierarchical dynastic realm." It can be argued that this dimension corresponds to the sense in the faith community of being divinely ordained and destined (*Imagined*, 6–7).

Asad challenges a simple identification of the Muslim *ummah* as imagined community, because "it is neither limited nor sovereign, for unlike Arab nationalism's notion of *al-umma al-'arabiyya*, it can and eventually should embrace all of humanity" (*Formations*, 197–98). Independent of views about the eschatological determinism of Islam, this research suggests that the concept of the Muslim community does function in terms of Anderson's imagined community for the women in the mosque program. See also Anisah Huda's comparison between *hijab* and a national flag (chapter 7, "Clothes and Covering").

12. Anderson, *Imagined*, 44.

13. Kanno, *Imagined*, 246; Bayat, *Neoliberal*, 10, 19.

14. Popular Egyptian preacher. The *New York Times* magazine described him in 2006

tajwid class I attended told me of a program on the *Al-Fajr* satellite station that explained the principles of *tajwid* in English; and another woman could enumerate different international Muslim teachers and the satellite channels and times I would be able to listen to them. Anisah Huda, in a lecture listed satellite channel progammes, with their content, days, and times, that she recommended for the women. The women's consumption of media shaped their sense of belonging to an international community defined by pious Islam.

Kraus describes how "the cognitization of the Other among the Islamic based associations in the UAE (United Arab Emirates) is rooted in the discursive tradition of *dar al harb* and *dar al Islam,* in which the enemy embodied *dar al harb* and the 'Islamic world' *dar al Islam.*"[15] For the women in the mosque program, reports of conflict in the media sharply formed their awareness both of the wider community of Muslim sisters and of those outside it. The *du'a* prayers concluding the *dhikr* preceding the lecture usually included prayer for Muslims or "our Muslim sisters" in countries in the region that were experiencing strife, such as Palestine, Iraq, or in the wider world. Anisah Huda's *du'a'* and lectures often referred to the need for wider Muslim unity,[16] and sectarian and geopolitical division was ascribed to foreign influence. She told the women:

> Foreign occupation has caused problems. In Iraq, what brought the problems and divisions? Occupation. Before that they didn't have divisions—Shi'ite and Sunni lived and married together. Who sowed the divisions between the Shi'ite and Sunni? It was all one country. Previously it was all the regions of Syria—now it is Jordan, Syria, Lebanon, the different emirates, Kuwait, and Lebanon—[these are] the lines of occupation.

When some Western countries withdrew support for the Hamas administration in Gaza following its election,[17] Anisah Huda and another female lecturer at the mosque encouraged women to donate to the Palestinian people. Troubles in Afghanistan and the bombing of a school in Pakistan were linked with US influence. And the atmosphere in an Islamic New Year

---

(April 30) as "the world's most famous and influential Muslim television preacher," and the *Times* Magazine 2007 and *Prospect Magazine* rated him respectively as thirteenth in the world's hundred most influential people, and sixth most influential intellectual.

15. Krause, *Women*, 113.

16. This was usually engendered by media reports of Muslims bombing mosques or communities of other Muslim sects, such as in the Sunni–Shi'ite conflict in Iraq.

17. Funding continued for the Palestinian Authority in the West Bank.

celebration at the mosque was somberly shaped by outrage at media reports of the reprinting of the Danish cartoons of Muhammad.

Grid–Group and Communal Response

The particular expression of imagined community is formed by connectivity and hierarchy in this cultural context. The Danish cartoons of religious figures, notably including Muhammad, Prophet of Islam, provoked anger around the Muslim world. Muslims talked about Islam being oppressed and attacked. Mockery of the Prophet of Islam was seen as a direct assault on their faith, their very identity as Muslims. Their feelings of disgust and horror, of having something precious to them desecrated, almost of being violated, were real and strong.[18] At the time of the cartoons, in different places, Muslims demonstrated, rioted, and burned flags, embassies (Syria), churches, and even people (Nigeria). However, the reactions were not uniform.

The meeting at the Garden Mosque in February 2006 was the usual weekly meeting, but they had planned to make this one a celebration of the Muslim New Year. The place became increasingly crowded as more and more women poured in, and instead of the usual festive mood at celebrations, the atmosphere was somber. There was an hour of songs of praise to God and about Muhammad, and then Anisah Huda got up to talk. She spoke of how we are living now amongst enemies of Islam and of the Prophet of Islam, and people who are enemies of all religions, of truth and history. But then she went on to look inwards, in painful self-examination, as she described the ways in which their own community and culture were failing to live up to the ideals of Islam. Yes, they were under pressure from the West. However, these attacks should make them examine themselves stringently in order to live in a way that was more according to the precepts of their faith; and so be able to stand against the pressure.

Others reacted more directly against the source of the cartoons, against both the author and the country that had permitted it. I talked about it with my neighbor, with whom I had spent many hours drinking countless cups of Arab coffee, sharing laughter or tears with her, as we discussed family, neighborhood, and wider concerns. My normally warm, generous-minded friend swore that if the author of the cartoons was in front of her, she would take pleasure in killing him personally. This defamation of the Prophet of Islam was like a direct attack on God who had sent him, and it was up to any

---

18. There was a further similar response to the 14-minute video clip "The Real Life of Muhammad" which was uploaded onto YouTube in 2012.

right-minded person to take action against such an affront, both for the sake of the honor of the Prophet of Islam, God, and the community, and to stop it happening again. It even threatened to open up a rift in our friendship. My sympathy for their hurt wasn't a proper response—I should be concerned for the dishonor done to God and to his messengers.

People in Western countries in turn reacted to what they saw as an irrational response, an aggressive attack on free speech. In some Western countries the cartoons were reprinted in newspapers or even on t-shirts (thereby further escalating the furor). Poking fun at religious figures is acceptable, almost required, in secular parts of Western society, as part of "the tradition of satiric self-examination and irreverence." It was viewed as "only a cartoon." Only a few people suggested any awareness of the depth of hurt and violation felt by many Muslims over the cartoons. And many Muslims in turn believed that the proclaimed defense of "free speech" just masked another attack on their faith and their world.[19] Some months later Anisah Huda told the women attending her lecture,

> People wrote about the Prophet. Muslims cried, shrieked, wept—and they [non-Muslims]] broadcast it more. Human rights—don't Muslims have the right to respect for their Prophet and their religion? I'm sorry that some Muslims talk about democracy, human rights. Millions are upset, wept, have been affected. Despite all that, where is Islam's rights?

Grid and Group

For this debate, seen predominantly in communal terms by Muslims and non-Muslims across the world, Grid–Group cultural theory, in elucidating the variety of responses to publication of the cartoons, also offers a perspective on the way in which imagined community was functioning within the mosque program. Grid–Group theory describes patterns of belief, ritual and moral control across societies. The position of a group or society is predictive of how they understand God, community, and self. The Grid–Group analysis helps anticipate the strength and different nature of the responses, the different rationalities behind them.

Grid–Group theory emerges from Douglas's suggestion of two intersecting axes or pivots[20] "as tools for describing in a more controllable

---

19. Marlette, *Cartoon*; Miller, *Respect*, 37; Hasan, *Realizing*, 36–37.

20. Douglas draws on Bernstein's analysis of the transformative effect of speech systems on individuals as the basis for her cultural framework (Douglas, *Purity,* 21–38, 90).

fashion the way that social pressures reach an individual and structure his [sic] consciousness." The vertical axis, designated "Grid," indicates the extent to which a person's identity is defined by their position or role in life. A strong grid society is characterized by a wide range of roles and rules, and by shared values across the society. The horizontal axis, labeled "Group," indicates how much a person's behavior is determined by group pressure. A strong group society requires a higher degree of conformity. Religion may be used to regulate what people do. Identity is determined by group belonging (whether through birth or initiation) and adherence to the group's rules. A society that is a weak group is more individualistic: membership of groups may be voluntary and membership does not affect a person's identity. Social groups can then be positioned within four quadrants derived from the intersection of the two axes. This analysis makes reference to two of the four quadrants: High Grid and High Group, and Low Grid and Low Group. Appendix 1 offers further elucidation of Grid–Group theory, including the other quadrants.

Societies that are High Grid and High Group are hierarchical in nature. In these societies, there are strong boundaries. The group is more important than the individual. There are set rituals and ways of relating to God and each other. For people who live in these societies the universe is just: moral and punishing. Moral failings are equally sin against God and the community. Ritual activity often involves prayer, fasting, sacrifice to the deity. There is a routine piety towards authority and its symbols, which are seen as efficacious in themselves.

For Muslims from hierarchical societies—strong grid and group—an attack on a symbol is an attack on what it represents, on the reality behind it. My neighbor lived in a very traditional area, where her husband's extended family met all together every week, where kinship allegiance retained priority. There was strong control by the group and commonly accepted ways of relating to its members, from the patriarch of the family to the newest comers. In this cultural context a cartoon attacking the Prophet of Islam is an effective attack on God who sent him and on the community which follows him, and should be met with punishment for wrongdoing.[21]

---

21. See also Turner's description of how in the past "the body of the king has often been regarded as the symbol or metaphor of sovereignty, so that an attack upon the king's body was equivalent to a violent assault on the society as a whole" (*Body*, 18).

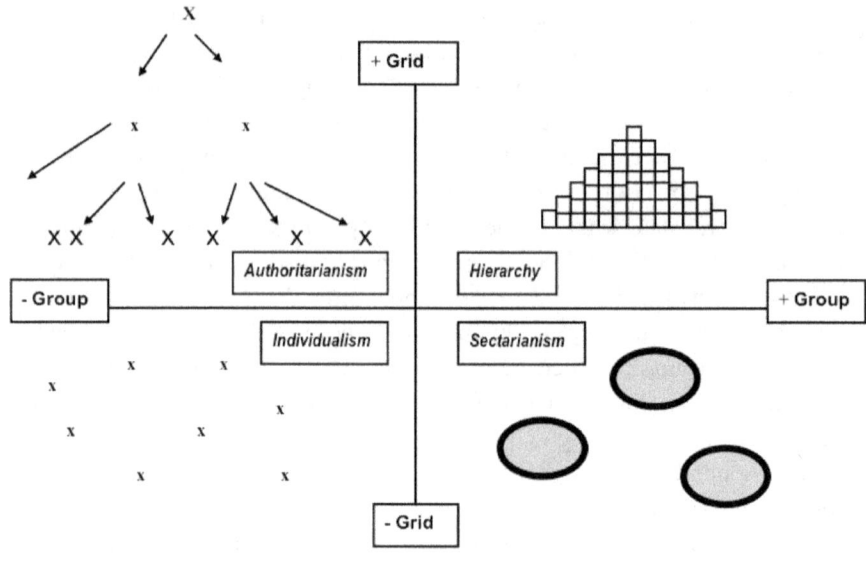

Figure 1

Diagonally opposite the hierarchical quadrant are the Low Grid and Low Group societies, where self is more important than the community. There is more sense of self-discovery and escape from others, along with less regard for rituals. Symbols only have expressive value. Religions are not moral regulators and there is less emphasis on a system of reward or punishment in this world or the next. Western societies are generally in the lower left quadrant, individualistic, low grid and group. With little regard for ritual and external symbols, the meaning is given priority over the form. The emphasis is on the internal, on self rather than others, and there is little stress on systems of reward and punishment in this world or the next. Matters of religion have generally been relegated to the private realm of inner experience. So external religious or other forms carry less value, and can consequently be attacked or denigrated with relatively little reaction or angst on the part of the faith adherent. The individual is responsible for her or his own opinions and actions and carries the consequences for them alone.[22]

    22. Other examples show the same pattern of responses. The response of Western Protestant Christians to Andres Serrano's controversial 1989 artwork "Piss Christ" (a photograph of a crucifix submerged in urine) was fairly muted: yes, it was offensive, but every individual has a right to their own belief, and it was "only" an external symbol, not the reality. However, Middle Eastern Coptic Orthodox Christians who came to the West from more traditional and hierarchical societies (and remained within the same church context) were deeply mortified at this desecration of their faith. They had come

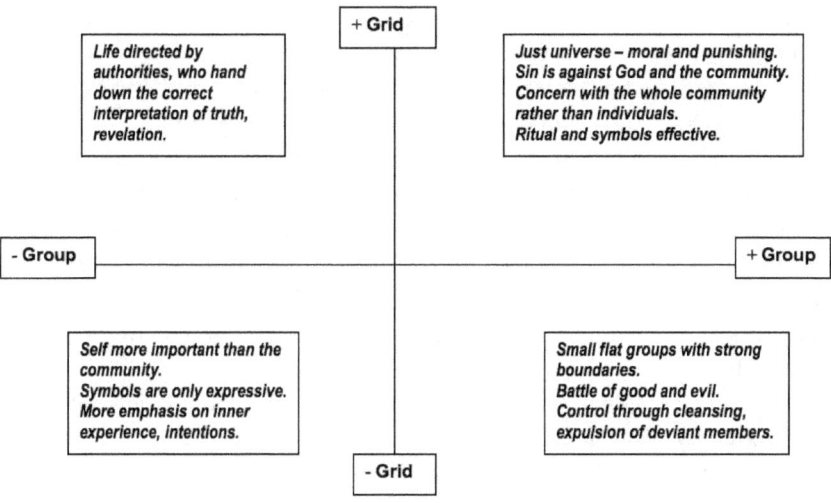

Figure 2

Anisah Huda, leader of the women's program in the mosque was from a more upper-class, educated and internationally connected family. She experienced less pressure to conform to the group, and with others in her family was able to accept and promote some new interpretations of traditional texts. There was also more emphasis on internal meaning to the symbolic forms (correlating with an underlying Sufi influence in the mosque). While still in a hierarchical society, she was positioned lower in both grid and group than my neighbor's family. Anisah Huda's response of anger at the cartoons also included an internal dimension, seeking a solution through turning inward, and examination of self and the community. Others from traditional hierarchical social positioning of high grid and group, where wrongdoing, or offence against God and community is perceived to incur automatic penalty, felt strongly in agreement with the sentiments of my neighbor: "No matter what such leaders say, the Muslim people will not keep silent" (in the face of this insult). The community is viewed as prior to, and responsible for, the individual. So the Danish government was seen as

---

to the West in search of religious freedom, only to encounter an image more offensive than anything they could have imagined. Similarly in Britain some years ago, caricatured puppet presentations of Christ provoked demonstrations. There was little reaction from Western British Christians. But Muslims living in Britain, who still existed within traditional hierarchical family networks, reacted angrily at what they saw as the unacceptable mocking of a prophet of God, and therefore of all who honored him.

directly responsible for the cartoons and for punishing their author. Posters encouraging a boycott of Scandinavian products remained displayed and renewed for several months after the cartoon furor.

In the initial responses from the West to all the ferment over the cartoons, the Vatican was one of the only voices suggesting that free speech should be limited by respect for others' faith. One of the few Western organizations still characterized by hierarchy, and the importance of symbol and rituals, it shares a similar social space to many of the Muslims protesting against the cartoons. Notably, Jewish writers also were fairly united in condemning the cartoons, out of their awareness that attacks on the symbols of a religious or ethnic group can easily become attacks on members of the group itself.

As societies change, at times of unrest and rapid social shift and less commonality of values, there is a move to more internalization of faith. Where life and society are stable and control established, there is more agreement on moral values, more adherence to the external forms of faith. One position is not necessarily more spiritually or socially advanced than another. So Douglas comments on the trend to a more interior, less ritualistic understanding of faith: "What is taken to be a more advanced, enlightened doctrine appears merely as the usual expression of a less differentiated experience of social relations."[23] Grid–Group cultural theory as an analytic tool can help us to predict the responses of a group, to anticipate and make sense of people's different responses, both our own and others. However, people do not occupy absolute positions; their responses are relative to one another. We can also expect that people of different faiths, for example Muslims and Christians, who share the same sociocultural space, will also share conceptual space about the place of ritual and symbols, interiority and exteriority, in faith practice.[24]

Exteriority and interiority are a measure of Grid. The dimension of Group invokes discussions of the role of community in determining behavior, both in defining the ideal, and in constraining behavior. In the context of this axis, Joseph is among writers who argue against the normalizing of the "bounded, autonomous, and separate self" (low Group), and for recognition of more relational (high Group) concepts of selfhood, for "notions of

---

23. Douglas, *Purity*, 113.

24. Lindgren notes: "However, these similarities do not necessarily mean that Muslims' and Christians' prayer experiences are identical, because the experiences are affected by, among other things, differences in the semantic field of the religious words and the context of the sacred narratives. Thus, the way the narratives about Muslim prayer experiences are structured might hold true for Christians' narratives as well, but the narratives become distinctly 'Islamic' in their intertextuality" (*Muslim Prayer*, 170).

maturity that valorize rather than pathologize the embeddedness of self and other, . . . selves in which embeddedness still encompasses agency."[25]

People in high-Group or collectivist societies, "from birth on are integrated into strong, cohesive in-groups, which through people's lifetimes continue to protect them in exchange for unquestioning loyalty." The interests of the group are typically given precedence over the interests of the individual. Decisions and actions are cooperative. Values that maintain group harmony, such as filial piety and patriotism, are more highly esteemed. In a society where the individual looks to the interests of the group, a focus on autonomy and individualism appears deviant and detrimental. The group shares responsibility with the individual for moral behavior.[26] Allegiance to faith rather than family does not necessarily signify a desire for individualism or low Group: rather it suggests a change in the community of primary loyalty and determination.[27] The community of allegiance defines the potentiality of the subject, in terms of identity and moral behavior. For the women attending the mosque, they were moving beyond a collective identity defined purely in terms of family, to the mosque community.

Challenging a focus on self-realization and emancipation, Mahmood asks:

> How might the notion of freedom be recast in such a context where the distinction between a subject's true desires and social conventions cannot be so easily assumed, where submission to certain forms of [external] authority is a condition for a subject achieving its potentiality?[28]

Thus Mahmood argues for "uncoupling the notion of self-realization from that of the autonomous will." In a high-Grid and Group (hierarchical) society, "self-realization" may come from fitting one's appropriate place in the hierarchy.[29]

25. Joseph, *Relationships*, 2.

26. Hofstede, *Cultures*, 76, 80–89; Malina, *New Testament*, 58–59; Mallouhi, *Miniskirts*, 133; see also Mahmood, *Feminist*.

27. Neither does the shift in primary allegiance from family to faith in itself signify a less intense or even less violent response—see Bano's (*Leadership*) analysis of the dramatic events around the Red Mosque in Islamabad in 2007. For Anisah Huda, family and sociocultural configuration and the process of changing allegiances or values combined to place her in a different social place to my neighbor.

28. Mahmood, *Rehearsed*, 845.

29. Mahmood, *Feminist*. Douglas comments that, "the relation of self to society varies with the constraints of grid and group: the stronger these are, the more developed the idea of formal transgression and its dangerous consequences, and the less regard is felt for the right of the inner self to be freely expressed. The more that social relations

The women's perception that the wider community of Islam was under attack deepened their sense of allegiance to and identity with it. Anisah Huda urged the women to make use of media such as CDs and the internet themselves and to learn other languages, to be able to respond to accusations against Islam, and answer those who "want to undermine Islam by any way and study day and night to find points of weakness."

The mosque community felt the effect of local as well as international pressure, where allegiance to the mosque was pitted against government policy. Regional politics and restrictive state security apparatus offered little place for opposing political parties, with the consequence that mosque networks were one of the few spaces where opposition to the regime could occur.[30] This seems to have been the reason that the government curtailed mosque opening hours for a month or so, and some of the entrance gates were locked. Anisah Huda warned the women in the lectures about the changed times of access.[31]

Membership of the Wider Community

Visiting Muslims from other countries also amplified the local women's sense of wider imagined community. As I arrived one day, three buses had pulled up to collect men and women of Asian appearance who were leaving the mosque. On another occasion a visiting Chinese Muslim woman told the women in the mosque program of her search to read the Qur'an and understand it in Arabic, a search which had taken her first to Pakistan and Turkey; and then her joy at being able to join with women studying the Qur'an in Arabic in Syrian mosques. Anisah Huda exhorted the women of their need to know about "our sisters in China or other places.... Where is the *ummah*, one body? How can the body live if it's not feeling [for all the parts]?" Anisah Huda herself travelled regularly to the Emirates to teach Muslim women there. At times this crossed confessional (Sunni–Shi'ite) boundaries. Anisah Huda's house included items linked to Iran as well as the Emirates: an Iranian magazine (*Mahjubah*) was distributed at the mosque,

---

are differentiated by grid and group, the more the private individual is exhorted to pour his passions into prescribed channels or to control them altogether" (*Purity*, 113).

30. Flint quotes authorities as varied as Al-Qadarawi and Erdogan to suggest that there has always been a close connection between mosques and *jihad* (Flint, *Church*, 659).

31. When I visited Anisah Huda in 2010, she told me that the government had forbidden foreigners (both Muslims and non-Muslims) to visit local mosques. This may have been a temporary edict, like restricting mosque hours. Anisah Huda and Ebtisam surmised that it was perhaps to restrict wider Islamic links beyond national boundaries.

and the women were invited to attend events at the nearby Iranian cultural center.

The Muslim *ummah* was also defined in relation to other monotheistic faiths. At times Anisah Huda contrasted Islam with her perception of Christianity in order to show the former as superior, for example suggesting the veracity and historicity of the Qur'an versus the gospels. At other times she highlighted religious commonality: "There's pressure on all religions, Jews, Christians, Muslims." On her return from teaching in the Gulf, she told me, "I mentioned you to show that Muslims and Christians aren't in conflict everywhere, but here in Syria we relate, I mentioned you by name each time I spoke." Sometimes she sought to clarify misunderstandings, for example, the Christian understanding of Trinity as not entailing God's physical procreation of Jesus.[32] While my presence may have engendered some of her discussions, Anisah Huda was very clear in her position in relating to non-Muslims: she didn't try to get someone to become a Muslim or to change faith—her role was to explain Islam and leave it up to the listener. During a conversation about the nature of the unity of God, when one of the women quoted a verse to me, Anisah Huda told her, "When you're dealing with non-Muslims, you deal with logic and mind, not 'it is written.'" While Anisah Huda was relatively openhanded in promoting Islam to non-believers, she took a stronger position vis-a-vis people who had been insiders, and chosen to leave the *ummah*. "Some people say, if there's no compulsion in religion (*la ikrah fiy al-din*), how can it say to kill the apostate (*al-murtadd*)? The object is one who wages war on *dar al-Islam*, the apostate who wages war."[33] (Citing *al-Baqarah* 2:256.)

The women had a clear sense of the wider community of Islam and of Muslim women to which they belonged. Perceived pressure on that community from outside groups intensified their loyalty.[34] Moghadam and

---

32. *Al-Ma'idah* 5:116 suggests an understanding of Trinity with Mary as God's wife.

33. When I asked for clarification in another lecture of "an apostate who attacks Islam," Anisah Huda explained that it would include those who said that the teaching of Islam was wrong. This definition leaves no space for those seeking to evaluate the claims of different religions or worldviews.

34. Maalouf comments in his insightful book, *On Identity*, that "people often see themselves in terms of whichever one of their allegiances is most under attack." (13, 22) Perhaps the sense of external pressure finds more resonance in countries like Syria, where Western weapons and, often, Western soldiers have sometimes been the immediate cause of destruction of property and lives in neighboring countries, and refugees have flooded across borders to jostle for place and livelihood alongside the local community. Now, in a tragic reversal, the stream of refugees is reversed, including people from this mosque community who have sought refuge elsewhere from their country's convulsions.

Joseph both discuss the use of the iconic category of "woman" as essentialized symbol of national, kinship, and religious imaginary communities: "Resistance movements, particularly political Islamic movements, also have used women's bodies and behavior for imagining their political community in opposition to dominant national visions." Where imaginaries of women are central to the discourse of community, they "become the revered objects of the collective act of redemption."[35] When I asked Anisah Huda about the significance of the Muslim community or *ummah*, she said wistfully that the Muslim *ummah* was sick, not like the strength and glory of the time of Muhammad and the first caliphs. For Anisah Huda and the women she trained, the need for renewal or strengthening of the wider Muslim imagined community gave weight to their commitment as Muslim women to *da'wa*.[36]

Local Mosque Group

Imagined community is realized materially in local gatherings or networking.[37] The women in the mosque program were concrete expression of the wider community of women defined by adherence to Islam, so that the basis of gathering and fellowship now included faith rather than (only) family. By having parties at the mosque for community feasts that were normally celebrated in the context of extended families, the women were being implicitly encouraged to make the mosque gathering their place of community. These celebrations included *Eid al-Adhah* and *Eid al-Fitr*, the Islamic New Year, the month of Muhammad's birthday, and also Mother's Day. Other

---

35. Joseph, *Gender*, 6; Moghadam, *Gender*, 4.

36. Vindication of Islam necessitates *da'wa*. Although Anisah Huda cites Muhammad's forbearance during the years of persecution in Mecca, Islam does not contain the route of glory *through* weakness and death, but is validated by victory. "We sent no Messenger, but to be obeyed" (*al-Nisa'* 4:64). Cragg quotes Ibn Khaldun in his *Prolegomena*: "If the power of wrathfulness were no longer to exist in man, he would lose the ability to help the truth become victorious. Then there would no longer be *Jihad*, or glorification (i.e. acknowledged establishment) of the word of God."

Cragg continues, "Later, Ibn Khaldun makes an interesting contrast with Christianity which, though it sends apostles to carry a message, does not, in his view, constitute a 'missionary religion' precisely because it had no *Jihad*. For him, to be seriously 'a faith' religion must enjoy benefit of power as proof both of its own sincerity and of its competence to be effectively sincere" (*Muhammad*, 32–33).

Fazlur Rahman concurs: "It is a part of the Qur'anic doctrine that simply to deliver the Message, to suffer frustration and not to succeed, is immature spirituality ... If history is the proper field for Divine activity, historical forces must, by definition, be employed for the moral end as judiciously as possible" (*Islam*, 16, 21).

37. Flint suggests that the international *ummah* is expressed in the *hajj*: at city or local level, it finds its expression at the mosque (*Church*, 665).

occasions, such as Valentine's Day (*Eid al-Hub*), which was being enthusiastically promoted by the local commercial sector, were dismissed as un-Islamic and inappropriate.

Anisah Huda actively encouraged the women to strengthen links of support with each other outside the mosque. At an *Eid al-Adhah* celebration, she talked to the women about "the importance of attending the mosque as an expression of love for each other, showing God's love: the need to come [to the mosque], to ask after each other, even to visit, at least to telephone each other." She told me:

> The program is all in the mosque. But it's not forbidden for us to visit a sick sister, we bless the sister who is a bride, we congratulate the sister who has bought a house, and the sister who has given birth; these matters concern social relationships and amicability but this is not an organized program.

At the conclusion of lectures, she would sometimes encourage women to pray (*duʿaʾ*) for, or to go and visit, someone bereaved. "Visit Sister X. The husband of our sister, father of our daughters, Y, died the first day of the feast. They have been in the mosque thirty years. Visit her, give her a present from the mosque." The mosque community was also effective beyond the borders of Syria: Anisah Huda encouraged a young bride who was about to travel to the Gulf with her husband for his work, to link up with other graduates of Anisah Huda's mosque program who were there.

The women accepted the nomenclature of extended family. One, greeting me before the start of the lecture, mentioned her sister, indicating the young woman beside her, and told me, "In God—we're all sisters—she, me, you, all of us here."[38] Muslim women in the UAE also gain a sense of family through Islamic centers. "There is a strong sisterhood here. Each woman wants for others what she wants for herself. . . . We act as a family." Many of the women in the UAE expatriate community feel isolated and lonely while their husbands work long hours, and the Islamic centers offer a needed sense of family and community.[39] What is notable about gatherings like Anisah Huda's program is the same emphasis for women living *within* the context of their existing extended families. The mosque family was not being invoked as substitute for absent family networks, but for present ones.

In a lecture, Anisah Huda emphasized primary allegiance to faith rather than kin: "If a woman loves her family, her husband, her mother—if

---

38. I was included here in the extended sisterhood. The speaker may have been defining it in terms of those attending the mosque. Some women who saw me attending regularly assumed I was an enquirer or convert.

39. Krause, *Women*, 119.

she angers God and pleases her husband ... isn't it *shirk*? ... We should say, 'I love my parents; I love the truth more.'" However, involvement in the mosque program often spread along existing network lines. Anisah Huda encouraged the women; "Some sisters like to bring their daughter, sister, friend." Family and faith are inextricably linked: mother and daughter, or sisters, would attend the same mosque. And family groupings would meet for faith activities: I sometimes joined women gathering to "seal" (recite the whole of) the Qur'an, with sisters, sisters-in-law, and mother-in-law meeting together to read, and then share a meal. And the same family, during their weekly gatherings as extended family, would sometimes read portions of the Qur'an, for example, *al-Ana'am* 6 for healing when someone was sick. However, in the latter context, the gathering was defined by family lines, whereas, in the mosque, family may attend but the gathering is defined by faith lines.

The Place of the Mosque

Women had traditionally met in homes for social and religious gatherings. Anisah Huda told me that the major move of women's religious activities into mosque space had happened within the last decade in Syria. This move allowed more supervision from government internal security and from male clerics:

> It was a good move from the government to open the mosques, better than having lessons in houses where anyone can teach what she likes in homes and no one is able to challenge her or ask her ... but in the mosque she speaks in front of the people gathered and anyone who wants can enter ... It's better to open the mosques to them than having people do lessons in houses, where we don't know what they're teaching.

As well as allowing authorities to supervise the content of the teaching more, the movement into mosque space facilitated the growth of community grounded in creed. The fact of being in the mosque, as well as the activities, enhanced religious identification for women and girls attending; and the physical lay-out enabled both the space for large group celebrations for feast times of the faith, and also multiple activities for different groups in the various rooms and spaces. Khadijah attended Anisah Huda's Tuesday lectures, but would come early so her daughter could come to the *fiqh* class that was from 2:00–3:00 p.m. She told me about the different classes for various ages and for adults. While these ran throughout the year, the summer months also included intensive classes for children. Females of all ages found their place in faith practices within the mosque.

The women felt the beneficial effect of wide communal participation in the more strenuous aspects of faith practice, when hundreds of women might gather together to pray, with the same number of men or more in the main room of the mosque below. I asked Anisah Huda about the nightly *tarawih* prayers in Ramadan at the mosque. She told me:

> In Ramadan we pray twenty *rakaʿ* every day and we read two or sometimes three divisions [*juzʾ*] of the Qurʾan every day. This is hard: if we wanted to pray three divisions in our home, we'd get tired and couldn't endure it, we might pray a section. This is not something that's easy for someone: however in the mosque, praise God! ... In the *tarawih* God gives unusual strength. We pray twenty *rakaʿ* and we continue for three hours sometimes, and we go out happily. We come to the following day and I, every day when I see [the leader] go on longer, I say no one will come tomorrow: but when we come we find more people than were there before!

Kalsum was explaining the Night of Vigil (*laylat al-qadr*)[40] to me, when the women attend the night prayers (*tarawih* and then *qiyam al-layl*), ending with prayers an hour before sunrise (about 3:00–4.30 a.m.):

> It's about weeping and submissiveness [*al-khashuʿ*]. God comes down to the first heaven and answers prayers. It's seclusion [*khalwah*], you and God alone. You feel as if you're flying, pray till tears come, it's a strange feeling, tears come suddenly. You pray to God, feel with everyone, love everyone, feel soft, forget worries: what I feel at night, I try to follow in the day, as I am able.

For the women in the mosque program, corporate involvement facilitated both endurance and ecstasy.

Including Dress

Mode of dress is a particular public way of being, signaling community allegiance. In Syria a wide range of dress could be seen in the streets, from

---

40. Most often translated as "Night of Power," Ebtisam preferred "Night of Vigil." Al-Hilali and Khan have "Night of Decree," in the *surah* of that name (*Al-Qadr* 97). Believed to be the night when the Qurʾan was first revealed, prayers on this night are thought to have special effectiveness.

contemporary, tight-fitting Western wear through to the more traditional all-covering black ʿ*abaya* or coat and black head-covering with black *mandil* pinned over the lower half of the face or fully covering it. At the mosque the prevailing dress was the full-length overcoat and headscarf that covered all but the face, tightly gathered to hold in any recalcitrant strands of hair that threatened to escape into view:[41] this was the indicator of membership in the pious educated group. Most of the younger women wore white *hijab*; older women usually preferred black or dark blue.[42] The all-covering coat concealed a range of clothes, from conservative long skirts through to trousers or blue jeans. An older professional woman who had come to mosque lectures in a trouser suit with mid-thigh-length top; after a while she began wearing a prayer skirt over her trousers. The evening *tarawih* prayers during Ramadan, attended by women who didn't come to the mosque at any other time of the year, showed more variety of dress, often with prayer skirt and perhaps top covering trousers and shirt. But for women who regularly attended the mosque, their clothing (long coat and *hijab*) fulfilled the requirements of covering for public modesty and for *salah* (whether private or public), indicating their primary adherence to the identity of conservative Muslim piety.

Syrian families can exert strong pressure on members to conform to behavioral norms. How closely did the mosque community enforce norms of conduct and comportment on its members? Communal authority is realized in restraining behavior as well as endorsing proper behavior. Such restraint may take different forms. Group behavior has a normative effect. As noted above, one woman attending lectures adopted a prayer skirt as more modest than her pantsuit trousers. A young woman arrived at the mosque teaching session one day in denim jeans and jacket, long hair loose and flowing, clutching a prayer cape and skirt. A warm greeting from a few of the young women did little to dispel her self-consciousness as she sat in a room full of women all in full-length manteau and close-covering *hijab*. She didn't appear again in that garb. Entering one day, I greeted an older woman, whose eyes flicked up to my scarf, and then away again quickly as if she had seen something indecent. In a reflected surface soon after, I noticed a substantial lock of hair showing from under my scarf. Such unspoken censorship encourages adherence to group norms. Hegland describes the

41. A frequent, almost unconscious gesture from Anisah Huda and the women, was to check the perimeter of the scarf round the face for any strands of hair that might need tucking back. I found myself doing the same.

42. The subdued hues which dominated here are in contrast to the variety of prints and colors which make pious dress such a colorful fashion statement among many Egyptian women; Anisah Huda commented on the difference.

"warm invitations and gentle social pressure" she experienced attending women's mourning rituals in Pakistan, which sometimes translated into "constant social pressure to attend," for the Shi'ite women involved—along with convention-guiding dress, music, and language.[43]

Sarah Islam describes the pressure exerted on women within the conservative Qubaysi women's movement in Syria. This functioned horizontally through small home-based study groups where "the movement was able to develop small, close-knit networks of committed students who would monitor each other's behavior in terms of maintaining religious, behavioral, and clothing norms, as well as provide spiritual and social support for each other." And there was also vertical reinforcement: "Similar to Sufi orders, the Qubaysi teaching structure is hierarchical. Each local study circle is placed under the authority of one anisah, or Qubaysi female teacher. This anisah is subordinate to the instructions of an anisah superior to her in authority."[44]

Other more outspoken pressure invoked fear of the afterlife. In the early years of this millennium, the woman's carriage in the Cairo metro increasingly featured stickers telling passengers, "*al-hijab qabl al-'azab*" ([wear] *hijab* before [facing] torment). During my fieldwork, Syrian press reported conservatively dressed women going into cafes during Ramadan in a major city and telling the proprietors that they should close during daylight hours or else face being roasted in hell.

Ceremonies in the mosque program, celebrating girls who had put on the *hijab* or memorized the Qur'an, certainly encompassed the "gentle social pressure" that Hegland describes.[45] However, this was not to the extent of Qubaysi norms of subordination and monitoring. While Anisah Huda taught principles of proper religious behavior and dress, she encouraged the women to choose for themselves on many issues. The variety of clothes under the encompassing long coat did not demonstrate uniform adherence to the long skirt and comprehensive undergarments that some of my conservative neighbors wore each time they went out. In the same way, when Anisah Huda taught on the proper characteristics to look for in selecting a spouse, she encouraged the women to take it as the basis to think and choose for themselves. "Why should I tell her to marry a particular person or not to marry him; or to buy a house in a given place or not to buy, or to go or not to go?" Anisah Huda emphasized the women's need to learn and

---

43. Hegland, *Rituals*.

44. Islam, *Qubaysiyyat*, 167–68. See also Ibrahim, *Qubaysi*; Zoepf, *Syria*; Weismann, *Sufi*.

45. Meltzer and Nix, *Light*; Hegland, *Rituals*.

to think and make choices for themselves, rather than looking to senior authority or peer norms for their decisions.[46]

The mosque community guided norms of behavior and dress. However, Anisah Huda and her spouse were more liberal than many families in the choices they offered their daughter[47] and this emphasis on choice and empowerment within boundaries, rather than tight control, was reflected in her teaching to the women in the mosque program.

Communities in Tension: Negotiating Another Allegiance

The women found community and identity with other pious Muslim women through the mosque congregation. At times this community commitment came into conflict with the requirements of their kin family. The tensions the women felt between family demands and mosque attendance were most clearly expressed at *Eid* celebrations, when women shared the microphone to talk about their involvement in the mosque program. Problems with children and resistance from spouse or mother-in-law were routinely mentioned as challenges for being able to attend regularly. Women sometimes talked to me about their husbands' behavior that didn't conform to proper Islamic observance. In a lecture Anisah Huda mentioned, "husband, children, mother-in-law, sisters-in-law," as part of the "pressure that makes [a woman] strong."

Teaching in the mosque program sometimes concerned family relationships, such as the injunction for justice between parents and children and between husband and wife/wives. Anisah Huda often urged the women to learn, to use their minds rather than following other people's opinions, and she encouraged the young women to agree on mutual rights with the prospective groom before marriage.

However, the tension was not just between cultural kin expectations and loyalty to the mosque community, but also within the latter's teaching. The women's mosque movement finds its place within the wider resurgence in Islamism, which insists on women's primary role as mother and nurturer of family (and thereby the extended community of *ummah* or nation):

> Although in Islam, there are many ways to open the doors of Paradise, the vehicle especially chosen for the woman is that of pregnancy, childbirth, nursing and conscientious rearing of her

---

46. See chapter 8 for further discussion on this.
47. See Chapter 6.

children. ... For every ounce of effort, be it physical, emotional or mental, exerted in this direction, the mother is elevated to a higher position of esteem in the eyes of her family and society, and has thereby gained a place for herself among the successful in the Hereafter.[48]

While some interpret this as restricting women's activities to the home,[49] others suggest that women can be involved in work outside the home or in *da'wa* providing their primary home responsibilities are adequately carried out first.[50] Anisah Huda's teaching and example placed her in the latter group:

The man is outside all the day working; when he comes home, she cares for him, obeys him. In Islam the woman is permitted to, but not required to work. She is the one who gets pregnant, gives birth, breastfeeds, weans, cleans the child, teaches—the man works outside and she is inside—and obeys what he requests. But this obedience is also limited—she is not required to obey if he requests something that is *haram*, it's not absolute obedience.

In this view there is a tenuous balance between Muslim women's role as obedient servitors in the home, and as pious subjects:

By the fulfilment of marriage, and consequent motherhood, the Muslim woman has completed a great part of her religion. The

---

48. Schleifer, *Motherhood*, 58; Krause, *Women*, 122. The woman without children is conspicuously absent in this purview. Notably Zeinab al-Ghazzali claimed that her inability to bear children left her "free to devote herself to the path of God" (Mahmood, *Politics*, 182). However, Ahmed (*Women and Gender*, 200) and Shehadeh (*Women*, 133) see al-Ghazzali's example as contradicting her own teaching on the role of Islamic women, citing her stipulation to both her first and second husbands that her role in *da'wa* had priority in the marriage.

49. See "Communities of Kinship" above. Maududi insisted that "the basic principles of the social system of Islam [restrict] the woman's sphere of activity to her home" (*Purdah*, 103). See also Al-Musnad, *Fatawa*, 314 in Saudi Arabia. Shehadeh (*Women*) suggests this view from al-Banna and Qutb in Egypt (20, 71–72), and Mutahhari in Iran (119). See also Egyptian Sheikh, Wagdy Ghoneim, recorded in Meltzer and Nix, *Light*.

50. For example, Hasan Ismail al-Anisah Hudaybi, successor to al-Banna as Supreme Guide of the Muslim Brotherhood: "The woman's natural place is the home, but if she finds that after doing her duty in the home she has time, she can use part of it in the service of society, on condition that it is done within the legal limits which preserve her dignity and morality" (cited in Shehadeh, *Women*, 18). Shehadeh indicates that this position is supported by Islamist leaders such as Zaynab al-Ghazzali in Egypt (128), Khomeini in Iran (94), al-Turabi of the National Islamic Front in Sudan (152–53), al-Ghannoushi in Tunisia (179), and Fadlallah in Lebanon (202). See also Schleifer, *Motherhood*, 89.

remaining part lies in the obligations incumbent on all adult Muslims, male or female. Although as a wife and mother, she may have to delay such obligations as prayer, for example, in order to attend to urgent needs of her husband or child, she is still held fully responsible for the completion of her religious duties.[51]

Both cultural tradition and Islamist teaching on women's domestic role offered a challenge to their involvement in the mosque program. Mosque attendance is not essential for women for *salah*, and the right of women to go to the mosque to learn could be (and often was) contested by their families. But this is always in tension with women's vocation—their family responsibilities. The pious Muslim woman holds in tension her duties of piety with the household duties which are her primary role, and the former cannot supersede the latter. For the women attending mosque classes, their most immediate sphere of responsibility and that on which they were primarily judged, was their success in the domain of home and family.[52] The teleological goal of self-formation of the devout Muslim woman in this mosque is embodied in regulations of modesty and purity, and in her place and responsibilities within her immediate family.

In such a context, Anisah Huda generally responded conservatively, telling the women in the program that doing one's duty at home ("the service of home and children, teaching the children, caring for their food, cleaning") was worship in its own right. However, invocation of the Muslim *ummah* as primary base of community and identity meant that the Qur'anic injunction to all believers to seek knowledge[53] could be adduced to support the women's involvement in mosque classes.

Anisah Huda asserted to me that the husband had no right to forbid his wife in matters of faith:

> It's the husband's duty to not forbid his wife to attend the mosque and not forbid her from visiting her family and parents. But if she's forbidden she has to choose whether to resist and clash with him or whether to be quiet until he changes, . . . but if learning is taken at the mosque and she needs to go to the mosque, the spouse doesn't have the right to forbid his wife from what God has enjoined. The husband's rights don't go across the command of God—he has specific rights to request and these are personal special matters to sit with her, to sleep with her, to consult with her, . . . but for him to order her in her prayers and her worship,

---

51. Schleifer, *Motherhood*, 60.
52. Vanderwaeren, *Muslimahs'*, 317.
53. *Ta-Ha* 20:114. "And say: 'My Lord! Increase me in knowledge.'"

he doesn't have the right in this, there are boundaries he doesn't cross.[54]

The teaching of Anisah Huda, as with other *da'iya*s, did not place primary focus on the wife as obedient subject to the husband[55] (although she did not dispute this within the limits specified above) but rather on the woman as devout subject. Allegiance defined in terms of the Muslim *ummah* and God's requirements rather than primarily in immediate familial terms gave the women room to maneuver, and to redefine existing patriarchal norms, whether within family or mosque. Obedience to God encompassed (but could not be superseded by) obedience to husband. The women did not directly challenge the religious and cultural traditions insisting on husband's authority and the priority of domestic space and responsibilities for women.

Thus Mahmood describes an Egyptian woman attending a *da'wa* program in the face of her husband's opposition, by dint of being especially

54. Anisah Huda specified that the wife should not work against her husband's wishes. However, she insisted that involvement in *da'wa* was different from a full-time job requiring the wife to be out of the house all day (Interview with BBC journalist Nawara Mahfoud). Her own husband was supportive of her *da'wa*, but maintained that domestic service had priority: "I fully support my wife in her work. She has been serving us for twenty years. This is the least we can do to repay her. But this doesn't mean, however, that a woman shouldn't know her duties. A man goes out and works hard and gets weary, for his family. He should be able to find rest when he returns to his house" (Meltzer and Nix, *Light*.).

55. Al-Baqarah 2:228; Al-Nisa' 4:34. *Ahadith* cited in this connection include the following:
"Allah's Messenger said: 'The wife is the guardian over the house of her husband and his children.'" (from the *hadith* collections of Al-Bukhari and Muslim); and, "If I were to command a single person to bow in prostration to another person, I could have commanded a woman to bow down (in obedience and respect, not in worship) to her husband." (from Abu Dawud's *hadith* collection). Allah's Messenger also said: "If a husband calls his wife to his bed, but the latter refused to fulfill the call (for any reason other than a lawful one), which drives the man to become upset with his wife, then angels will curse such a wife until she gets up in the morning." (from Al-Bukhari and Muslim) He furthermore, said: "Their (husbands') rights over you (wives) is that you do not allow anyone whom they dislike onto your bedding and you do not allow anyone whom they dislike into your house." (from Al-Tirmithi's *hadith*). Allah's Messenger said: "The best woman is the one who when you look at her, you are pleased; when you order her, she obeys; if you are absent from her, she guards herself and your property." (from Al-Tabarani's collection) Allah's Messenger stated: "A wife is not allowed to observe fast (other than fasting in the month of Ramadhan, the prescribed, unless she has his permission. She may not allow any one to come into his house, unless he permits." (from al-Tirmithi) Al-Tirmithi also reported from Umm Salamah, the mother of the believers that Allah's Messenger said: "Any woman whose husband dies while he is pleased, happy and satisfied with her (acts, attitudes and behavior) will enter Jannah (Paradise)."

diligent in completing all her household responsibilities on the days she attended the program, at the same time as reminding him of his own obligations to be more devout. She notes, "Paradoxically, Abir's ability to break from the norms of what it meant to be a dutiful wife[56] were predicated upon her learning to perfect a tradition that accorded her a subordinate status to her husband." Her noncompliance to her husband "did not represent a break with the significatory system of Islamic norms, but was saturated with them, and enabled by the capacities that the practice of these norms endowed her with."

Other examples include Shaima, a volunteer preacher in an Egyptian village who offers advice to women on their rights and duties in Islam, which enable them to resist pressure from family members (including being married against their will). Young women from Indian subcontinent families in the UK are able to resist family pressure by using "their increased textual understanding of Islam to context the traditions and restrictions imposed on them by their parents:" as do Muslim women in European youth associations.[57] The identity of the pious Muslim woman reinforces the role of domestic subordination as divinely mandated.

However, by setting wifely subordination in the context of faith submission rather than family, women find ground to challenge family demands that are based on traditional norms of cultural patriarchy. In learning about their rights and responsibilities as Muslim women, rather than solely as members of extended families or ethnic groupings, women find a stronger position from which to negotiate life issues such as marriage or divorce.

In teaching women Anisah Huda had encouraged them to give their daughters opportunity to learn and interact with the world, and her own readiness to challenge cultural norms for the sake of the wider *ummah* is seen most clearly in her own family in her unusual decision to send her daughter Enas abroad for study, to give her the opportunity to be better equipped to speak for Islam.

> When I planned to send my daughter, this was something not common among us in Syria, to let a girl travel at eighteen years to study . . . it was not present at all, and against our customs, traditions, and environment. But my intention was . . . for her to be a successful, respected Muslim who could address foreigners and correct [misconceptions about Islam] with the weapons of

---

56. By going against her husband's wishes in attending the *da'wa* program (Mahmood, *Politics*, 179, 186ff). Similarly Anisah Huda recalls in her youth working all night sometimes to finish her household duties in order to be able to do *da'wa* (Meltzer and Nix, *Light*).

57. Minesaki, *Gender*, 404–7; Afshar, *Feminisms*, 278; Minganti, *Challenging*, 384.

knowledge and language, to lecture and speak in many of the universities of the world.

However, generally she was cautious about direct conflict with social norms, as seen in her encouragement to the women whose families opposed their attendance that domestic service was as valid a worship as coming to the mosque (see above). She does describe to BBC journalist Nawara Mahfoud one instance of telling two sisters (of over thirty years old) to take work against the wishes of their father as he was getting older and would be unable to provide for them, and they had little prospect of marriage at that age. But she immediately goes on to say that she wouldn't encourage a woman to work against the wishes of her husband: "his word is sacred." As Kalmbach suggests, in a conservative society, it is necessary to live in (and encourage others to) a way that does not flagrantly contravene social norms, in order to retain a hearing.[58]

The women attending the mosque program were subject to a variety of forms of community constraint, whether national, cultural or familial. Mahmood notes that:

> The task of realizing piety placed these women in conflictual relations with a variety of structures of authority: some grounded in instituted standards of Islamic orthodoxy, and others in norms of liberal discourse; some in parental and male kin authority and others in state institutions.

As Mahmood points out, these pressures are best not read from the framework of constraints on individual autonomy.[59] Rather we should see them as competing communities of allegiance, invoking their own sources of authority and model behavior.

Kanno and Norton note that all imagined communities have "defining sets of 'rules and regulations.'" An imagined community assumes an imagined identity. Some identity positions restrict opportunities; others may open enhanced possibilities for "social interaction and human agency."[60] While both kin and mosque community endorse the domestic role of women, allegiance to the mosque community offered the possibility of social interaction with, and support from, women beyond the family, and a legitimate sphere of learning and performance within the religious domain as well as the domestic.

---

58. Meltzer and Nix, *Light*; Kalmbach, *Social*, 39, 51.
59. Mahmood, *Feminist*; *Politics*, 11–15.
60. Kanno, *Imagined*, 224; Norton, *Identity*: 414–15, 422.

Communities in Contact: The Place of *da'wa*

A shift in allegiance is seen when there is tension or conflict between fidelity to the mosque sorority and extended kin community. It is also evident when the women's mosque community becomes a base from which to do *da'wa* to one's original extended family and friends.

Da'wa, as "the invitation, addressed to men [sic] by God and the prophets, to believe in the true religion, Islam,"[61] may be addressed to non-Muslims. However, it is primarily understood and practiced as a call to other Muslims to observe piety and proper Islamic conduct.[62]

Life passages, shaping women's lives, are primary expressions of community. Anisah Huda prepared some papers (*durus fiy al-munasibat*: Lessons on Occasions) and gave them out as parts of lectures on proper ways to participate in events of crisis or joy, such as the death of a child, or a marriage, and to promote the cause of God. One paper on a speech to give at a wedding began:

> I congratulate the honored bridal couple and their families and felicitate you on this blessed wedding, encompassed in the recollection of Allah and obedience to him. For all work begun in the recollection of Allah will be blessed and fruitful, and everything that doesn't start by remembering God will be cut off and curtailed.

The paper cautions the reader at this point: "The speaker should be smiling, with sensitive behavior appropriate to the context, addressing the families and bridal couple in complimentary terms."

Other papers suggested how to respond to a death or the birth of a child or what to say at a graduation. Islam notes that the Qubaysiyyat prepared "short pamphlets on areas of popular interest or daily practice for the masses on topics like weddings, beautification, marriage, and childrearing."[63] As with norms of daily behavior and dress, ways of marking celebration or grief or passages of life, are shaped within family customs.

---

61. Canard cites *Ibrahim* 14:44: "And warn mankind of the day when the torment will come to them; then the wrongdoers will say: 'Our Lord! Respite us for a little while, we will answer your call (*da'watak*) and follow the Messengers'" (*Da'wa*, 168; Mahmood, *Politics*, 57).

62. Analogous to Old Testament prophets, whose primary mission was calling the children of Israel back to true faith practice. Oracles to the nations and the book of Jonah are examples of prophetic calls to people outside the community of faith, but the majority of the prophetic writings are to the (sometime divided) nation of Israel/Judah.

63. Islam, *Qubaysiyyat*, 174.

The mosque community both suggested its own guidelines for appropriate negotiation of communal rites of passage, and also instructed the women on how to move beyond involvement as a family member or friend to make use of these occasions for *da'wa* to the participants, training them in appropriate exhortations at such times to encourage people in pious practice and attitudes.

While *da'wa* to Muslims occupied most of Anisah Huda's time, non-Muslims were clearly within her ambit, to be encouraged towards the *ummah* faith community. She made time within a full program to sit with foreigners and explain Islam to them. At the least she viewed the internet and other media as a vehicle for greater interaction and understanding between Muslims and non-Muslims, seeking more knowledge both of using the internet and of English language for herself and women in the program, and attempting a bold initiative to use it as a medium of conversation between Syrian Muslim youth and young people in other countries. Similarly women in the mosque program would ask me if I had Islamized yet, or tell me of other foreigners who had become Muslims, with the clear implication that I should follow their example. The women's allegiance to the mosque community and the wider *ummah* shaped a missionary attitude both to their extended families and to people outside the *ummah*.

Conclusion

This chapter has explored the allegiance of women beyond their primary identity within extended family networks to the imaginary community of Muslim women, embodied in the community of women in the mosque program. Media promotes particular Muslim identities, contributing to shaping awareness of the extended but bounded community of the Muslim *ummah*. The sociocultural factors of hierarchy and connectivity (grid and group) shape the expression of community and of response to those outside the community. Mosque gatherings create an alternative community to the extended family through times of shared celebration and pious practice: visiting based on relationships of faith practice, not just family, is encouraged. The mosque teaching constructs the desired behavior of a pious Muslim woman in her daily life, dress, and family interactions. While mosque teaching touches every detail of daily life and relationships, it also reinforces the priority of domestic space and gendered subordination. Within this relationship hierarchy, the identity of the pious Muslim woman may open up a place to maneuver within family relationships. However, this moral or religious high ground is gained through the demonstration of exemplary adherence to the required norms. *Da'wa* as the basis of relationship to others, whether Muslim family members and friends or non-Muslims, suggests a shift of the women's allegiance to identity within the mosque community and extended *ummah*.

6

Ideal Leader

Today we will see the way we can arrive to conformity with the Prophet (PBUH).

Sayidna Ibn Omar did what the Prophet did. One day the Prophet was walking along a path and stopped for a little while in one place and then continued. Ibn Omar came along there and stood in the same place and then continued on the path. See this love! ... Ibn Omar loved him and followed him in all details. (Teacher in the mosque program, commenting on *Al-Nisa'* 4:69)

For the *daʿiya* is the mediator of God to the people and the successor of the Apostles. (*liʾannah al-daʿiya safir Allah ila al-nas wa khalifat al-rusul.*) (Mosque lecture handout)

Introduction: Leadership, Authority, and Mimesis

COMMUNITY, WHETHER FAMILIAL, LOCAL, national or transnational, is characterized by some form of leadership. Discussion of leadership patterns may come under a larger rubric of social relationships, or be couched in terms of the type of authority they wield. Looking more explicitly at religious power and jurisdiction, Gaffney takes Weber's categories of charismatic, dominant, and rational leadership to describe Muslim preachers in Egypt in terms of saints, warriors, and scholars. El-Fadl's book on authority and Islamic law distinguishes between coercive authority and persuasive authority.[1] Bano and Kalmbach define Islamic

---

1. Douglas, *Purity*; Gaffney, *Prophets*; Bano and Kalmbach, *Women*, 3. El-Fadl (*Speaking*, 18) says: "Coercive authority is the ability to direct the conduct of another person through the use of inducements, benefits, threats, or punishments so that a reasonable person would conclude that for all practical purposes they have no choice but to comply. Persuasive authority involves normative power. It is the ability to direct the

religious authority in textual terms, asking "who has the right to interpret religious texts and apply them to the lives of followers."[2]

In the previous chapter I noted that a shift in one's primary community of allegiance requires belief in an alternate community, defined by particular ways of being and behaving. These ways of being and behaving may be exemplified in a particular person as leader or exemplar for the group. Such a person becomes the focus for allegiance and the mimetic ideal for members of the group. Hence, I suggest an alternate understanding of leadership and influence, based on the mimetic ideal and the desiring subject, where the influence of the leader is determined by the extent to which they embody and shape the desired community values and way of being, through their personal characteristics or abilities, and access to power and resources.

Mimetic Paradigm

Hafez, following Joseph's description of Lebanese women, uses the notion of "desire" to explore the subjectivity of activist Islamic women in Cairo.[3] Girard takes the relational nature of desire further in his insistence that all desire is mediated by the mimetic principle: that our desires are not spontaneous, but rather are prompted by imitating another "model."[4] Human desire is then mimetic, and also triangular, with mediator or model who evokes the desire, the desiring respondent (or disciple), and the object (material or immaterial) which is desired.[5] Drawing his observations initially from literature,[6] Girard takes Don Quixote's emulation of Amadis as ideal knight to describe mimetic theory:

---

belief or conduct of a person because of trust."

2. Bano and Kalmbach, *Women*, 3.

3. Hafez describes "'desire' as the multifarious wants and needs that underlie subject formation ... [as] an ongoing process rather than an ultimate objective" (*Islam*, 5). Joseph (*Learning*, 79) discusses "how the desires of female and male subjects both become animated by culturally specific notions of subjectivity that embed desire within relational matrices."

4. In Alison, *Girard's*.

5. McDonald, *Violence*.

6. Originally a historian, Girard based his theory on his observations from the literature he was teaching. He then went to the fields of anthropology, psychology, and religion for further elucidation and examples. He continues, in mimetic theory, to describe the conflict arising from mimetic rivalry, and its solution, the scapegoat mechanism, which he suggests is the basis of myths, culture, and religion (Andrade, *Girard*; Kirwan, *Girard*, 20).

> The disciple pursues objects which are determined for him, or at least seem to be determined for him, by the model of all chivalry. We shall call this model the *mediator* of desire. Chivalric existence is the *imitation* of Amadis in the same sense that the Christian's existence is the imitation of Christ.... The mediator is there, above that line [joining object and subject,] radiating toward both the subject and the object....
>
> We shall speak of *external mediation* when the distance is sufficient to eliminate any contact between the two spheres of *possibilities* of which the mediator and the subject occupy the respective centers. We shall speak of *internal mediation* when this same distance is sufficiently reduced to allow these two spheres to penetrate each other more or less profoundly.[7]

Mimesis differs from imitation in that it is always acquisitive, driven by desire for the competence or power perceived in the model. It is culturally shaped, in that culture and community determine, not what our basic needs are, but how we meet them—through imitating others. "Desire itself becomes informed by a realm of symbols that instruct participants in a given culture how and what they are to desire."[8]

Mimesis is then fundamental to desire and to learning.[9] When a given community finds its characteristics and values best embodied in a particular individual, that person becomes the model or *Other*, the mimetic ideal, who mediates the desires of community members.

The influence or authority of the ideal leader may be perceived in terms of El Fadl's "persuasive authority," which "involves the exercise of influence and normative power upon someone. Persuasive authority influences people to believe, act or refrain from acting in a certain fashion by persuading them that this is what ought to be." El Fadl is concerned to note that the surrendering of personal judgment and independent reasoning to another person's judgment may be a form of coercive authority.[10] However, Girard's theory questions independent judgment at the level of desire, through his argument that the shape of all desire is fundamentally learned, and therefore mimetic.[11] In talking in terms of desire and mimesis, we are

---

7. Cited in Williams, *Reader*, 34, 39. Excerpts are taken from the first chapter of Girard's first book, *Deceit, Desire, and the Novel*. Original emphasis.

8. Williams, *Bible*, 7, 8.

9. In a performance-based understanding of learning, the model or mimetic ideal becomes the standard for defining a correct rendition. This is the basis for what is often categorised as "rote-learning" (Dale, *Rote*).

10. El Fadl, *Speaking*, 19, 20, 22.

11. Alison, *Girard's*; McDonald, *Violence*; Andrade, *Girard*.

asking about the influence of leadership in *forming* the aspirations of the follower or disciple, rather than merely conformity of behavior to the leader's persuasion.

From the reverse perspective, Gaffney, noting the "multiple and coexisting concepts of knowledge as well as their competing modes of validation" within Islam, concludes that "a preacher's influence in a local context depends fundamentally on the concepts of knowing that are found there and on how these qualities are understood to be portrayed."[12] The power or effectiveness of a leader can be determined according to the extent to which they embody (and shape) the desires of the community. Girard notes the possibility of what he describes as "double mediation" where "the model becomes the imitator of his imitator and the imitator becomes his model of its model." In internal mediation this leads to mimetic escalation and conflict.[13] However, another form of "double mediation" or reverse influence can also occur in external mediation, where if the model leader or founder is sufficiently remote, characteristics expressing community values may be ascribed to him or her.[14]

Community and Leader, Ideal and Actual

As the imaginary community finds concrete realization in the local mosque community, so the mimetic ideal is found primarily at two levels for this community: in the person of Muhammad, Prophet of Islam and exemplar Muslim, and in the local leadership of Anisah Huda.

Muhammad is clearly an example of external mediation, where there is no risk of rivalry between model and desiring subject: the distance between the two is too great. However, the acquisitive dimension of mimesis remains. This can be seen in Taussig, intriguingly writing at a similar time but independently of Girard and his school.[15] He describes

> the mimetic faculty, the nature that culture uses to create second nature, the faculty to copy, imitate, make models, explore difference, yield into and become Other. The wonder of mimesis lies

---

12. Gaffney, *Prophet's*, 35.

13. Muller, *Interview*.

14. See Stowasser's discussion of the variation in content and meaning of Qur'anic "images" and "models" according to the interpreter's culture and time (*Women*, 21).

15. There is no mention or recognition in Taussig's evocative book of what Girard had been writing. Taussig's reflections on mimesis derive from his observations in Central and Latin America, and Walter Benjamin (1892–1940) is prominent among the writers on whom he draws.

in *the copy drawing on the character and power of the original, to the point whereby the representation may even assume that character and that power.* . . . I believe it is as necessary to the very process of knowing as it is to the construction and subsequent naturalization of identities.[16]

I suggest that imitation of the exemplar at both levels, of Muhammad and also of Anisah Huda, offer the disciple both power in negotiating life in this world, and the possibility of access to the next world.

Muhammad—Ideal Leader

The Muslim is defined by recitation of the creed: *la illaha illa Allah wa Muhammad rasul Allah*—"There is no god but God and Muhammad is the Messenger of God."

Each lesson in the women's program in the mosque began with an invocation to God and prayer for Muhammad: *Bism Allah al-rahman al-rahim wa ʿala sayyidna wa habibna Muhammad al-salah wa al-taslim*—"In the name of God the Compassionate, the Merciful; and on our lord and beloved Muhammad be prayers and peace."

Islam is as much focused on and identified by Muhammad, Prophet of Islam, as it is by its worship of the God by whom Muslims believe he was sent. Worship of God is defined by the practice of the Prophet. Islam is founded on the Qur'an, believed to be received through Muhammad, and on the words and acts of Muhammad. Official Islam is based on the five practices.[17] These basic practices are further described, refined, and detailed in literature that has built up richly over the centuries. Each practice and its development must ultimately find its roots in the sanction of Muhammad, whether in deed or word, through the *ahadith* literature or the Life of the Prophet (*sirat al-nabi*). The *ahadith* themselves are authenticated through a chain of witnesses that must go back to Muhammad. The practice of orthodox Islam is a detailed codification of behavior firmly grounded in Muhammad.

---

16. Taussig, *Mimesis*, xiii-xiv. Emphasis added.
17. Reciting the creed, praying five times daily, fasting during Ramadan, paying the *zakat* (2.5 percent of one's wealth) and making the pilgrimage.

Practices of Life and Faith

The women in the mosque program attended lectures on Muhammad and on the Qur'an, richly illustrated with stories of his life and that of his Companions. They were exhorted to follow his example in attitude as well as action. Memorizing the Qur'an was a foundational part of the program at all ages, followed by memorizing books of *tafsir* (interpretation). However, there was another dimension to life and faith which showed itself at the end of lectures in occasional questions about the use of magic or *jinn*: a dimension that was non-textual, or else based on a different use of text, as in Mahjubah, the Iranian English-language magazine for Muslim women given out at the mosque, which instructed its readers:[18]

> Whoever writes these seven verses (*Ayat*) with Saffron, musk and Rose water on the Eid of Nowrooz and drinks, it [sic] will be safe from sickness, problems and sufferings.
>
> Peace be on Musa and Haroun (*Salamum Ala Musa wa Haroun, 37:120*)
>
> Peace be on Nuh among the nations (*Salamum ala Nuh fi al Alamin, 37:79*)
>
> Peace be on Ibrahim (*Salamum Ala Ebrahim, 37:109*)
>
> Peace be on Ilyas (*Salamum Ala Al Ya sin, 37:130*)
>
> Peace; a word from a merciful Lord (*Salamum Ala Qolan men rabe Rahim, 36:58*)
>
> Peace be on you, you shall be happy; therefore enter it to abide (*Salamum Alaikum tebtom fadkholuha khaledin, 39:73*)
>
> Peace it is till the break of morning (*Salamum hia hata matlael fajr, 97:5*)

The magazine also cited the founder of Egypt's Muslim Brotherhood to support reciting particular verses at specified times a set number of times in order to receive blessing:[19]

---

18. Issues of *Mahjubah* can be found at http://www.mahjubah.com/.

19. Lenning describes *barakah* or blessing as fundamental to Jewish, Christian, and Muslim thought, and including the ideas of "beneficent force, efficient power." He cites Parrinder's definition of *barakah* in Islam as "a mysterious and wonderful power, a blessing from God." Possessed by the saints, "the prophet Muhammad possessed it in the highest degree.... Barakah is seen in miracles, holy places and people, prayers, blessings and curses" (*Blessing*, 9-10). In this book *barakah* refers to blessing and power as similes.

In Imam Shaheed Hasan Al-Banna's Al-Ma'thurat, there are a number of *hadith* verifying the verses quoted in it as a daily wazifa, generally along the form of: "X reported that the Messenger of Allah (PBUH) said, If anyone recites these verses at this time this number of times, they will . . . [received blessing], or some other praise of the verses and their benefit."[20]

One of my first visits to Anisah Huda's home was when she invited me to join with a few other expatriate women while she explained Islam to us. Her husband and daughter Enas had just returned from the *'umrah* (lesser pilgrimage to Mecca), as a reward for her daughter's high school marks. She told us of the beliefs of Islam (belief in God, his prophets, his books, angels and the day of judgment, and also fate), and taught us too about the pillars or practices of Islam, which she listed as saying the Creed, Praying, Fasting, Giving, and Pilgrimage, and also Jihad. Then she offered us water that her husband and daughter had brought back from the spring of Zamzam at Mecca, and told us to offer a petition as we drank it, because God would answer it. Blessing or merit could be gained through belief in and practice of the central pillars of Islam; but the water also offered special efficacy to elicit response or blessing from God by virtue of its origin.

Drinking verse-washed water or water from Zamzam, repeating verses at special times for a particular number of reiterations, these were part of a wider range of customs not always mentioned in books introducing Islam, but part of daily life for many of the women I met in the mosque or visited in their homes, and for Muslims throughout the world. Practices, such as reciting the Qur'an right through for *barakah* (blessing);[21] reciting particular Qur'anic verses or other invocations two or three, seven or a hundred times, at prescribed times in the day or year; writing the names of the prophets on paper, then submerging the paper in olive oil for anointing an afflicted part of the body or in water for drinking with medicinal intent, were also well-used ways of accessing blessing, healing, protection or forgiveness, that women described to me.

---

20. *Mahjubah*, Inside cover: Vol. 23, No. 3 (229) March 2005/Safar 1426. The same practice is supported in widely-used Muslim devotional books, such as "Private Devotions for Morning and Evening from the Qur'an and Sunnah" (Al-Qahtani); "More than 1,000 Sunan for every Day and Night" (Al-Husaynaan); and the ubiquitous "Fortress of the Muslim/حصن المسلم" (Al-Qahtani).

21. This is particularly practiced over the month of Ramadan, or sometimes after someone has died. However, it is not uncommon for a group of women to meet together and take sections each to read concurrently until the whole Qur'an has been recited.

Further popular practices included use of amulets and other protective devices against sickness or envy/the evil eye.[22] It was routine for some of the women, as for Muslims in many other places in the world, to make a motion of wiping their faces with the palms of their hands at the end of *du'a'*, bringing the flow of *barakah* (blessing/power) from the recited words back on to themselves.

These practices and other rituals may seem far removed from official delineations of Islam, from the theological schools of law and the debates studied in colleges. But they are deeply ingrained in everyday life for Muslims in every continent, described in books from Lane to Musk and also Rahman.[23] Their very ubiquitousness can be puzzling to the observer: the life of the most orthodox practitioner of Islam includes elements that can look to have magical associations. Anisah Huda specified intercession as especially effective while drinking the water of Zamzam or on the Night of Vigil. She stipulated that while wiping the face after *dhikr*, saying certain phrases seven times, reciting the Qur'an, could all be effective in healing, they should be done in association with consulting doctors and taking medicine, basing her position on the example of Muhammad. A division between what appear to be conventional religious practices and those that seem to have overtones of magic or manipulation, into high or low, official or popular religion, does not adequately explain the universal appeal of the latter, nor their apparently seamless integration into a continuum of faith conduct, "an indivisible, functional whole for believers."[24]

The crucial place of Muhammad as Prophet of Islam and exemplar par excellence of the faith offers a framework to understand the place and basic

---

22. Fear of envy, or the evil eye, is widespread around the Mediterranean region and further afield. Old English lists of herbs (and contemporary Wiccan ones) mention particular herbs as protection against the evil eye. The tenth commandment, against envying a neighbor's possessions (Exodus 20:17), is probably based on an early link between the evil eye and envy, as one of a list of prohibitions against actively harming others. See Malina, *Insights*, ch. 4, for an extended discussion of envy and the evil eye in the context of biblical cultures and its basis in collective cultures characterized by an understanding of limited good. So also the Prayer of Thanksgiving in the Coptic *Book of Hours*, which is repeated seven times daily with the Lord's Prayer, places "envy" at the beginning of a list of surrounding dangers from which the supplicant asks God's protection: "All envy, all trials, all the work of Satan, the counsel of wicked men, and the rising up of enemies, hidden and manifest, take them away from us, and from all Your people, and from this holy place that is Yours." (*Agpeya*)

The evil eye, rooted in envy of another, has intriguing undertones of correspondence with mimetic desire.

23. Lane, *Manners*; Musk, *Unseen*; Rahman, *Islam*; 152–53.

24. Burnett, *Unearthly*; Musk, *Unseen*; Christian, *Folk*, 372; Gaffney, *Prophet's*, 29.

unity of Islamic practices, the meaning and function of customs both within and beyond the central pillars of Islamic faith.

Muhammad is named as final seal of the prophets, the one who brought the Qur'an, read as the conclusive and universal revelation to humanity. From his close position as God's emissary, his words and actions become normative for the rest of humankind. To become a good Muslim is to become like Muhammad: "for a true Muslim there is no greater proof for settling arguments than authentic *ahadith* and practices of Prophet Muhammad."[25]

This gives us a lens through which to view Muslim practice, whether prescribed or popular, as ways in which to copy or connect back to the example and person of Muhammad. Rather than being two separate categories of orthodox and popular religion which exist in puzzling cohabitation in faith practices, they can be seen as one body of behavior which seeks to establish a connection with the source of faith and power.

The Messenger of Islam is the unifying principle of Muslim practice. To follow Islam, then, is to worship God through imitating Muhammad's precepts and following his practices.

Muhammad's place as mimetic ideal takes us back to explore the nature of mimesis, whereby to imitate is to seek to take on the character and attributes of the original or template. Anisah Huda told the women, "We need to connect all his *ikhlaq* (character/morals) to ours." To love Muhammad is to follow him "in *haram* and *halal*, in his character." Taussig writes of the use of the mimetic or imitative faculty in "granting the copy the character and power of the original, the representation the power of the represented."[26] Through imitating Muhammad, the Muslim may take on his character or characteristics, and so access something of the flow of *barakah*/power that Muhammad received.

To explain the power of mimesis, Taussig returned to Frazer's two principles as the basis of much religious convention and practice. Frazer describes them:

> First, that like produces like, or . . . an effect resembles its cause: and, second, that things which have once been in contact with each other continue to act on each other at a distance after the physical contact has been severed. The former principle may be called the Law of Similarity, the latter the Law of Contact or Contagion.[27]

25. Saqib, *Guide*, 4.
26. Ibid., xviii.
27. Frazer, *Golden*, 11.

Muhammad, as perfect exemplar of Islam, mediates God's power[28] to his obedient followers through his intercession. And Muslims demonstrate their conformity through living the Muslim life as Muhammad did, seeking to acquire his character, emulating his example in order to draw from his power and proximity to God.

IMITATION

Mimetic practice, which Frazer has named the "Law of Similarity," begins from the premise that through faithfully imitating an original, the imitator or imitation may take on something of the nature of the original. The principle of imitation is the basis of the main pillars, or duties of Islam. These pillars, and in particular the details of their performance, are drawn primarily from the *ahadith*, or traditions of Islam, rather than from the Qur'an itself. Thus practitioners of the five daily prayers take Muhammad as their source, both in the general practice and its particulars. Describing the closely-connected authority of the Qur'an and Muhammad's example, Anisah Huda told the women twice that "the *sunnah*[29] of the Messenger came to us in the same way the Qur'an came to us."

> The model for how to pray was the Blessed Prophet Muhammad. He brought the Qur'an to us and put its teachings into practice. The Qur'an and his Sunnah, or example, are intertwined together in a symbiotic link. They cannot be separated as the Qur'an itself declares over and over: "Obey Allah and obey the Messenger." And one of the things the Messenger of Allah told us was, "Pray as you have seen me praying." Therefore, the first Muslims made it a point to note every feature of Salah and every method of how to perform it.[30]

The actions, and also the appropriate attitude in prayer and how that attitude is expressed, are recommended on the basis of the original pattern of Muhammad. It is required to approach prayer with the right intent (*niyyah*) in the heart, but Saqib also cautions us, "*Niyat* by words is not approved by Prophet Muhammad."[31] The mandatory number of *raka'* (prostrations

---

28. In Muslim prayer manuals, Padwick suggests *barakah* stands for "a kind of power, a spark of divine power attached ... pre-eminently to the personality of the Prophet" (*Devotions*, xxvi).

29. The *sunnah* of Muhammad are defined as "his sayings and doings, later established as legally-binding precedents" (Wehr, *Dictionary*, 433).

30. Emerick, *Islam*, 120.

31. Saqib, *Guide*, 11. However, Abdullah instances Islamic leaders who support

in *salah*) at the different times each day are carefully based on Muhammad's example, and so also the precise number of extra *raka'* that can be performed each time and whether they are done before or after the required *raka'*. And so it continues into every detail of life, beyond the prescribed actions and prayers even to non-mandatory matters like cleaning teeth. Saqib cites the *hadith* about using the *siwak* (tooth-stick):

> It is a good practice to clean the teeth with a tooth-stick, or a toothbrush, before performing *Wudu*. In this way you can avoid many diseases which are caused by unclean teeth. As mentioned in the *hadith* : 'Aisha' (*radiy Allah 'anha*) reported Allah's Messenger as saying: "The use of tooth-stick is a means of purifying the mouth and is pleasing to the Lord as well."[32]

The reason to clean the teeth with a *siwak* is not primarily hygiene but rather the example of Muhammad: the hygienic logic serves but to validate the wisdom of Muhammad in laying this down. Similarly in all aspects of existence, Muhammad's followers sought to establish a precept or example from him to guide their own conduct, giving rise to thousands of *hadith*. Through rigorous adherence to Muhammad's behavior and words, the devout Muslim seeks the favor of God by following the example of his most illustrious prophet. In making his life conform as closely as possible to Muhammad's life, the Muslim gains a greater chance of gaining some part of the blessing and power accrued to the Prophet of Islam.

Through the minutiae of the physical practices of Islam—standing, bowing, prostrating in prayer, and the ritual washing; the abstinence from bodily pleasures of eating, drinking, smoking, and sexual intercourse during daylight in Ramadan and other times of fasting; the circumnavigation and kissing of the black stone at Mecca, walking seven times between the hills of Safa and Marwa and stoning the pillar, in the pilgrimage—the Muslim creates in his or her own body their identity as Muslim, as one who follows as closely as possible in the steps of Muhammad. Taussig suggests that mimicry offers the possibility

> to get hold of something by means of its likeness. . . . the two-layered notion of mimesis that is involved—a copying or imitation, and a palpable, sensuous, connection between the very body of the perceiver and the perceived.[33]

---

saying *niyyah* aloud (*Religious*, 277).

32. Saqib, *Guide*, citing Ahmad, Darmi, and Nasai, 11.
33. Taussig, *Mimesis*, 21.

Muslims construct in their lives what it is to be followers of the Prophet of Islam, joined at the one time and often place with others, and through mimetic embodiment, with the Prophet himself as source and model. "Habit offers a profound example of tactile knowing ... because only at the depth of habit is radical change effected, where unconscious strata of culture are built into social routines as bodily disposition."[34] This knowledge is created as part of the wider Muslim community, who participate in the faithful recreation of the actions and life of the Prophet of Islam in daily detail in community, where knowledge and identity are embodied both socially and physically.

Contact or Contagion

The Law of Contact or Contagion rests upon establishing a physical connection with the original. It is not necessary to have a current connection—it is enough that there is a connection made, whether former, or stretching throughout time. It is based on the assumption "that things which have once been in contact with each other are always in contact."[35] It is seen in its simplest form in Islam in the *isnad*, chains of witnesses that must authenticate each tradition, reaching from witness to verified witness, right back to the Companions and wives of Muhammad or to the Prophet of Islam himself. Authentication rests on some kind of contiguity, of a physical link with the original.

Alternate lines of authority come through the Sufi *tariqa*s, which trace their ancestry back (most often through Ali) to Muhammad.

Another form of contagion is found when the names of Muhammad and other prophets are written on a piece of paper and immersed in oil for anointing or water for drinking for curative effect, as noted earlier. The physical representation of the names of power, or of Qur'anic verses, transfers the power of the original through the medium of paper and ink, oil or water, to the sufferer. Muhammad is the Messenger through whom the Message, the Qur'an, is received. It is the Qur'an which validates Muhammad as God's chosen Messenger. Believed to be the pre-existent word of God, the Qur'an is the source of the power which marks Muhammad. So the physical realization of the Qur'an, whether aural/recited, as verses, or in a bound book, also enables sympathetic connection with the original (held to be in heaven with God).

---

34. Ibid., 21, 25.
35. Frazer, *Golden*, 12.

Copy and Contiguity

However, as Frazer notes, the principle of contact usually also involves imitation. The aural recitation of the Qur'an is both a physical manifestation of its presence, but also combined with imitation of Muhammad who was commanded to "Recite!" and spoke the Qur'an in the form he believed he received it. So too with the rituals of pilgrimage, including drinking water from the sacred spring of Zamzam: as Muslims follow the practice and precept of Muhammad, walking in their bodies in the same physical space and patterns that he walked in, we have "imitation blending so intimately with contact that it becomes impossible to separate image from substance in the power of the final effect."[36]

A group of women gather for the "sealing" *khitmah* (complete recitation) of the Qur'an, each one taking one or two or more portions to read until every portion has been recited by someone, all reciting at the same time in a just-audible murmur. On the table in the middle are some bottles of water with their lids off. This gathering may just be an excuse for the women in the extended family to get together and bring particular blessing on the house in which the recitation occurs. Or it may be done with intent to bring God's blessing on a new business venture of one of the families; or a friend in hospital will ask them to do it, and pay for the food they enjoy together over a good gossip at the end. And the bottles of water are taken home, with extra blessing for those who drink them. This is not an un-Islamic pagan ritual, but rather an accessing of the power/*barakah* of the Qur'an and the Messenger through whom it came, by the physical recitation and imitation of the Reciter, which is transferred to the place where it happens, to those participating, and to the water over which the recitation takes place. This is the law of contagion, or connection, closely intertwined with imitation of the Prophet of Islam—the two together empower and bring blessing to their practitioners.

The use of the Arabic language itself, as the only language in which the true Qur'an is accessible and the language of daily prayer even for the approximately 80 percent of Muslims who do not have Arabic as their first language, also stems from the effectiveness of following the example of Muhammad. If the worshipper reads or prays in another language, the imitative link is weaker. In *tajwid* (Qur'an recitation) classes, many of the lessons are spent in training even native speakers of Arabic how to vocalize the Qur'anic letters and words in a way which is believed to be a more authentic rendition of how Muhammad spoke. The very configuration of

---

36. Frazer, *Golden*, 12; Taussig, *Mimesis*, 53.

the vocal organs, dialectic precision, confers more power/*barakah* on the reciter of the Qur'an, both imitating and entering into the recitative power of the Prophet of Islam.

Donning defining clothing, whether the male robe (without stitching) for the *hajj*, or the head covering for the woman (the descending head shawl and long skirt of the prayer outfit, or the embracing scarf and full-length coat of the conservative Sunni woman), is both copying (imitation, either of Muhammad or that which he enjoined on his wives) and contact. In putting it on, the Muslim is establishing physical contact: "the touch, the feel, like putting on a skin . . . here [their] very body becomes the vehicle onto which mimetic appearance becomes three-dimensioned, becomes optics in depth."[37]

All the practices of Islam, orthodox or popular, can thus be read as actions which bring the actor/s into connection with the original, the Message and Messenger, and their associated power/*barakah*. All practices, whether the central five pillars or more diffused and sometimes localized rituals, are ways of connecting with Muhammad: through imitating his example, through the historical links of the *hadith* chains, or through other means of contact and contagion. The corporate dimension of so many pious practices is evocative of the imaginary community of the Muslim *ummah*, the body of Islam emerging from the life and message of Muhammad who is the supreme embodiment of Islam.

Connecting With the Source of Power

This brings the practices of Muslims into a coherent whole. That which connects a Muslim with the Prophet of Islam, whether through meticulous copy or contagion, enables them to more fully participate in his life and example, therefore to become a good Muslim, with a fuller hope of acquiring the merit needed to evoke God's mercy and enter heaven—thus the ever-present need concerning the hereafter is met. In the same way, by diligent imitation or by establishing some form of contiguity with the Prophet of Islam, the Muslim can enter into the flow of power/*barakah* that came to and comes through Muhammad, which is needed in the daily concerns of life and health, for protection against evil forces, and to negotiate success in business, relationships, and the complexities of life.

This coherence suggests an understanding of how some more peripheral practices may be defined as Islamic or non-Islamic. The classification depends on the source of power that is being accessed. For the devout

37. Taussig, *Mimesis*, 191.

Sunni, only that which takes us back directly to the Messenger of Islam (or his Companions) and his Message is permissible. This also translates into a rejection of anything that looks like *bida'* (innovation), that goes beyond Muhammad's example or words. If it is not clear what the source of the innovation is, then the power derived from it is suspect.

Other Muslim groups may allow a wider definition of sources of power. For the Shi'a, it can include those of Muhammad's bloodline—their lives and examples (for example, Fatima) provide an acceptable basis for citing and imitation, their lives and deaths (particularly Hussein) are reenacted, and their tombs become a source of contagious blessing. Similarly, Sufi chains set up a connective association of blessing and authority traced back to their founder.

Small amulets with verses from the Qur'an are usually acceptable ways to access power for protection or healing, in the imitative writing out of the verse and the physical connection through wearing them. However, the extensively used *hijayib* (writing from the Qur'an or magic squares of letters or numbers on a piece of paper that is then tightly folded, sown into a small square of material and kept on the body for protection or power) is stigmatized by official practitioners of Islam, because of its link with the occult, an unacceptable source of power to the devout monotheist.

The month of Muhammad's birthday (*Rabia' al-Awwal*) is a time of increased religious gatherings and *dhikr*s. The regular teaching timetable at the mosque pauses to focus on the Prophet of Islam and teach about his character, morals, and behavior. The measure of the Muslim's life is the degree of connection with the source of Islam, imitating Muhammad in all details, and finding or establishing contiguous links to him through his name, companions, precepts or practices.

Model Muslim Women

Muhammad is the external mimetic ideal and source of power/blessing for the imaginary community of the Muslim *ummah*. But where roles are often presented in gendered terms, and particularly when regulations concerning purity and pollution so constrain women's participation in rituals of faith, what shapes the daily life and identity aspirations of Muslim women? I had anticipated that in the teaching in the women's mosque program, there would be a focus on women in the Qur'an and around Muhammad. Pierce comments:

> In recent decades, some Muslim scholars have explored how a re-evaluation of classical historical narratives may interrupt

> certain dominant gender assumptions and give rise to greater gender justice within Islam.... The stories of prominent women in Islamic history have been retold in order to inspire and justify the acceptance of wider spheres of female authority.[38]

Certainly Anisah Huda was well able to cite the example of eminent women in Muslim history when talking to foreigners. In the lecture she gave in her house to three expatriate women, she cited a book *tahdhib al-tahdhib* (*The Refined of the Refined*) about many of the prominent historical people of faith in Islam, which after its fourth recension still included 580 women, and quoted the example of Umm al-Darda,[39] who used to teach in the Ummayad mosque, and whose lectures were attended by both women and men, including the king himself 'Abd al-Malak bin Marwan. She also quoted a *hadith* about 'Aishah, that Muhammad said to "take half your religion from this *humayra'* (red-cultured woman)."[40] In response to questions from her expatriate audience, Anisah Huda could describe the examples of Umm Waraqah being permitted by Muhammad to lead her household in prayer when the man was sick,[41] and Umm Salma giving Muhammad advice when his men rebelled.[42] When I asked her in a private interview about her ideal woman, after she spoke at length about her mother as exemplar, she also mentioned 'Aisha', Khadijah, Hafsah, and Fatimah, along with Nusaybah and 'Aishah's sister, Asma' bint Abu Bakr.[43] All these women were described in terms of how they served Muhammad.

Anisah Huda noted also the female Companions of Muhammad and many daughters of scholars, hundreds of them especially in the first three centuries of Islam, and more than 88 women who transmitted *ahadith*. However, I heard little mention of these examples in her lectures to the women.

---

38. Pierce, *Remembering*, 346.

39. Umm al-Darda is extensively referenced in Nadwi's (*al-Muhaddithat*) book on woman scholars in Islam. See also Nurbakhsh, *Sufi*.

40. Despite the frequency with which it is quoted, this *hadith* is not well supported. Al-Islam, "Traditions," 2; al-Turayri, "Islam Today."

41. This *hadith* is found in Abu Dawud, Book #2, Ḥadīth #0591. However, its application, that women can lead mixed prayer, is disputed: for example, see Yahya, "What did the Prophet do?"; Al-Munajjid, "Ruling."

42. Found in Sahih Bukhari, Book #50, Ḥadīth #891.

43. 'Ali Qutb, *Women*, 151–55; Ibn Sa'd, *Women*, 196–199. See also Jaschok and Shui, *History*, 230).

Women's Vocation

"When we had reared our children and finished our vocation and married them off..." ("*wa-rabbayna 'ayalna wa-khalasat **risalitna** wa-gawaznahum*...")

The speaker was a middle-aged Egyptian woman, attending a literacy class. Her extended discourse reflected classic ring structure, shown even in this excerpt where the middle of the three phrases carries the central import of the sentence,[44] as she described her role in bringing up and marrying off her children with the same term that is used to describe Muhammad's vocation as prophet—*risalitna* (our mission, or vocation).[45] As Middle Eastern women's primary community was their extended family, so they saw their primary role, their mission, in family terminology of caring for their children. Anisah Huda explained, "In Islam the woman is permitted to, but not required to work [outside the home]. She is the one who gets pregnant, gives birth, breastfeeds, weans, cleans the child, teaches." When I ask Middle Eastern women about their ideal woman, the first answer is almost invariably their mother. The primary community of family locates the mimetic ideal in familial terms, where the ideal woman is the one who succeeds in her given mission of bringing up her children creditably and marrying them well.[46]

A lecture given by Anisah Huda on Mother's Day (a public holiday) included a brief mention of the wife of Pharaoh, where she was bracketed immediately with Mariyam (Mary),[47] "who endured everything because of 'Isa, the blows and words of the Jews against her. So there are Asya,[48] Mariyam, Fatima, and Khadijah—four outstanding women." Stowasser suggests that

---

44. Ring structure (sometimes described as "chiastic" structure) has been described most in the context of ME writings. However, Douglas comments: "Ring composition is found all over the world, not just in the Middle East" (*Thinking*, Loc. 57, 185). I had not anticipated finding it in the spoken discourse of an "illiterate" woman; however we can expect that common literary discourse forms would have their origin in speech patterns. See also Walker's (*Decoration*) analysis of ring structures in Biblical and Qur'anic texts.

45. Dale, *Women*, 317.

46. Jane Austin shows us a parallel in her character, Mrs Bennett: "The business of her life was to get her daughters married" (*Pride*, 4).

47. This is from the link between the two women in *al-Tahrim* 66:11–12. No allusion was made to the preceding negative example of the wives of Noah and Lot (66:10).

48. Islamic tradition gives the name of Pharaoh's wife as Asya (Stowasser, *Women*, 59). Mariyam, mother of 'Isa, is the only woman mentioned by her name in the Qur'an.

the Qur'an's female exemplars came to serve as "models," symbolic entities representing past human experience, but also called upon to shape present and future human reality; their symbolic function was and is that of "models of" and also "models for" the Islamic way of life.[49]

However, this was the only time I heard women in the Qur'an publicly instanced as models in the mosque, and it was specifically in their function as mothers (in relation to Moses and 'Isa), along with Fatima and Khadijah in the same role. In the same lecture, Anisah Huda referred to the *hadith* that "Paradise is under the feet of mothers" commenting "Islam raises (the mother) to a place that men don't dream of. If there were only this one *hadith*, is this among any other nation?[50] This is raising women, her rights, the freedom of women." She went on to quote the *hadith* on honoring one's mother.[51] However, such a model offers no place to the single or childless woman: women receive honor in relation to their offspring, not in their own right.

While the woman "becomes the projection of the inadequacy of society, shackled with the burden of failure and weakness … at the same time, her role as mother is symbolically elevated" as "the source of love and compassion, symbol of sacrifice, … center of honor, of human purity."[52] Female exemplars were cited in reference to their maternal role.

Precedents or Paradigms?

Beyond the preceding instance, in Anisah Huda's mosque lectures to Muslim women I heard little mention of historical Muslim women as mimetic ideal. In addition to Muhammad as paradigm, mention was made of many different Companions and Muslim rulers, and a whole paper/lecture was given on notable (male) *'ulama'* as examples. When women were included among the many men cited, it was not so much as models or exemplars for

---

49. Stowasser, *Women*, 20–21.

50. This Hadith is attributed to the *hadith* collection of Al-Tirmidhi. It is not found in al-Bukhari, Muslim, Malik's Muwatta or Abu Dawud; and is not consistently deemed a strong *hadith*.

51. Narrated Abu Huraira: A man came to Allah's Apostle and said, "O Allah's Apostle! Who is more entitled to be treated with the best companionship by me?" The Prophet said, "Your mother." The man said. "Who is next?" The Prophet said, "Your mother." The man further said, "Who is next?" The Prophet said, "Your mother." The man asked for the fourth time, "Who is next?" The Prophet said, "Your father. " (Al- Bukhari: Book #73, Hadith#2)

52. Haddad, *Islam*, 11.

the women;⁵³ but rather as illustrations of particular Muslim principles (as in the preceding examples of Umm Waraqah and Umm Salma), whether positive (the woman who confronted the Khalif 'Umar) or negative ('Aisha herself could make mistakes [in opposing 'Ali]). Thus Anisah Huda described "a woman, who was a doctor, defended the Prophet of God and fought. . . . With many blows, she didn't fall,"⁵⁴ to critique a sheikh who refused to teach a woman.

Anisah Huda encouraged girls graduating from Qur'an classes that women could be scholars, teachers, guides, could rule or arbitrate; and even raised the question of whether women are allowed within *shari'ah* to become president.⁵⁵ In conversation with expatriates she could denote the examples of women in Muslim history who had led mixed prayer or taught both women and men in the main Damascus mosque. However, explicit public espousing in her lectures of women as models of religious authority to teach or lead prayer in mixed groups may have been too risky in the conservative climate in which she taught.

The absence of Muslim women as exemplars in mosque lectures may also be because when "all of God's prophets and messengers, from Adam to Muhammad, were men,"⁵⁶ historical Muslim women were not of sufficient prophetic stature or conformed to the mimetic ideal to be effective external mediators in offering access to blessing/power to disciples. Their optimum role was that of serving God's prophets and messengers. However, they were also too removed to function as internal mediators to the women who followed them in the faith community.

If there was minimal focus on prominent women within Muslim sources and history in the mosque program teaching, more recent Muslim women leaders such as Nazira Zayn al-Din in Syria and Zaynab al-Ghazali in Egypt received no mention. Although Zayn al-Din promoted women's interpretation of the Qur'an, in doing so she directly challenged the importance of veiling, to which Anisah Huda is strongly committed. Al-Ghazali takes a very similar stance to Anisah Huda, but there is mixed response as to how much she exemplified the domestic submission which she taught,

---

53. In contrast with Egyptian Zaynab al-Ghazzali, who described how her father would say to her, "'Do you choose Huda al-Sha'rawi or will you become Nusaybah?' And I would say to him, 'I will be Nusaybah.'" Quoted in Shehadeh, *Idea*, 122.

54. Nusayba bint Ka`b (also preceding note). She is probably referred to as a doctor here because she is said to have initially gone to the battle to bring water (succor) to those in need, and then moved to Muhammad's side and started fighting to protect him (`Ali Qutb, *Women*, 184).

55. Meltzer and Nix, *Light*.

56. Stowasser, *Women*, 20.

as well as the commitment to *daʿwa*. It may be that the mimetic example of women leaders who are so close geographically and historically is more open to examination and contestation. Similarly there was no direct reference to other contemporary women leaders in Syria, most notably the al-Qubaysi movement which developed from the Al-Nur Mosque with which Anisah Huda had been involved. Girard's model of mimetic rivalry within the context of internal mediation suggests the risk of public engagement with those who are close mediators of desire.

The daʿiya—Embodied Model

As Girard suggests, the desires and identity aspirations of Muslims acquire form as they are mediated through their local model or immediate mimetic ideal. Traditionally many Muslim women have found their model among the women in their immediate or extended family. However, identity within the mosque community offers a mimetic ideal that is defined in terms of function within the faith community rather than family. Shaykhah Ghina Hammoud in Lebanon links being a leader and role model for the women she teaches, with her own practical experience in "ordering the good or forbidding the bad."[57]

When Anisah Huda tells the women, "You are the *khalifat* of God[58] on earth," she is placing Muslim women in relationship to God, as opposed to their position in kin patriarchy where the woman is always subordinate. So also, Jaschok and Shui write about female imams (*ahong*) in China:

> When some of the most articulate and forthright women *ahong* ponder a direct relationship between God and women, to the exclusion of male intermediaries, they not only question the immutability of a "celestial patriarchy," intervening thereby in its secular subtext of a more worldly gender hierarchy, but they also begin to determine their own existential and social worth.[59]

As allegiance to the imaginary community is best expressed through its local embodiment within the mosque, so too the shape of loyalty to Muhammad as ideal Muslim finds form through the teaching and example of local leaders. Anisah Huda, through modeling leadership and teaching in the mosque sorority, had an influence that exceeded her words and tuition

---

57. Maher, *Veiled*.

58. Wadud translates *khalifah* in this context as "vice-regent" or "moral agent" (Qur'an, 23:102); see particularly her discussion in *Jihad*, 32–37.

59. Jaschok and Shui, *History*, 236.

in evoking desire in her disciples beyond a solely familial role. The growing presence of Muslim women teachers is offering Muslim women a new mimetic ideal, a new shape to their aspirations and identity.

When women gave testimonies in *Eid* celebrations about coming to the mosque programs, Anisah Huda's name was frequently mentioned as a reason to attend. While Anisah Huda resisted this ("I don't want any woman to come because of me or because of any other woman, but because this is God's house—[regardless of] whoever greets her or doesn't greet her") at other times she used her own behavior as example for the women. So she described to the women how she left a wedding celebration early ("I stood outside in the cold for half an hour") because the kind of songs and dancing made it an inappropriate context in which to remain.[60] A woman who had had Anisah Huda as teacher in another mosque school told me how she had started attending this mosque program because she liked her teaching, it was "*waʿi, ḥadath*" (aware, modern). And another commented, "Anisah Huda respects herself and all others. Her teaching is very *hadirah* [civilized]—that's Islam."[61] For these women, Anisah Huda represented a form of Islam with which they could identify—both conservative and "aware, modern." She exemplified further possibilities for their own roles within the community. A *tajwid* teacher told me that she had accompanied Anisah Huda when she was going to a sheikh, and as a consequence, asked to attend classes with the sheikh too, and also graduated with an *ijazah* to teach. Anisah Huda's own presence and example as a religious teacher was an implicit challenge to the oft-quoted *hadith* that women are deficient in intelligence and religion.[62]

Mahmoud, in her discussion of the rise of *daʿwa* as a movement within Islam, comments:

> In many ways the figure of the *daʿiya* exemplifies the ethos of the contemporary Islamic Revival, and people now often ascribe to this figure the same degree of authority previously reserved for religious scholars.[63]

---

60. Maher, *Veiled*, 33.

61. See Deeb's discussion on the use of "civilized" as synonymous with "modern" among Shi'ite women in Lebanon, and the questions it raises about who defines "civilized" and in what terms (*Piety*, S114).

62. Al-Bukhari, Book #6, Ḥadīth #301, and Book #24, Ḥadīth #541. The latter also includes

Muhammad's saying that "the majority of the dwellers of Hell-fire were you (women)."

63. Mahmood, *Politics*, 58; see also Gaffney, *Prophet's*, 33.

Anisah Huda was conscious of the import of her role: "*Da'wa* isn't easy work. You are between people and God [*fa 'inti takuni bayn al-nas wa bayn Allah*]. I ask God Almighty to make me worthy of it."[64] In lecture notes that she had prepared for women at the mosque, Anisah Huda wrote, "For the *da'iya* is God's mediator to people and successor of the Messengers [*li'annah al-da'iya safir Allah ila al-nas wa khalifat al-rusul*]."

Woman as "God's mediator to people" and "successor of the Messengers" is a startling, almost shocking, shift from the familial sphere of women describing *risalitna* (our mission) in maternal terms, as being to raise and marry children. The role of notable women in Muslim history was to serve prophets and messengers. But here vocation in the context of the faith community locates the woman who is a *da'iya* in the place of mediator between God and people, and successor or caliph to the apostles (*khalifat al-rusul*). The model of the *da'iya* offers women the possibility of an honored position within the mosque and wider religious community, rather than solely in the domestic domain.

Khalifat Allah is a phrase that in Qur'anic terms embraces all humanity (*al-Baqarah* 2:30).[65] And Qur'anic verses such as *Fussilat* 41:33, *al-'Imran* 3:104, 110, *al-Tawbah* 9:71 are used to emphasize that all Muslims, women and men, are to be involved in *da'wa*.[66] Anisah Huda told the women, "We need to be witnesses, present in every situation, a witness to Islam and Muslims" and encouraged the women to read widely and disseminate material on Islam. However, while *da'wa* is enjoined on all Muslims, the significance (and prophetic connections) of the position of *da'iya* is evident in Anisah Huda's description of the training offered at the mosque. She told the women:

> We will teach girls for free, in English and computers, those who are outstanding [*mutamayizin*], specialized people, to be cultured *da'iyas* [*da'iyat muthaqafat*]. Like the prophets, [they should present] the best picture, of someone aware, tactful and neat. The *da'iya* [should have] a good image among people, the best picture among people. No prophet has defects. There are special characteristics for a *da'iya*—not all people can be one.

Khalifat al-nabi, 'successor to the prophet', carries a higher significance than *khalifat Allah*, which is a vocation for all humans. Likewise, all (Muslims) are adjured to do *da'wa*, but it requires special qualifications to be a *da'iya*. On an earlier occasion Anisah Huda had described the qualifications

---

64. Meltzer and Nix, *Light*.
65. Wadud describes it as "fundamental and essential to being human" (*Gender*, 33).
66. Mahmood, *Politics*, 58.

for someone to be a *shaykh* in a mosque as "studying the Qur'an and the *shari'ah*." She herself had memorized the Qur'an as a young girl, studied the *shari'ah*, and studied in al-Nur mosque.[67] Then twenty-three years ago she had begun offering classes in memorizing the Qur'an and interpretation in a couple of mosques. She was seventeen at the time.

However, while men and women require the same basic qualifications to become a *da'iya*, women *da'iyas* have restricted responsibilities because of their gender. Mahmood notes that women participating in *da'wa* in the Egyptian context are not allowed to do so among men, according to prohibitions against women delivering the Friday sermon or leading men in collective prayer. She links this to the Qur'anic verse *al-Nisa'* 4:34, where men are guardians of women, so women "should not serve in significant positions of leadership over men" and to the belief that a woman's voice is *'awrah* (defective, or to be concealed) particularly in situations related to prayer, when it could incite sexual feelings in men.[68] Anisah Huda did not challenge these constraints: and took care that the sound from the microphone when women were speaking or singing could not be heard in the main male section of the mosque (although the reverse was a frequent occurrence). However, she located the restrictions on women leading mixed prayer in the context of ritual pollution rather than aural distraction: "The woman could not always lead [mixed prayer] because she was prevented from praying privately when she was menstruating, let alone leading others in prayer." In China, *nu ahong* do not lead worship or perform the call to prayer; nor are they "involved in weddings or chanting scriptures at the graveside," because of the risk of "*bidaerti*" or innovation/unorthodoxy with women's mosques and teachers.[69] So too Rausch and Hassan discuss the constraints faced by *murshidahs* (women preachers and spiritual guides) in Morocco, and by female preachers in Turkey. Likewise Professor Su'ad Saleh's discussion of her futile application to the Islamic Research Council in Egypt, despite Grand Mufti Tantawi's insistence that for membership, "if she has memorized the Qur'an and the Sunna of the Prophet, and understands jurisprudence from the four schools of Islamic law, and everything

67. Although Anisah Huda is normally referred to as a *da'iya* (preacher) rather than a *shaykhah*, she didn't repudiate the implicit link when asked about her own path to becoming leader in the women's mosque program.

68. As for men, so for women: "The da'iya must practice what she preaches, and her exhortations must be in accord with the Quran and the Sunna, undertaken with wisdom and sincerity of the heart, and performed for the purpose of pleasing God rather than for personal gain or popularity" (Mahmood, *Politics*, 65; see also Al-Musnad, *Fatawa*, 340–41).

69. Jaschok and Shui, *History*, 93, 159.

associated with legislative rulings, there is no difference between men and women." Norton argues that the question "Who am I?" can only be understood together with the question "What am I allowed to do?"[70] While the reasons offered vary, Muslim female religious teachers commonly find their role is restricted or contested.

Becoming a *da'iya*: The Making of a Missionary

Beyond the qualifications, what goes into the making of a Muslim missionary,[71] teacher or *da'iya*? Anisah Huda is in a line of women who stand out in each of their generations for their education. She describes her mother, Yazda al-Sayyd: "Back in her time, many women were illiterate. Many people didn't know how to read. In her village in Lebanon there was only her and another girl who knew how to read. People would celebrate by putting them on a horse and parading them through the village." Anisah Huda recalls being one of only four or five girls who had memorized the whole Qur'an in her *shari'ah* school when she was growing up: "Now there are thousands." At present Enas, who had memorized the Qur'an when she was between three and ten years old, is unusual among her peers in being allowed as a young woman to go abroad for tertiary study. Anisah Huda, noting that this wasn't widely acceptable "in our society," commented: "In allowing Enas to travel, our intent was that she become a world-class *da'iya*,[72] to answer questions on Islam, God willing. To be a world-class *da'iya*, she needs to know the languages and cultures of others." Even though Enas's studies are "secular," the intent is *da'wa*. Enas reflects on generational attitudes:

> When my mom was my age it was impossible for a girl to travel and to study abroad. And study what? Politics! Politics? A girl? That is not common! There are still people from the other generation, and from my generation, who are still living on the old ideas, the old understanding. I can see that I can serve Islam

---

70. Rausch, *Women*; Hassan, *Reshaping*; Maher, *Politics*; Norton, *Identity*, 8.

71. Both the persuasive and practical aspects of *da'wa* suggest this as an apt translation. See also Gaffney, *Prophet's*, 33; Glassé, *Encycylopaedia*, 127.

72. The need for social sciences as well as religious knowledge in mission was developed by Rashid Rida (1865–1930), early advocate of contemporary understandings of *da'wa*. Thus, in Egypt "significantly, it . . . is secular universities—not the state-run Islamic University of al-Azhar where the 'ulama'are usually trained—that have produced the most prominent da'iyat (both male and female) of the last century" (Mahmood, *Politics*, 62, 64).

better if I study politics, or if I study economics or media—but my mom didn't have a choice—she had to study Islam.[73]

Women who have achieved prominence have often been able to do so through male relatives: Nadwi in his book on women scholars in Islam notes that "many were daughters of men bearing the title 'qadi', 'imam', 'hafiz.'"[74] Anisah Huda records her gratitude to her mother for letting her spend time at the mosque and in study instead of seeking her help in the house. Her mother recalls being encouraged by her husband: "Don't make [Huda] work—just let her study and teach." On another occasion, Anisah Huda described how her father would gather the family at home to pray together in the mornings and often in the evenings, with "him, my brothers, and us [women] lined up behind; afterwards he would teach us." She told me of her father's petition at the ka'ba that his children would become *da'iyas*. Her brother, Dr Muhammad al-Habash, internationally known as an Islamic scholar, encouraged Anisah Huda, who had her program at the mosque where he was *imam*.[75]

Within the women's mosque movement, now women are enabling other women to become leaders. Now Anisah Huda passes on her own passion for education to the women she trains. She insists, "The school at the mosque doesn't take the place of normal studies. I don't like any sister to come to the mosque who isn't studying. If she was in school and dropped out, I work hard to have her return to school and study anew." Meltzer and Nix show an interview with Amina, who attended Anisah Huda's mosque lessons, and now gives classes at her local mosque. Amina described how she dropped out of school at fifteen years and worked hard in the fields. Then she went back to school, although it was difficult, and was now in her third year of university. Against all her village norms, thirty-eight and single: "Now people respect me. They now call me "Anisah" [Teacher] Amina." Similarly Anisah Huda describes two sisters, thirty and above, living unmarried and in poverty with their father. Despite the father's opposition, Anisah Huda found work for them both. When identity is defined in terms

---

73. Meltzer and Nix, *Light*, 1, 13, 25-6.

74. Nadwi, *Al-Muhaddithat*, XII. See also Halima Krausen's sponsorship by Imam Razvi in Hamburg (Spielhaus, *Making*), and Umm-i-Hassan's support from her father-in-law and husband in Islamabad (Bano, *Conclusion*). In Egypt, Zaynab al-Ghazzali was encouraged by both her father and later Hasan al-Banna (Shehadeh, *Idea*, 122–23) and Dr Su'ad Saleh is from a family of Islamic teachers (Maher, *Veiled*). The same trend of male patrons (not necessarily relatives) is evident in Smith's book on women in mission in the history of the Christian church (*Women*).

75. Anisah Huda also mentioned two brothers in other countries who were both *da'iyas*, and a sister in a different city who taught Islam both in Syria and internationally

of faith, and not only family and reproduction, both single and married women can find purpose. Maher records Amal, a school teacher, describing how Anisah Huda "had a big influence through her teaching. Her teachings are the basis for my life": as Anisah Huda encourages Amal to see her own role in "teaching future generations" in mimetic terms of *da'wa*.[76]

Authority and Representation

The mimetic ideal of *da'iya* does not nullify the familial model of mother so much as extend it. Anisah Huda insists that her work of *da'wa* doesn't come before her domestic responsibilities. "I will be judged first on my home and my children." Her husband corroborates, "I always say that my wife is exemplary in everything, an example in her work inside the house and outside the house, and everywhere. . . . At home she is an exemplary wife."[77] The women in the mosque program are taught to be loyal to their parents and more loyal to religious truth. "We should say, 'I love my parents; I love the truth more.'"

So also, the qualifications required for a woman to be one of the leaders in the mosque program include personal ability to relate to people and children, as well as religious knowledge. She is required

> to have memorized the whole Qur'an [not necessarily in *tajwid*]; to know about our religion, so she can answer any questions; and to have a good personality, which means she should be calm, patient, treat people well. If a mother brings little girls and they don't know what to do and move around or make a noise, she [the teacher] needs to relate well to them. (Ebtisam's notes)

Gaffney develops his typology of saints, scholars, and warriors to describe Islamic preachers in Egypt. *Da'iya*s also wield authority in different ways. Mahmood contrasts the "scholarly" approach of Hajja Faiza with the more informal style of Hajja Faris, and later the strict fear-evoking mode of Hajja Samira (all teaching in different mosques and neighborhoods in Cairo). Each of these "pedagogies of persuasion" finds its basis in different communities of followers (most notably with Hajja Faris, whose supporters have prevented efforts to have her removed from her position as *da'iya* because of her lack of knowledge of the authoritative religious sources).[78] The influence wielded by these women is in relation to the extent to which

---

76. Meltzer and Nix, *Light*, 51–55; Maher, *Veiled*, 14.
77. Meltzer and Nix, *Light*, 51; Maher, *Veiled*, 32.
78. Mahmood, *Politics*, 92.

they represent the mimetic ideal for their communities of hearers, both in the social understanding of knowledge and mode of persuasion,[79] and in their comportment and lived practices of faith and life. So Halima Krausen maintains her position and influence as female *imam* in a Hamburg mosque through focusing on writing and teaching, delivering Friday *khutba*s only if the whole congregation accept her in this role (although her written *khutba*s are widely disseminated) and not seeking to lead mixed-gender prayers.[80]

Anisah Huda refers to a definitive time in her life early in her ministry, when "religious leaders" surrounded her with "criticism, discouragement, and scolding."[81] In an interview with me, she described the same time in her life as a time when she consciously turned away from an authoritarian model emphasizing fidelity to and dependence on the rulings and views of individual *da'iya*s, which sought to influence students "as if they were following me and not following God." This is a process of negative mimesis, where the follower seeks to become the opposite of the model, and thus is still shaped in reference to it.

Hence, while Anisah Huda sees the role of *da'iya* in prophetic terms, she is clear that she prefers to exercise her role in an exemplar or mimetic, rather than an authoritarian framework:

> We can't describe the work of *da'wa* in terms of leader and followers, ruler and ruled. The male religious leader is a brother to the people, and the female religious leader is a sister to the people. She can order them to do good works and forbid them from doing bad ones, she can organize and arrange things, but all this is built on love and willingness. She can't force anything, I cannot impose my opinion or decision on anyone. It all happens through love, as long as they have accepted me as a leader, and they take me as an example.[82]

Anisah Huda constantly encouraged women to learn and think for themselves, to make their own choices. However, women commonly came to her to ask for advice in family and marital issues.

In the women's *madrasah* in the fateful Red Mosque in Islamabad, Bano similarly identifies Umm-i-Hassan's role in providing a source of shelter in relationship and domestic tensions for the girls who came to her. Umm-i-Hassan defined the teacher–student relationship in terms of a "spiritual" mother–daughter bond. In invoking the family link, Umm-i-Hassan

---

79. Gaffney, *Prophet's*, 34–35.
80. Spielhaus, *Making*.
81. Meltzer and Nix, *Light*, 22.
82. Maher, *Veiled*, 33.

was acknowledging its foundational place in the lives of the women even as she called for an alternative allegiance.[83] Bano compares Umm-i-Hassan's authority with that of the *Anisah*s in the Qubaysi organizational structure in Syria and internationally; and her focus on details of personal life and grooming with the *ustani*s (women teachers) in Indian village *madrasah*s, inculcating by example urban forms of comportment.[84]

For women in the mosque program, the *da'iya* models an alternate mimetic ideal grounded in a framework of faith rather than predominantly family. The desires of the disciples may be mediated through various forms of persuasion or instruction. The *da'iya* represents in herself a way of dressing, being, and relating to others that they desire; and beyond that, a place of influence, able to draw on the authority of Islamic texts, with potential for a role and purpose beyond the boundary lines of marriage and reproduction.

Conclusion

The measure of leadership and influence can perhaps be best seen through its mimetic effect in shaping the desires and behavior of adherents. In different degrees, both Muhammad, Prophet of Islam, and Anisah Huda mediate the desires of those who look to them. Through imitation of their pious practices, they present those who follow their example and teaching the possibility of power to negotiate the next life. They also offer power for this life, whether in accessing *barakah*/blessing to deal with life's uncertainties, or in offering a role and purpose that, while fulfilling family priorities, is not circumscribed by them, but offers the possibility of influencing one's own fate and that of others. The position of *da'iya* takes women beyond the constraints of kin patriarchy, though still restricted by gender, to responsibility designated in prophetic phraseology. Allegiance to the imaginary community is enabled through fidelity to the founding or prophetic ideal leader. At the same time the local leader both embodies and shapes the desires of community members, mediating their aspirations, and thus the virtues or power which they seek to emulate in the founding figure.

---

83. In 2007 the Red Mosque was the centre of a military operation by the Pakistani government to crush a protest there, resulting in (a state figure of at least) eighty-nine deaths (Bano, *Conclusion*, 510, 518–521).

84. Islam, *Qubaysiyyat*; Jeffery et al., *Leading*. Also Hafez's description of an Egyptian village women's project: "To them, Amal was a model of Islamic womanhood that they all wished to emulate. Urban, educated, and obviously more financially prosperous than they were, she embodied qualities to which the village women aspired. They believed that the program would make them just like her" (*Islam*, 141, 148).

7

Performative Practices

Anisah Huda said that the Prophet had come to a house and found the man sick, and the woman was educated, and he had said that she could lead the household in *salah*. So in principle a woman could lead (mixed) *salah*, but generally the man would be the leader in *salah*, as he could always lead. But the woman could not always as she was prevented from praying privately when she was menstruating, let alone leading others in *salah*.

She quoted a verse from the Qur'an that men and women are from the same soul (*nafs wahid*) and therefore of the same essence; and said that they were equal in reward/merits and punishment (*al-thuwab wa al-'uqab*). If they committed the same offence they would receive the same punishment. But there were differences in their duties (*al-wadha'if*).

Introduction

WE CAN THINK ABOUT how people and individuals are formed in terms of their desires, which are shaped within the context of their relational network and of cultural understandings of what it means to be a person.[1] Girard develops the idea that desire is formed within relationships through his proposition that all our desire is mimetic, not spontaneous, mediated by another "model."[2] Allegiance to a community can thus be understood through individual desire for competence or power which is perceived to characterize members of that community. The mimetic ideal who embodies the desired characteristics is most often the leader of the community. In the previous chapter we noted how the local leader both personifies and shapes the desires of community members, mediating

---

1. Hafez, *Islam*, 5; Joseph, *Learning*.
2. Alison, *Girard's*; McDonald, *Violence*.

their aspirations. Allegiance finds focus in the ideal model, or leader, who shapes community desires. Allegiance is then demonstrated in particular ways of being and doing, exemplified by the mimetic ideal, that embody the values of a community and form the practicing individuals within it according to the desired ideal.[3] We can describe these ways of being and doing as performative practices. "Practices" refers to their habitual and reiterative nature. "Performative" suggests both their enacted and formative character. Performative practices are ways of inhabiting particular historical and cultural contexts of place and time. These practices refer both to specifically "pious" and also everyday acts, ways of dressing, walking, talking, and the guiding scripts that shape them.

The Muslim community becomes visible and is reproduced in the communal imitative actions of its adherents. The Muslim *ummah* finds particular (self-) definition in *arkan al-Islam*, the five (or six) pillars or practices of faith.[4] Allegiance to Islam finds realization in adherence to a local community expression of faith. Muhammad as mimetic ideal is interpreted through the example and teaching of particular leaders. As the imagined community finds shape in the local gathering, so Islam is embodied in particular performative practices which give expression to specific local community experiences, values, and life priorities.[5] And these ways of being and practices are gendered: while men and women are "equal in merits and punishments," there are "differences in duties," which shape the practice of Muslim women.

---

3. Similarly Gee uses the term "Discourses" to describe "ways of coordinating and integrating words, signs, acts, values, thoughts, beliefs, attitudes, social identities, as well as gestures, glances, body positions, objects and settings. A Discourse is a sort of "identity kit" which comes complete with the appropriate costume and instructions on how to act, talk and often, write, in order to take on a particular social role that others will recognise" (*Literacy*, 6).

4. Ibn 'Umar replied, "O son of my brother! Islam is founded on five principles, i.e. believe in Allah and His Apostle, the five compulsory prayers, the fasting of the month of Ramadan, the payment of Zakat, and the Hajj to the House (of Allah)." (Al-Bukhari, Book #60, Hadith #40; Sahih Muslim, Book #001, Hadith #0021) Anisah Huda included *jihad* as another pillar. Others place *jihad* as one of the three duties, along with *da'wa* and "encouraging good while forbidding wrong" (Emerick, *Islam*, 51; also Mahmood, *Politics*, 58).

5. Mellor and Shilling comment that "religiosity is not just a matter of beliefs and values, but is to do with *lived experiences, practical orientations, sensory* forms of knowing and patterns of *physical* accomplishment and technique that impact upon day-to-day lives in far-reaching ways. ... These bodily aspects of religion are central to its capacity to integrate individuals into social and cultural unities, but also crucial in illuminating the limits of social and cultural influences relative to human embodiment" (*Religious*, 217).

Writing about religion and the body, Coakley asks "*how*, exactly, do corporeal 'practices' mediate social meanings and even transform them (or *vice versa*)?"[6] In this chapter I ask how some of the gender-specific performative practices and their meanings are reshaped within the mosque community. Asad and Mahmood have taken up Mauss's description of *habitus* to describe pious formation, leading to the desired *telos* or ideal mode of being.

Values of the kinship groupings are taken up into a divergent *telos* for the mosque sorority, acquired through particular performative practices. I discuss these performative practices, or ways of being, in relation to dress, and to how the women inhabit both domestic and mosque time and space around *salah* and the annual fast and feasts. I also discuss requirements of ritual purity and defilement, with the activities permitted and proscribed, and the possibilities for female leadership.

Individual Body in Social Formation

Mauss was one of the first within ethnography to discuss the somatic enactment of culture through habitual mimesis, incorporating the most basic of human activities (he included ways of walking, swimming, digging as examples of culturally-shaped action sequences). From Aristotle, Mauss used the term *habitus* to describe these "techniques and work of collective and individual practical reason"[7] or "techniques of the body." While *habitus* has since been prominently associated with the writings of Pierre Bourdieu, Asad and Mahmood have returned to Aristotle's use of the term in ethical pedagogy for more conscious practice of moral cultivation.[8] Mauss described the body as "man's first and most natural instrument. Or more accurately, not to speak of instruments, man's first and most natural technical

---

6. Coakley, *Religion*, 8.

7. Asad, *Genealogies*, 75; Mahmood, *Politics*, 135–39. Similarly Vygotsky, discussing the culturally-specific nature of learning and its link with (children's) development, states that "the development of consciousness is the development of a set of particular, independent capabilities or of a set of particular habits." Imitation enables human learning, which "presupposes a specific social nature and a process by which children grow into the intellectual life of those around them" (*Interaction*, 31, 34).

8. Winchester (*Embodying*) prefers Bourdieu's development of *habitus* as dispositions in the "socially informed body," in his discussion of religious practices of adult Muslim converts in the United States. His argument for a stronger position for subject agency than Asad or Mahmood may reflect the Western context of his research. (See Mahmood. *Politics*, ch. 1, especially 10–22, for her critique of the liberal idea of individual autonomy that has shaped discussion of "agency.")

object, and at the same time technical means, is his body."⁹ Asad, building on Mauss to explore human behavior in terms of learned capabilities (with the suggestive example of the "professional pianist's *practised hands*"), describes the human body as "the *self-developable* means for achieving a range of human objects—from styles of physical movement (for example, walking), through modes of emotional being (for example, composure), to kinds of spiritual experience (for example, mystical states)." A view of the human body as the principal means of formation, "man's first and most natural instrument," in the context of Asad's discussion of medieval Christian monasticism, suggests that "the inability to 'enter into communion with God' becomes a function of untaught bodies."¹⁰

Mahmood proffers Ibn Khaldun's use of the term *malakah* (natural disposition) as a link between Aristotle's description of *habitus*, and the contemporary *daʿwa* movement, noting that "while a virtuous habitus is acquired through virtuous habits, the two are not to be confused," because *habitus* becomes a permanent, behavior-regulating part of a person's character. She critiques Bourdieu for ignoring the pedagogical process through which *habitus* is acquired, referring to women's intentional use of pious practices to acquire pious disposition, within the Egyptian women's mosque movement.¹¹

Asad and Mahmood have helpfully highlighted the conscious use of disciplines of piety in self-formation. However, a focus on the purposeful use of performative practices should not lose the significance of the mimetic

---

9. *Techniques*, 73, 75–76. First given as a lecture in 1934, published in French 1935 and again 1968. Like Taussig, Mauss had earlier noted the connection between "technical action, physical action, [and] magico-religious action," where "techniques of the body" are "effective and traditional" actions. Douglas used Mauss's analysis in her discussion of the cultural determination of social expression (Grid and Group: see chapter 5 of this book) (*Natural*, 72–73, 76).

10. *Genealogies*, 76–77; *Remarks*, 47–48. Here Asad refers to Mauss's (*Natural*, 87) concluding suggestion that "at the bottom of all our mystical states there are techniques of the body . . . I think that there are necessarily biological means of entering into 'communication with God.'" It is not clear where "communication" became "communion."

11. *Politics*, 136–39; see also Krause, *Women*, 122–24. In reference to *salah*, see also Padwick, quoting an Indian Muslim in *The Light*, Lahore: "It is not a mechanical drill, but the various postures of humility in *salah* indicate complete external or bodily submission to God which conforms with the spiritual submission, and this is a necessity since man has a body as well as a soul which exercise great influence on each other through their movements. The submissive movements of the body in this prayer produce equivalent submissive movements in the soul." (*Devotions*, 8. See also Cragg, *Mind*, 82, and Winchester, *Embodying*, 1762, on contemporary North American converts to Islam.)

ideal which gives particular shape to the enactment of the disciplines in a specific social context or community.[12] Returning to Mauss:

> What takes place is a prestigious imitation. The child, the adult, imitates actions which have succeeded and which he has seen successfully performed by people in whom he has confidence and who have authority over him. The action is imposed from without, from above, even if it is an exclusively biological action, involving his body. The individual borrows the series of movements which constitute it from the action executed in front of him or with him by others. It is precisely this notion of the prestige of the person who performs the ordered, authorised, tested action vis-a-vis the imitating individual that contains all the social element.[13]

Performative practices are movements, series of actions, ways of being in space and time, which are "borrowed" from the ideal leader(s) or prestigious person who embodies communal values. *Whether performed consciously or unconsciously, they denote the performer's community of allegiance.* Mahmood takes up Foucault's analysis of ethics, particularly his "techniques of the self,"[14] or conscious "operations one performs on oneself in order to become an ethical subject" and the *telos* (or mimetic ideal), the "mode of being one seeks to achieve within a historically specific authoritative model."[15] The *telos* gives shape to the narrative script determining the form and meaning of performative practices which embody community allegiance.

12. In Asad's critique of Geertz, he cites Geertz's comment, "To visualize was to see, to see to imitate, and to imitate to embody" (Geertz, *Interpretation*, 130) and responds, "In my analysis of monastic rites, I try to show that observation and imitation, although important, were not sufficient for the effective operations of power. The formation/transformation of moral dispositions depended on more than the capacity to imagine, to perceive, to imitate . . . which, after all, are abilities everyone possesses in varying degree" (*Genealogies*, 134). Precisely: the universal mimetic principle underlies cultural transmission, whether conscious or otherwise, within which relations of power are produced.

13. *Techniqes*, 73.

14. Foucault defined these "techniques of the self" (adopting/adapting Mauss's "techniques of the body"?) as "the procedures, which no doubt exist in every civilisation, suggested or prescribed to individuals in order to determine their identity, maintain it, or transform it in terms of a certain number of ends, through relations of self-mastery or self-knowledge. . . . What should one do with oneself? What work should be carried out on the self? How should one 'govern oneself' by performing actions in which one is oneself the objective of those actions, the domain in which they are brought to bear, the instrument they employ, and the subject that acts?" (*Ethics*, 87).

15. Ibid., 30.

Family: Embodied Honor, Shaping Behavior

Within traditional kinship patriarchies, the community virtue of family honor is scripted to the body of the woman in biological and also "bodily and social virginity," safeguarded through "physical threats," together with "the segregation of gender spaces and the active mobilization of the institution of social gossip and reputation. 'Because you are a girl, and people will talk if you do this,' is rhetorically how Arab women come to acquire their gendered subjectivity."[16] Kressel discusses the strength of the concept of "the Arabic notion of *ird*, and its related frame of thought that encodes femininity with shame."[17] For women whose primary community of allegiance is their extended kin, the dominant diegesis then becomes a performance of modest modes of walking, talking, encompassing what they wear and what spaces they enter, which secures the reputation of female and family. Family members are accountable to enforce appropriate behavior: Joseph discusses the role of brothers as responsible for their sisters.[18] In women's family discussions evaluating potential or new brides, modest social behavior is the necessary characteristic within which aptness in domestic duties, and physical attractiveness (within the boundaries of permissible viewers[19]) then also ranked high as significant attributes.

The same trope of family honor may underlie apparently religious behavioral injunctions. Thus a woman who had grown up in a traditionally conservative suburb of Damascus described to me her family's lack of concern about whether or not she was performing the five daily *salah*, compared with their insistence that she wear *hijab*, as a marker of bodily and social modesty.

---

16. Abud-Odeh suggests that Arab women "are supposed to perform a 'public' virginity with a certain body 'style,' the body moving within a defined and delimited social space. Each one of the above borders, the vaginal, the bodily, and the social is enforced through a set of regulations and prohibitions that the woman is not supposed to violate" (*Honor*, 923–24). Ahmad notes that, for women in Pakistan, "any activity deemed culturally inappropriate thus results in the loss of honor, and not just hers but also her family's, and eventually her nation's" (*Transforming*, L.681, 2130).

17. Kressel, *Shame*. Malti-Douglas quotes El-Saadawi's childhood "sensation that my body was *'awra*" (*Women's*, 121). The English translation of El-Saadawi's book translates it as "Shameful! Everything in me was shameful, and I was a child of just nine years old" (*Memoirs*, 10). See also deSilva on how social honor and shame are represented in the physical body (*Honor*, 31–52; also Malina, *New Testament*, 51–52). Where family shame is more defined in female activity, there is always the possibility that the script may turn into the tragic genre.

18. *Intimate*, 134.

19. These included other women, and *mahram* males within one degree of relationship (father, brothers, husband, sons).

Within the kinship patriarchy, the *telos* is that mode of behavior which brings honor to the family; and it is gendered. Women learn through imitation and family constraint the techniques of the body—the appropriate ways to sit, walk, dress, respond to others, according to the norms of that kinship community. Common values and even basic biological acts find particular expression within specific communities.[20]

Mosque Community: Behavior and *ikhlaq*

A shift from family to faith gathering as primary community of allegiance implicates a different *telos* according to a particular mimetic ideal, and a different set of performative practices. Through these practices, members inhabit time and space in ways specific to their community. The community-defined basis of the *telos* or mode of being is clear in Mahmood (reminiscent of Mauss, above):

> The kind of agency I am exploring here does not belong to the women themselves, but is a product of the historically contingent discursive traditions in which they are located. The women are summoned to recognise themselves in terms of the virtues and codes of these traditions, and they come to measure themselves against the ideals furbished by these traditions.[21]

For women in the mosque community, honor was still salient, but in the context of the wider Muslim *ummah*. Honor of the *ummah* was closely tied to Muhammad, and (to a lesser extent) to what was happening to Muslims in other countries. In the light of the publicity around the Danish cartoons, Anisah Huda exhorted the women:

> People wrote about the Prophet.[22] Muslims cried, shrieked, wept—and they broadcast it more. Human rights—don't Muslims have a right to respect their prophet and their religion? ... This situation—if you think that you and your children are fed, clothed, alright—but we have a greater concern than clothes, car or house: the honor of Muslims. Iraq, Lebanon, Palestine, are on our borders.

---

20. See El-Saadawi's *Two Women in One*, which begins and ends with perceptive descriptions of how the women walk and stand. See also Ahmad *Transforming*, L.2230.

21. *Politics.*, 32.

22. This seems to have been a response to the publicity in the Muslim world about Pope Benedict's Regensburg lecture on 12 September 2006, when he quoted a comment made with reference to Muhammad by a Byzantine emperor at the end of the fourteenth century.

However, the dominant cultural discourse of honor becomes subsumed within a larger *telos* of pious behavior as Muslims, defined in terms of *ikhlaq al-Islam* (Islamic virtues/morality). Anisah Huda's solution to defamation of Muhammad was not to reclaim honor through vengeance, but through increased moral behavior, including cleanliness, punctuality, order and integrity. "Economic and political strength is limited; *quwat al-ikhlaq* [the strength of morality] is the greatest;" because "*al-ikhlaq bitirfa' al-'umum*" (moral behavior elevates nations). Muhammad was adduced as the exemplar of virtue, in reverse attributive mimesis: so the women were exhorted to follow "*ikhlaq al-nabi*" (the moral behavior of the prophet). Moral behavior was also suggested as the preeminent criterion for assessing bridal suitability in a reframing of familial cultural norms: more long-lasting than beauty, it could also encompass social modesty.

Being and Behaving in Everyday/Everynight Life[23]

Being part of the mosque community entailed ways of being and behaving, of particular gendered relationships in home and society, as with women's groups in the UAE, where "Concentration was on . . . penetrating society with a particular view of morality, well-being, and mode of living discursively enabled through the polity of the *ummah*."[24] The presence of increasing numbers of women *da'iya*s means that both the religious teaching that women receive and the questions that they ask are more likely to relate to their daily concerns, to issues of life, family relationships and duties, and dress (see chapter 5). The women expected the teaching received in the mosque community to go beyond text and dogma, to pertain to every part of how they lived their lives. Similarly Rausch notes the dual role of *murshidah*s in Morocco in giving lessons which transmit knowledge of Islamic doctrine and practice, and also in "facilitating conversations about problems and issues of a more personal nature, such as spousal relationships, domestic violence, infidelity, parental love, and the upbringing of children

---

23. This expression was coined by Dorothy E. Smith in her writings on institutional ethnography. In a recent book she writes, "'I think, therefore I am' has been spoken by men; 'I do sex, I give birth, I care for children, I clean house, I cook, therefore I am not' has been the unspoken of women . . . What has been repugnant, dangerous to the purity of the world of enlightened intellect, has been the presence of the mortal body that women's presence inserts, our breach of the divide that insulates mind's recognition that it has, dwells in, is not separable from, a body" (*Institutional*, 22–23). Women's occupation of mosque and religious teaching space, coming from and speaking into women's lives and daily (defiling) activities, is part of Smith's "breach of the divide."

24. Krause, *Women*, 139.

and adolescents; or of broader interest such as ethics, worship, and devotional practices."[25]

Mosque lectures often encompassed teaching involving the marital and family realm. Instances included how to respond to the desire of teenage daughters to go out by themselves, the basis for choosing a groom, or a bride (for a son or brother), the appropriate place of Eastern ("belly") dancing, disciplining children, and rearing confident daughters. The mosque teaching challenged cultural norms of wealth and attractiveness in choosing a spouse, by suggesting piety as an alternative and higher qualification. Mothers were told when to encourage their daughters to take up *hijab*, and how to persuade them if they were reluctant. The month of Muhammad's birthday occasioned lectures on his character and morals (*ikhlaq*) in daily behavior as example for the women. On occasions specific lectures were offered on topics such as bringing up children and answering their questions. And the women wrote down questions about everyday life topics on pieces of paper to be answered at the end of lectures, including questions about taking contraceptive pills, having marital relationships while still breastfeeding, the age to start wearing *hijab*, having *jinn* help with housework, giving bribes, and magic.

Questions of intimate daily life addressed to sheikhs on talkback shows are not new. What is significant here is the reading of religious texts from women's perspectives as the basis for its application in women's daily lives. This offers Muslim women a new way of being within the *ummah*, where faith is not defined by default in male terms or by only male authority. Anisah Huda encouraged the women not to unthinkingly accept others' opinions. "You want to know who to marry, you ask the sheikh—what's he got to do with it? The sheikh is for teaching about religion and religious judgments. If he has studied politics and economics, alright, ask him about them: if he hasn't, ask someone who has."[26] Within the mosque program, the texts were read by women, as women, in the context of their everyday life relationships and issues.

Performative Practices in the Mosque Community

Dress and *salat*, feasts and purity, are part of the women's everyday worlds, whether in home or mosque. However, they find redefinition in allegiance to the mosque community, as part of *ikhlaq al-Islam*.

25. *Women*, 76–77.
26. Wadud cites Abdur-Rauf in a similar vein (*Inside*, 51).

Clothes and Covering

Form

Values of morality and modesty are performed through dress and behavior, and take particular cultural shape according to the communal context. In the women's piety movement, female modesty as a family value is transcribed as religious ethic in the *hijab*.[27] Mahmood records the "extraordinary degree of pedagogical emphasis . . . on outward markers of religiosity—ritual practices, styles of comporting oneself, dress," in the Egyptian women's mosque movement.[28] Anisah Huda and her daughter themselves practiced different conservative expressions of *hijab*: Anisah Huda more traditional in dark blue or black scarf and manteau, Eman in white *hijab* and lighter colors (and sometimes a knee-length coat outside the mosque). Modesty was communally expressed for women in the mosque program by full-length and headscarf in one of two or three modes of wear, with older and younger women differentiated by hue. In Pakistan, Ahmad describes how women in the al-Huda movement adopt *hijab* and *'abaya*s as public garb, a nonindigenous "Arab import" form of dress.[29] Religious ethic may privilege particular cultural expressions, where a local (Middle Eastern) form becomes the universal (and uniform) signal of allegiance to a wider imaginary community. However, Anisah Huda taught the women that pious values could find different cultural expressions:

> *Hijab* originally referred to the curtain that the Prophet's wives were behind—we use it now to refer to the scarf. The *mandil* [black cloth covering the face] is cultural tradition. A woman in one place may wear full covering of face and body because that's the culture—in another she may wear trousers and that is religious. The important thing is that she covers her hair and her body shape. Maybe 90 percent of the scholars say women don't need to cover their face—maybe 10 percent say they should.

---

27. The requirement of *hijab* is often linked to *al-'Ahzab* 33:53, 59 and *al-Nur* 24:31. Requirements for covering are also specified in terms of *'awrah*, as noted elsewhere in this chapter. The Sunni schools have different rulings: "The Maliki Madhhab considers the whole body—except the face and hands—to be *'Awrah* [that which must be covered]. The Hanafis suggest likewise." While "some (mostly Shafi'i and Hanbali) favour covering the face and hands, too" (Khattab, *Muslim*, 17).

28. Mahmood, *Politics*, 31.

29. Ahmad, *Transforming*, L.55, 1794.

Meaning

Anisah Huda encouraged girls to begin wearing *hijab* when they had reached puberty and their body began developing. In contrast to some young women in Syria who wore *hijab* together with tightly-fitted clothing, in the mosque program, the headscarf became a symbol of a total commitment to concealment of form.[30] She cautioned them,

> *Hijab* is not just covering your head, but all the clothing—*la yashif wala yasif* [don't see and don't describe/outline]. If you're wearing over-tight jeans and top, even if you cover your head, it's not *hijab*. Clothes [should be] concealing, loose, wide, and long.[31]

Hijab can carry a range of different meanings as well as forms: this has been widely discussed in other publications.[32] Certainly pious observation for women in the mosque program did not exclude attention to a wide diversity of smaller details of cut, material, and buttons in the all-encompassing manteau that signaled degrees of fashion or wealth.[33] They were quick to notice and comment approvingly when I wore a more fashionable version of the all-covering overcoat. The girls in the mosque program contemplating taking up *hijab* saw it first in pragmatic terms of protection from being bothered by men, and also as required by Islam (*fard*). However, in the ceremony celebrating putting on *hijab*, Anisah Huda invoked it as the "flag of Islam":

---

30. The popular explanation that the women gave for this was to liken the woman to a precious jewel which is protected, so that she may only be admired by her husband. This metaphor locates the woman as a possession of the man. It is a (more passive) shift from the emphasis on woman as the source of chaos and danger, exemplified in Maududi: "Woman is raised to prominence in a manner and with the result that a storm of immorality and licentiousness follows in her wake. She is made a plaything for carnal indulgence, she is actually reduced to the position of the Devil's agent, and with her rise to 'prominence' starts the degeneration of mankind in general" (*Purdah*, 2). See also El Saadawi's description of the dangerous "turbulent force" inherent in female sexuality (*Hidden*, 40).

31. Compare with Ismail's quote from hip-hop journalist Adisa Banjoko: "Our *deen* [religion, in Arabic] is not meant to be rocked! ... I see these so-called Muslim sistas wearing a *hijab* and then a bustier, or a *hijab* with their belly button sticking out. You don't put on a *hijab* and try to rock it!" (*Islamism*, 7).

32. Notably Ahmed, *Quiet*.

33. Similarly Arthur notes how in a conservative Mennonite community which required a strict uniform dress code of its women, the women carefully utilised differences in tucks, pleats, yokes, and darts in dress design, to signal individual expression of different norms of conformity, while still keeping it within the boundaries required by the ministers (*Deviance*, 75).

> The *hijab* is an emblem. It signifies that I belong to the school of Islam. A flag symbolizes the state, and this *hijab* symbolizes Islam. So take care of it and beware not to taint it.... No one can inflict an insult on a flag because it is a symbol and an identity.[34]

This was a public commitment to a mode of dress and behavior designed to inculcate modesty that was also part of a wider program of performative practices associated with the mosque program. Anisah Huda's advice to the mothers, "If the girl doesn't agree about wearing *hijab*, be patient—tell her to wear it on some occasions," demonstrates her appreciation of the need to train the girls in becoming habituated to it.[35] For the young women, putting on *hijab* was a ceremony demonstrating both faith and also passage from puberty-to-womanhood; for the program leaders it was a significant step in enacting the performative practices signaling the young women's allegiance to the mosque community.

ʿawrah—Concealing Shape and Sound[36]

Religious and cultural requirements together determine expression of modesty in a particular context, within the preferred range of style, color, and audibility. Both bodies and also voices of women in the mosque program were subject to the need for concealment, whether for their own protection or for the men who might see or hear them. Sometimes Anisah Huda would check to make sure her voice or those of the women couldn't be heard in the main body of the mosque, or she would abandon the microphone if teaching in the balcony area overlooking the main mosque when men were present. On one *Eid* celebration she ended the program as the men were coming

---

34. Meltzer and Nix, *Light*.

35. Also Nama (Mahmood, *Politics*, 157–58): "In the beginning, when you wear [the veil], you're embarrassed and don't want to wear it ... But you *must* wear the veil, first because it is God's command, and then, with time, because your inside learns to feel shy without the veil, and if you take it off, your entire being feels uncomfortable about it."

36. Vom Bruck comments about Yemeni women: "On attaining physical maturity, a woman is said to be ʿ*aurah*, literally, that which is indecent to reveal ... One of the guiding principles of learning to be female is to conceal one facet of identity—the surface of the body –from non-*mahram* both at home and in the street." Women's perfume and voices are also part of their ʿ*awrah* (*Elusive*, 172, 178). Malti-Douglas notes that "in literary Arabic, this word signifies at the same time something shameful, defective and imperfect; the genitals; and something that must be covered" and cites Ibn Hanbal's declaration: "Everything in woman is an 'awra" (*Women's*, 121, 127). See also Munajjid, "Women's 'awrah."

to pray in the mosque below and "wouldn't want to hear our voices."[37] In contrast, the voice of men leading prayer or teaching was regularly heard over the loudspeakers in the women's section. As with women's bodies, the need for concealment of women's voices is because they can come within the category of ʿawrah, particularly when singing. Malti-Douglas examines early Arab-Islamic writers to conclude, "woman's hair (that should not be uncovered) and woman's voice (that should not be heard) come together under the heading of ʿawra, a notion embodying shame and imperfection, whose perimeters ultimately encompass the entirety of woman's body."[38]

In the face of these restrictions, the women's program controversially released a CD of *anashid* (religious songs) composed by a woman in the mosque program, and sung by some of the women there.[39] Ebtisam explained to me that because no one woman's voice could be distinguished, it was alright to have it in the public sphere. She had earlier written on my notes in reference to a question about the women singing in chorus in the mosque, "Even if (men) hear, there is no problem because they do not know who is singing. Anyway, religious songs do not evoke temptation. But that does not mean that it is allowed to sing in front of men because there are men who can sing, so there is no need for women." Anisah Huda concurred, but noted that some men strongly opposed women's voices being audible at all. In like manner, the photo of the chorus on the front of the CD was (intentionally) slightly out of focus, so that no one of the group of young women all dressed in white headscarves and similar manteaux could be distinguished, and no boundaries of revealing/concealing were transgressed. The production of the CD probed the boundaries of religious and cultural conventions.

While stipulations of modesty and concealment shaped the behavior of women in the family sphere as well as in the mosque program, in the latter they were part of a wider program of Islamic morality, rather than subsumed under (patriarchal) family honor. General uniformity in modest dress allowed some attention to individual difference. Paradoxically also the

---

37. This voice concealment is described also in "The Daʿiya—Embodied Model" in chapter 6.

38. *Women's*, 89–90. Some suggest that women's voices in themselves are not ʿawrah; however speaking in a "soft and alluring" or "melodious" voice is considered ʿawrah, based on al-'Ahzab 33:32. See also ibn Adam, "Female," and the debate around al-Qardhawi's recent *fatwa* in al-Shibeeb ("New") and Al-Musnad (*Islamic*, 340).

39. Nelson summarizes the debate in Islam about whether it is acceptable to listen to music or not, noting that both those who accept music and those who oppose it base their arguments on the same premise—"that music is a powerful and affecting force" (*Art,* 50).

wider group in the mosque allowed the public suppression of individual identity on the CD in a way that enabled more exposure of their talents.

Performative practices are lived within defined parameters of space and time: in the mosque community they were shaped by the trope of Islamic virtue, encompassing where and when you could be seen and heard, as well as other pious activities including *salah*, participating in *Eid*s and the Ramadan fast.

Covering for performing *salah* corresponds generally to covering required in front of non-*mahram* males.[40] When I visited women from the mosque in their homes, they met me in clothes that were colorful and fashionable, with attention to hair and face, in contrast to the plain concealment of form in the outside and mosque world. Modesty required that such details be concealed from non-familial men. Even in the privacy of their own home or a women-only environment (whether it be the tightly-shuttered local women's hairdressing salon, or carefully separated women's space at the mosque), *salah* takes women into "public" non-intimate space, so that their body and hair must be appropriately concealed when they pray. In formal *salah* at least, dress denotes distance between God and the (female) worshipper.

Salah

Quiet activity permeates the upper part of the mosque. Class groups of eight to twelve young women are sitting in circles on the balcony which overlooks the main mosque space. In the big hall four women are sitting, one is doing *salah*, a few are having their Qur'anic recitation heard. A woman puts her bag at the end of the mattress where I am sitting, steps back and begins her *salah*. In a few minutes a youthful male voice sounds the call to prayer. Women rise and walk through to the balcony. Numbers of women appear now going through from inside rooms—the last few pass through the room almost at a run. The woman praying at the end of the mattress continues her *salah*, finishes, picks up her bag and hurries after them. They form united rows of movement:

Allahu 'akbar (God is greatest)—and they bend at the waist.

40. Emerick describes the clothing requirements for *salah*: "For women, . . . from the ankles to the neck and down to both wrists [and] a head-covering called a Hijab, or scarf, should be worn" (*Islam*, 122). Some scholars add the specification that a woman's hands and feet should be covered during *salah* (Al-Musnad, *Islamic*, 112). See also Muslim, "Awrah."

Rise, kneel, and bow their heads to the ground, rise.

Bend, stand, kneel, and bow, sit up, bow, sit up.

Stand, bend, stand, kneel, and bow, sit up, bow, sit up.

Greeting to each shoulder.

The actions and times of *salah* are carefully specified within Islam based on the traditions of Muhammad's patterns of prayer. Here I discuss the relationship between *salah* and how women inhabit space and time.[41] While *salah* is required for women in their extended families, in domestic space it must find its place within and around family responsibilities and requirements of purity. Jansen suggests that young mothers may abstain from *salah* because purity stipulations are too difficult to maintain.[42]

However, women in the mosque community, in inverse focus, try to shape their other activities around diurnal cycles of *salah*. It may interrupt any other proceeding. Women break off in casual conversations to do their *salah*, but it can also take place while other religious activities are going on, whether teaching, *dhikr* or classes on Qur'anic recitation.

Salah is the constant punctuation to all the women's movements,[43] in the same way that the prayer call punctuates the aural world, signaling the move into a new time/prayer space. While women may not stop immediately to pray, they might pause to recite under their breath with the *muʿadhdhan*, or the petition enjoined on Muhammad,[44] sometimes with a finger upraised as a sign of respect to the prayer call.

41. El Guindi, *Noon*.

42. Jansen, *Religious*, 273.

43. When I asked Anisah Huda, she explained the gradations of duty and devotion within the five prayer times. Central is the prescribed *fard* prayer: "We need to pray it, and if we don't pray it we are punished." For the devout who pray the recommended *sunnah* prayers: "we receive wages and benefaction if we pray it," and it was also "commanded by the Prophet, and if we love the Prophet I [sic] will listen to his words." Women in the mosque program would often pray these *sunna* prayers when there was no time pressure on them to finish the *salah* quickly, particularly in the evening. And there is the optional *nafilah* prayer, which carries no set reward or penalty beyond that of devotion: "If we don't pray it, there's no penalty . . . We pray it when we're tense or upset and we should pray it in the preferred days, in Ramadan. And the benefit of this prayer is drawing closer to God." Saqib agrees, but adds, "Prophet Muhammad (pbuh) encouraged the believers to pray *Nafl* to help make up for any minor omissions or other defects in the obligatory prayer" (Saqib, *Guide*, 18–20; Emerick, *Islam*, 135).

44. "O God, Lord of this perfect call and of this established prayer, grant our master Muhammad the means of approach and honor and exalted and elevated status, and raise him to the praiseworthy position you have promised him: for you do not alter [your] promises." The Arabic is rich in rhyme and rhythm.

The activity of *salah* can consecrate almost any place for worship; a clean space, marked possibly by a prayer mat, or just by an object (a handbag) as the *sutra* (barrier), marking and protecting the space to kneel and prostrate, in front of the standing pray-er. But worship offered in the mosque gains more merits (*thuwab/hasanat*):[45] Saqib assures us, "wherever a Muslim might be he can offer his *salah* (prayer) but the reward of a *salah* (prayer) offered in a mosque is far greater than that offered in an ordinary place."[46] Cragg comments:

> Everyone's prayer mat is a portable mosque and wherever they choose to spread it they can find their *Qiblah* and worship God. ... Nevertheless, the noon prayer on Fridays is to be said as far as possible in the place of corporate prayer. When so said its four *raka'at* are reduced to two.[47]

But here Saqib and Cragg write only of men. Friday prayer, with its possibility of reduced *raka'at*, is when time and space in the Garden Mosque is reserved for men. More generally, my appointments with Anisah Huda and with Ebtisam were set around both the times of *salah* and their access to spaces in which they could perform it. Women cannot turn public places into prayer sites as men can. I have met women in sheltered places, even in old and ruined mosques, putting their handbag in front as a *sutra* (barrier) and prostrating on the bare and dusty stone floor; but they do not pray in public spaces with the same freedom as men. Requirements of modesty[48] constrain their freedom to turn outside space into spaces of worship; their primary place of *salah* is the home.[49]

---

45. Abu Huraira: "Allah's Apostle said, "The congregational prayer of anyone amongst you is more than twenty (five or twenty seven) times in reward than his prayer in the market or in his house." (Sahih Bukhari, Book #34, Hadith #330) Also: Narrated Abu Huraira . . . : Allah's Messenger said, "The reward of the salat (prayer) offered by a person in congregation is multiplied twenty-five as much than that of the salat offered in one's house or in the market [alone]. And this is because if he performs ablution and does it perfectly and then proceeds to the mosque with the sole intention of offering salat, then, for every step he takes towards the mosque, he is upgraded one degree in reward and his one sin is taken off [crossed out] from his accounts [of deeds]." (Sahih Al-Bukhari 10.30.647) In Khan, *Qur'an*, 373.

46. *Guide*, 17; Emerick (*Islam*, 122) quotes it as twenty-five times better.

47. Cragg, *Call*, 99.

48. And also cleanliness and ritual purity. Thus Saqib includes a bathing place in his list of forbidden spaces for *salah* (*Guide*, 17).

49. "Umm Humayd Sa'idiyyah (RA) said: 'O Prophet of Allah, I desire to offer prayers under your leadership'. The Holy Prophet (SAAS) said: 'I know that, but your offering the prayer in a corner [of your house] is better than your offering it in a closed room, and your offering it in a closed room is better than your offering it in

In giving priority to domestic space, there is no discussion of what is appropriate for the many Muslim women who work professionally. Ebtisam, who was a teacher, told me that generally she prayed at home, except in Ramadan. If one prayed with an imam (at the mosque), during Ramadan it offered seventy merits. Apart from Ramadan, even for professional women or those who lived close to the mosque, there was no expectation that women would go to the mosque to do *salah*. Mosque attendance was justified in order to learn, and the women performed their *salah* before or after (or for individuals, during) the different activities in the women's mosque program.

When they do pray in the mosque instead of in their homes, the physical location reinforces their place within this architectural focus of the wider community of faith. Coming to the mosque, men walk through the main door into the body of the mosque. The women go behind a curtain set across between the corner of the building and the fence, concealing the women's entrance from male eyes, and up to separate rooms. Once there, the women's section gives freedom for the performance of pious activities. In discussing where women sit during the *dhikr* and lecture, Ebtisam quoted a *hadith* where the Prophet said that the best row for the men is the first row, but the first row for the women [behind the men] is the worst,[50] adding, "But they have a separate place, so everywhere (in their section in the mosque) is OK." Although it is not *fard* for women to come to the mosque for *salah*, when they are there for other activities and join in *salah* together, they too receive the twenty-seven times extra reward. Standing shoulder to shoulder in tight rows for *salah* in the mosque, a performative practice act of both imitation and contact, in this deed of revering Deity they are most connected to faith community.

Even performed within the solitary corner of one's home, *salah* remains a corporate act, joining with the wider community in set patterns of prayer, at set times, facing the same direction. Gendered patterns are reproduced at home: if men join the women in prayer, the women pray behind. Anisah Huda advocated *sunnah* and *nafilah* prayers at home, "so that the home will be ordered by *salah* and *dhikr*":

---

the courtyard of your house; and your offering it in the courtyard of your house is better than your offering it in the neighbouring mosque, and your offering it in the neighbouring mosque is better than your offering it in the biggest mosque of the town'" (Imam Ahmad and al-Tarbarani; similar *hadith* in Abu Da'ud) (Khattab, *Muslim,* 2). The Maliki, Shafi'I, and Hanafi schools prefer women to offer their prayers at home; the Hanbali school recommends the opposite (Mahmood, *Politics,* 87). See chapter 1 for other *ahadith* permitting women to attend the mosque.

50. Abu Huraira said: "The best rows for men are the first rows, and the worst ones the last ones, and the best rows for women are the last ones and the worst ones for them are the first ones" (Al-Musnad, *Islamic,* 121–22).

> Of course this place in which you do *salah*, it is like a special mosque, the place of my worship. Of course there is a good impact. God willing, the believer will encounter that impact in every place: for example, I do *salah* here in the home and every prostration in the house has an impact on me. One time I did *dhikr* here, and another time here I did *du'a'*, and another time I humbled myself [prostrated] there—God willing, all the home will be a place of prayer and a mosque for me. However, this doesn't prevent me having a special place also: this is better, so when I sit in it, I feel more nearness [to God]; this is very special.

Practice and space interact for the pray-er. The performed practice of *salah* marks the way in which the women relate to God through time, space and the wider community, embodying their communal allegiance.

Feasts and Fasting

Eids

If diurnal rhythms are shaped around *salah* for women in the mosque program, annual rhythms in the wider community are calibrated by feasts and by the fast of Ramadan. Ramadan is a time for enjoying the evening breakfast meal with family members or friends. The beginning and the end of Ramadan are times when people make a particular effort to be with their relatives. *Eid al-Fitr,* which concludes the fast, and *Eid al-Adhah* (the Feast of the Sacrifice),[51] are times when families gather for a meal together and visit the members of the extended kin, usually starting with the eldest. For women, these times are marked by extra effort in hospitality, involving long hours in cooking, and also house cleaning, especially before a feast day.

The women's mosque program arranged special celebrations for women together in the mosque at the time of the major feasts, including the Islamic New Year. These celebrations typically began with a chorus of five or six women singing *anashid*[52] accompanied by a frame drum, a talk from Anisah Huda and contributions from other women—testimonies about their involvement in the mosque program, why they came and how they had benefited, and sometimes descriptions of family resistance to their attending. Sometimes there was a question-and-answer competi-

---

51. Near the conclusion of the annual time of *hajj*; the feast commemorates Abraham's willingness to sacrifice his son, and his offering of a ram instead. (*Al-Safat* 37:100–107)

52. Many of the *anashid* were composed by one of the women in the program.

tion, or edifying reading from a book, or poem presented by Enas. Women sat mostly on chairs instead of on the carpet, and there were light refreshments of a cold drink and biscuits or cake. In a context where feasts are preeminently times of family gathering, the location and content of these celebrations positioned the mosque community as the place for the women to commemorate religious feasts together, beyond the domain of home and kinship community.

Ramadan

For the non-religiously inclined, Ramadan is a time of family celebration and nightly feasting. In the evenings people relax eating and watching popular television soap operas with their family, or join friends to talk, relax, and perhaps smoke over the break-fast or later *suhur* meal at a restaurant, and then sleep.

For others, the month of Ramadan is when they "bank up" religious observance for the rest of the year. Ramadan is synonymous with sealing (completing) the Qur'an; women are seen reading the Qur'an in the mosque or in their homes, to recite it right through.[53] Women spend more time in cooking for the extended break-fasts each night,[54] people pray more, and even women who don't go to the mosque much or at all in the rest of the year will attend the evening *tarawih*[55] prayers after the *'isha'* prayer.

Similarly the pre-dawn (*suhur*) prayers typically attract large crowds of men and women to spend a few hours from about 2:00 a.m. in *salah*, listening to the Qur'an and to supplication led by the sheikh of the mosque; then they return home for the last light meal of the night after which the daily fast from food and water recommences. Again it is a time of intense emotional and physical engagement with the words of *salah*, supplication and scripture.

53. Rutter describes a similar scenario in Mecca nearly 100 years earlier (March, 1926): "A person walking in the lanes of Mecca on a Ramadan morning hears voices chanting the Koran in nearly every house. Many do their chanting in the cloisters of the Haram. Thus, with sleeping, reading and praying, the Muslims spend the long slow hours until sunset" (Eldon Rutter, cited in von Grunebaum, *Muhammadan*, 58).

54. Ebtisam quoted me the *hadith* that "Whoever feeds a fasting person will have a reward like that of the fasting person, without any reduction in his reward." (Al-Tirmidhi, 807, cited in Uthaymeen, "Islamic").

55. Literally "prayer of rest," named for the pauses after every four *raka'at* for personal prayer and recitation from the Qur'an. They may include twenty, thirty-two or forty *raka'at*. Glassé suggests "*tarawih*" is a "euphemism for one of the most strenuous exercises designed to tap into religious fervour" (*Concise*, 459; Gibbs and Kramers, *Shorter*, 573; Emerick, *Islam*, 155).

The *tarawih* prayers culminate in the Night of Vigil (*laylat al-qadr*) when they continue through the night to the early hours before sunrise. There is disagreement on exactly when the night is: Anisah Huda explained that although God told Muhammad the date, there was a quarrel between friends, and he forgot the date. Most suggest it is in the last ten days of Ramadan, on one of the odd-numbered days, with the 27th (evening of the 26th) preferred. Glassé proposes, "It is certain that this common belief originates in Manichaeism where the 27th day of the month of fasting is the celebrated anniversary of the death of Mani, for there are no Islamic sources for such an idea."[56] With the uncertainty of the actual date, Ebtisam was among those who elected to go on the 23rd, 25th, 27th, and 29th, until midnight, to ensure that the real night was covered.

> Anisah Huda tells me, "It's the Night of Vigil—intercede for your family, intercede for [she names my children]." . . . Another woman comes up to talk to Anisah Huda and greets me, telling me, "Intercede for me." A woman comes with bitter Arabic coffee in a flask and small cups. Anisah Huda stands, gives me some; all the women are getting up now.
> 8:50 p.m.—The loudspeaker is clearer now and we hear the *Fatihah* and the Qur'an read. All the women have formed themselves into rows. After a section of the Qur'an, they all move into the prayers, bow, kneel, prostrate, and continue. In between, women sit in groups and talk, some are reading the Qur'an. . . . Each prayer, there is a time of silence; and then the microphone voice says twice, "Peace be on you all with God's mercy," as the women sit and look to each shoulder. The chorus of men's voices is heard again from the main body of the mosque with Qur'anic verses, and the women sit, relax, chat for a minute. About six women are sitting at the back, not joining the *salah*. . . . Some girls are sitting at the back—two reading the Qur'an continually. Others sit a little wearily. The sitting girls rock slightly from side to side or back to front while the Qur'an is being read. One has prayer beads; another is reciting, lips moving slightly. . . . 10:45 p.m.—The sheikh tells us to ask God to heal all the sick; . . . then reads from the Qur'an. . . . The room is packed now—another male voice adds a call to pray for someone.

Anisah Huda exhorted the women for *laylat al-qadr,* "Repent, repent, weep, seek forgiveness. Tonight and after and after, pray for each other. . . . Try to come early—the library space will (also) be open. The ones who come late mightn't find a place inside. Come when you can." *Al-Qadr* (97)

---

56. Glassé, *Concise*, 310.

describes the night as better than 1000 nights, when the angels and the Spirit descend, and there is peace until dawn; and it is believed that anyone who prays on that night "out of faith and sincerity shall have all their past sins forgiven."

As the night wears on, rounds of *raka'at* continue, interspersed with recitations from the Qur'an and teaching from the sheikh: intercessions are offered, emotions are high, people are weary, space is tightly crowded, and participants gather strength from the congregated community to complete the arduous duties of *tarawih*, finishing in the darkness of the mid-morning hours, an hour or so before sunrise.

Laylat al-qadr, more than any other occasion except the *hajj*, is when pious acts (*salah* and *saum*), place (mosque), time (Ramadan and *Layal al-qadr*) and community membership converge in intense spiritual experience.[57] For these women, Ramadan is the most focused time of pious practice, a time for experiencing community solidarity with other women, for being in the mosque as well as in family homes for breaking fast. And it is a time of encountering the Qur'an heard expounded through the nightly sermons, orally recited, and physically experienced through the rounds of bodily standing, bowing, prostrating in worship that thread through its completion in recitation during this month.

Piety and Purity

> Verily the Muslims men and women, the believers men and women, the men and the women who are obedient, the men and women who are truthful, the men and the women who are patient, the men and women who are humble, the men and the women who give alms, the men and the women who fast, the men and women who guard their chastity and the men and the women who remember God much, God has prepared for them forgiveness and a great reward. (*al-'Ahzaab* 33:35)[58]

When I attended Anisah Huda's lectures to expatriate women in her home, she explained to us that men and women were from the same soul (*nafs wahid*) and therefore of the same essence; and said that they were equal in reward/merits and punishment (*al-thuwab wa al-'uqab*). If they committed the same offence they would receive the same punishment. But there were differences in their duties (*al-wadha'if*). This explanation locates

---

57. See Kalsum's description in "The Place of the Mosque" in chapter 5.

58. Further verses cited to support the fundamental equality of women and men in Islam include *al-'Imraan* 3:195; *al-Nisaa'* 4:1, 124; *al-Tuubah* 9:71–72.

any gendered difference in social roles and duties as opposed to pious practices.[59] Khattab is more cautious: while "in Islam, religious duties are to be performed by men and women alike, . . . having said that, there are some differences in the ways in which men and women are to go about performing these acts of worship, which sisters need to be aware of."[60] The differences include when women and men are in a state of ritual purity and able to complete religious duties.

Islam describes two categories of impurity (*najasah*). Minor impurity (*hadath*) proscribes the believer from *salah*, circumambulating the *ka'abah*, and touching the Qur'an. It is incurred by defecation, urination, secretion from the penis, flatulence, bleeding, sleeping, touching the penis, touching women, laughing, eating camel flesh, and some other debated categories; the believer becomes ritually pure by performing ablutions (*wudu'*).[61]

Major impurity (*janabah*) prohibits the believer from fasting and many authorities hold that it also proscribes entering a mosque, and reciting the Qur'an. It is incurred through menstruation,[62] ejaculation, sexual intercourse, childbirth and post-birth bleeding. Purification of *janabah* requires complete washing (*ghusl*).[63]

59. So too Jouili: "concerning `ibadat (Islamic laws governing religious observances), and unlike in the field of *mu`amalat*, (Islamic laws governing social relations such as family and civil codes), there is no difference in regard to gender. Women and men alike have the same duties and receive the same reward for accomplishing them, the same retribution for neglecting them" (*Religious*, 282).

60. Khattab, *Muslim*, 1.

61. Washing hands, feet, and faces, and rinsing out the mouth, ears and nostrils before praying. This must be repeated before each time of *salah*, unless nothing has occurred to defile the individual since their last ablution.

62. Qur'anic exegetes debate the place of Mary, mother of Jesus, and whether she had prophetic status. The purity given to her by God was exceptional, and al-Razi implicates this with "the necessary absence of menstruation in Mary which is also linked to her sinlessness" (Rippin, *Qur'an*, 268).

Menstruation is linked with defilement in many different cultural and religious contexts. Within Christianity today, in many Eastern churches, menstruating women may not take communion or enter behind the iconostasis. Women in contemporary indigenous African churches also face role restrictions on the basis of ritual purity (Crumbley, *Patriarchies*). De Troyer et al (*Wholly*) discuss issues of bleeding and purity for women in Jewish and Christian traditions. Diamant's (*Red*) compelling narrative of Dinah's story deals with defilement and fertility in the context of the Genesis records. Other contributions on menstruation and pollution include Hoskins (*Menstrual*) in Indonesia, Stewart and Strathem (*Power*) in Papua New Guinea, and Churchill (*Oppositional*) among Southeastern Indians in the USA.

63. Maghen, *Close*; Anwari, *Bodily*, 29. Coming into contact with physical impurities (bodily emissions of humans and animals, wine, dead bodies, dogs, and pigs all come under the category of *najasah*) causes impurity, and should be kept away from Muslims, clothes, and places of prayer. However, their effect can be washed away

Impurity is thus part of the daily human condition:[64] and washing for ritual purity is a routine part of piety for Muslims. The entrance courtyard to the mosque contained ablution facilities for men, and there was an ablutions room upstairs for the women. Gauvain, discussing the egalitarian nature of Sunni Islamic purity, notes, "According to Sunni Islam, no human being is deemed purer than any other, and none—*with the arguable exception of women*—is isolated or disadvantaged in any way through purity strategies."[65] A glance at the list of major impurities above shows that women[66] are far more implicated than men: we may estimate that for, at the very least, a quarter of their time when they are between about thirteen and sixty years of age (menarche to menopause) women are in a state of ritual pollution,[67] and thus proscribed from participating in pious duties described above.

I encountered the subject of ritual purity as a frequent part of women's discussions in domestic gatherings, sandwiched among recipes and household concerns, with its impact on much of their daily lives. Women have to decide when they are considered impure and when not, according to the conditions and length of their *hayd* (menstruation), and other

---

(Gauvain, *Ritual*, 342). Safran (*Rules*) examines debates by Maliki scholars about whether Christians are polluting. Shi'ite Islam includes *mushrikin* within the category of *najasah*, and some also include *ahl al-kitab* (Rizvi, "Najasat").

64. Hibbert, *Defilement*, 345–46.

65. Gauvain, *Ritual*, 350, italics added. Douglas's (*Purity*) understanding of pollution as derived fundamentally from boundary transgression (in her paradigmatic definition of dirt as "matter out of place") has been challenged by recent writers as not being applicable in detail to Sunni purity laws: see Gauvain's discussion of Reinhart, Maghen, and Katz's work. However, al-Ghazali's [d. 505/1111] explanation of the impurity of various body excretions supports Douglas's general theory. Guavain prefers to interpret the restrictions as "reminders, or symbols, of the seriousness with which *male and female sexuality* is taken by Islamic law and ritual" (Gauvain, *Ritual*, 343, 369, original italics).

66. Reflecting on Muslim women in China, Jaschok and Shui write: "Women . . . are faced with an in-built contradiction: in order to be a good Muslim, they must be good wives and mothers. The Muslim's duty of increasing her religious knowledge to attain perfect faith, to attend to the daily duties of purification and praying, are in daily life at odds with her inability to reconcile time-consuming domestic duties with the time-consuming task of learning, ablution and prayer" (*History*, 28).

67. Buitelaar notes that although "this only means that women are more often impure but certainly not inherently more impure than men, in practice women tend to be more strongly associated with impurity than men" (*Space*, 542; see also Roded, *Women*, 98–101). Al-Faisal links ascribed deficiency with fertility: "Women's deficiency lies in the fact that she becomes pregnant, gives birth and menstruates. This clearly means that motherhood is the cause of her deficiency! . . . these writers have forgotten to tell us whether we should deduce from all this that the barren woman is more complete than the one that is fertile, and whether women who do not menstruate are more complete than the other women" (*They*, 232–33).

considerations.⁶⁸ One acquaintance recounted how she had taken a pill to avoid menstruating during Ramadan; however, its impact on her body was sufficiently severe that she didn't take it again and returned to missing the fast during her menstrual period and making up the missed days at another time of the year, the normal practice for Muslim women.⁶⁹ Devout women commonly would only wear make-up and nail polish for special occasions or when menstruating, as face make-up washes off with each ablution and must be reapplied and nail polish is viewed as a barrier between the water and the person, preventing proper *wudu'*. So Wynn concludes, "Thus piety is constructed and enacted through bodily practices."⁷⁰

Ahadith collections include detailed sections on issues of impurity, as do collections of *fatwa;* similarly *fiqh* classes incorporate multiple sessions in scrupulous description of what constitutes states of impurity and purity, particularly with regard to degree and color of menstrual flow and other bodily emissions. Intricate details among the different schools of Islam, determined by medieval male scholars, determine women's practice of daily piety. Classes on rulings of purity were given early in the program to the women or girls coming to mosque classes, following a curriculum along the lines of *'ahkam al-'ibadat* (*Rules of Worship*), a small book available in mosques and bookstores in Syria, with sections on Purity, Salah, Fasting, and Pilgrimage. Its extensive teachings on purity include careful enumeration of various *najasah*, and of the kinds of water offering different degrees of purity. (A similar publication readily available in Islamic bookshops in the West is *'ahkamu dama' al-mara'ah al-tabiy'iyyah* [*Islamic Rules on Menstruation and Post-Natal Bleeding*], which offers detailed analysis of different conditions of discharge and what pious practices are permitted in each condition.) The impact of stringent rules of purity may be a partial explanation of the more prominent place of Muslim women in rites of passage where restrictions of purity are less applicable than they are to rites of intensity such as *salah* and Friday *khutbah* attendance.

Purity and Defilement in the Mosque Community

Every Muslim (woman) is always either within a state of purity or of defilement—they are primary binary categories of being which determine the individual's involvement in meritorious pious practices at any time. The

---

68. Anwar, "Bodily," 27; Philips, *Islamic*.

69. Fasting outside Ramadan, without the community participation and support, is generally viewed as more challenging (Jansen, *Religious*, 274).

70. Wynn, *Religious*, 271.

mosque community could offer both more clarity in definition and more possibility in negotiating the categories.

For Ghina Hammoud and her students in Lebanon, issues of purity and piety were easier to discuss with a woman. Ghina told an interviewer:

> Sometimes the women have questions to do with menstruation, or inter-menstrual or post-natal bleeding, on the issue of blood or menses, and they are shy to ask men: and I have experience in this, apart from the *fiqh* books. I have had menses or post-natal bleeding, or been in a condition of *janabah*, and I can answer them, without shyness, more than a man. Men sometimes get a bit embarrassed.

Her students confirmed it:

> I want to say that it's really nice to listen to a *shaykhah*, because as a woman she feels like I do, she feels for me. A woman's emotions are different to a man's. A woman's composition is not like that of a man. God created each gender with specific composition and feeling. So there are intimate things to do with women that I can only ask a *shaykhah*, I'd be shy to ask a *shaykh*. This is the difference. I feel more comfortable asking her questions, for example, on your menses, on bleeding and childbirth, when to do *salah*, when to stop doing *salah*, the things to do with religion.[71]

Requirements of modesty and purity shape performative practices in gender-specific ways. One of the benefits of female scholars and teachers is that women can ask them about such personal details without embarrassment about bringing such details into public (mixed gender) space where they don't belong. The teaching of these *daʿiya*s is characterized by attention to issues of women's intimate personal and family life, bringing them into the center of (women's) public teaching space. In doing so, they are able to combine their knowledge of original sources with application to contemporary Muslim women's life in "religious practice, dress, and interpretation."[72] A women's mosque community offers its members the freedom to ask their female leader, with her embodied understanding of daily life issues for the women, about intimate details pertaining to religious practice.

Some of the prohibitions concerning impurity are non-negotiable. However, Anisah Huda preferred to interpret the injunction against praying

---

71. Maher, *Veiled*; Minesaki, *Gender*, 396.
72. Kalmbach, *Introduction*, 17; Jaschok, *Sources*, 43; LeRenard, *From*, 125.

and fasting during menstruation as God's mercy, rather than indicating women's deficiency.[73]

> Now fasting and *salah* are tiring and exhausting and the woman during her monthly period loses a lot of her blood and her time, and fasting and even *salah* become extra exhausting, and so she isn't ready to pray and the blood which issues from her is unclean, but this matter is to do with worshipping God, so during her menstruation she doesn't pray.

Within the actual main mosque lectures in the Garden Mosque, I heard little discussion of issues of purity. This may have been because it was covered in introductory classes (likewise, there was no discussion of how to pray or follow Ramadan or make the *Hajj*).

Anisah Huda also challenged an over-preoccupation with details of purification. She told the women, "Islam came to give people first of all freedom," describing, "a convert [who] after four months wanted to return,[74] because for months they had been learning how to purify, how to pray. Does anyone have a shower without washing everything, being purified? It takes one lesson!"

With the wide-ranging debate and disagreement around defining the finer details of *taharah* (purity) in traditional *fiqh* (jurisprudence),[75] some negotiation among different schools of opinion is possible on issues such as

---

73. The oft-cited *hadith* that women are deficient in intelligence and religion is explained in reference to the ruling on giving witness (al-Baqarah 2:282), and to menstruation: Narrated Abu Said Al-Khudri: Once Allah's Apostle went out to the Musalla (to offer the prayer) of 'Id-al-Adha or Al-Fitr prayer. Then he passed by the women and said, "O women! Give alms, as I have seen that the majority of the dwellers of Hell-fire were you [women]." They asked, "Why is it so, O Allah's Apostle?" He replied, "You curse frequently and are ungrateful to your husbands. I have not seen anyone more deficient in intelligence and religion than you. A cautious sensible man could be led astray by some of you." The women asked, "O Allah's Apostle! What is deficient in our intelligence and religion?" He said, "Is not the evidence of two women equal to the witness of one man?" They replied in the affirmative. He said, "This is the deficiency in her intelligence. Isn't it true that a woman can neither pray nor fast during her menses?" The women replied in the affirmative. He said, "This is the deficiency in her religion." (al-Bukhari, Book #6, Hadith #301; and Sahih-Muslim, Book #001, Hadith #0142)

74. Ebtisam added to my notes here, "and leave Islam because people taught them a lot about purification forgetting about the things which are more important."

75. Maghen, as a generally sympathetic expositor, notes the "internal inconsistency and tortuous abstruseness of *tahara* jurisprudence and the bewilderment it occasions even among its own exponents," leading us to join them in the conclusive phrase: "*wa-Allahu a`lam!*"—"and God knows best!" (*Close*, 353–54).

whether menstruating women can recite some of the Qur'an,[76] and attend the mosque.[77] Anisah Huda explained to me:

> The woman, when she is menstruating, some of the [theological] schools and sayings of the scholars prohibit her entering the *masjid*, but some others say she can enter for essentials. So for me, coming to learn is essential; for others, it's not so essential that they always come and they don't safeguard learning sessions or worry too much about them; such a person would say that she wouldn't come during her menses. But for those who are never absent and who safeguard and follow [the sessions] with us, for such a one you could say that coming to the mosque is essential. We don't say to the girls to come; neither do we tell them not to come: she needs to decide, it's her decision.[78]

A woman attending the mosque program told me that coming to the mosque during one's menstrual period depended partly on the time and whether men were present or not, adding "some scholars say it is permitted and some say it isn't, so you choose what you think."

Ebtisam added to my notes here: "It doesn't depend on the time or on the presence of men except if she means that in the time of the prophet there was no means to keep clean, but in our times we have more than one means to keep ourselves and the mosque clean." This supports Maghen's reading of impurity derived through the actual *najasah* (unclean substance) coming in contact with the place or person.[79] In a contrary ruling, a prominent Melbourne mosque requires that all women in visiting groups not enter the main (male) prayer space, rather than asking them individually whether or not they are menstruating.

For women in the mosque program, ritual purity shaped their lives, determining what pious practices the women could carry out when, and their relationship to others in the community. Core purity restrictions on

---

76. Philips cites al-Bukhari and Ibn Taymiya to support the position that a menstruating woman can recite a Qur'anic verse (*Islamic*, 16–17).

77. A commonly mentioned *hadith* in the literature in support of menstruating women attending the mosque is: 'A'ishah said: The Messenger of Allah once told me to get his mat from the *masjid* and I said, "I am menstruating!" He replied, "Your menses is not on your hands." (Sunan Abu Dawud, Book #1, Hadith #261, and Sahih Muslim, Book #1, Hadith #587)

78. See Mahmoud's discussion of how women in the *daʿiya* movement in Egypt use the "space of disagreement among Muslim jurists," and her analysis of women's involvement in the process of debate and disagreement within the "pedagogical space of daʿwa," around use of canonical sources (*Politics*, 88, 101–106. See also Pemberton, *Religious*, 276).

79. Maghen, *Close*, 379–82.

pious practice were unchallenged, but they preferred to interpret the restrictions as God's mercy on women rather than as their deficiency.

Allegiance to the mosque community and the increased engagement with Islamic teaching through the mosque program, offered the women the chance to learn the intricacies of regulations around purity and defilement without embarrassment. And the women were able to challenge some of the rulings, such as mosque attendance, which in turn enabled increased involvement in pious practices within the community.

Leadership

Constraints on purity govern women's role in leading *salah*. At the time of Wadud's public leadership in 2005, I asked Anisah Huda about women at the head of a mixed congregation in *salah*.[80] In answer, she told me that the Prophet had come to a house and found the man sick, and the woman was educated, and he had said that she could lead the household in *salah*.[81] So

---

80. On a number of occasions in the past decade, Wadud and other women in the West have led mixed-gender congregations in prayer, or given the Friday *khutbah* (sermon). These include:

1994, Amina Wadud gave the *khutbah* before Friday prayer in Capetown, South Africa;

2004, Maryam Mirza gave the second half of the *Eid al-Fitr* khutbah in Toronto, Canada; and in the same year also in Canada, Yasmin Shadeer led the night *'isha'* prayer for a mixed-gender congregation;

2005, Wadud gave the *khutbah* and led Friday prayers for a mixed congregation in New York (March), as did Raheel Raza in Toronto (April), and Pamela Taylor at another mosque in Toronto (July). Wadud led mixed prayers at Barcelona, Spain (October);

2006, the former Mufti of Marseille requested that either Raza or Taylor lead him with a mixed congregation in prayer during his visit to Canada (February). Nakia Jackson led *Eid* prayers and Laury Silvers gave the *khutbah* in the USA;

2007, again Nakia Jackson led *Eid* prayers and Laury Silvers gave the *khutbah* in the USA. And Silvers gave the *khutbah* in Capetown and in Johannesburg, South Africa (May);

2008, Wadud led a mixed congregation in prayer at an Oxford College, UK (October);

2010, Raza led a mixed congregation through Friday prayers in the UK (Taylor, "First"; Colin, "Female").

81. The *hadith* generally cited as support for a woman leading men and women in prayer is: Narrated Umm Waraqah daughter of Nawfal: When the Prophet (PBUH) proceeded for the Battle of Badr, I said to him: "Apostle of Allah allow me to accompany you in the battle. I shall act as a nurse for patients. It is possible that Allah might bestow martyrdom upon me." He said: "Stay at your home. Allah, the Almighty, will bestow martyrdom upon you." The narrator said, Hence she was called martyr. She read the Qur'an. She sought permission from the Prophet (PBUH) to have a mu'adhdhin in her house. He, therefore, permitted her (to do so). She announced that her slave and slave-girl would be free after her death. One night they went to her and strangled her with a

in principle it could happen, but generally the man would be the leader in worship, as he could always lead, but the woman could not always as she was prevented from praying privately when she had her period, let alone leading others in *salah*.

At times of combined gathering at the Garden Mosque, such as for *tarawih* prayers, the prayers and teaching were always led by men, with their voice broadcast into the women's section upstairs. During the weekly women's program sessions, if the call to prayer sounded, the women would hurry to form lines on the balcony overlooking the main body of the mosque, and in the main upper hall, to join the *salah* along with the men below. However, if the call sounded during her teaching time, Anisah Huda would wait till the end of her lecture, and then lead the women in corporate prayer. Mahmood describes the same practice in a mosque in Cairo, where the Hajjah responds to criticism of her practice in leading women in prayer when there is a male imam available, by citing agreement in three of the four law schools (Shafi'i, Hanafi, and Hanbali) that it is permissible and better for a woman to lead other women in prayers.[82]

Beyond *salah*, in gendered societies, segregated space made available in the mosque facilitates female gathering (and therefore also female leadership). LeRenard suggests that in a partitioned society such as Saudi Arabia (and the conservative sector within Syria), "the expansion of female religious spaces—physical and virtual—is a *necessary* prerequisite for the construction of networks in which women can develop these qualities" (knowledge, activism, and charisma), so that "by contributing to the development of

---

sheet of cloth until she died, and they ran away. Next day Umar announced among the people, "Anyone who has knowledge about them, or has seen them, should bring them (to him)." Umar (after their arrest) ordered (to crucify them) and they were crucified. This was the first crucifixion at Medina. (Book #2, Hadith #0591) Al-Qadarawi comments on this: "It is reported by Imam Ahmad, Abu Dawud, and others on the authority of Umm Waraqah, who said that the Prophet (peace and blessings be upon him) appointed a muezzin for her, and ordered her to lead the members of her household (who included both men and women) in prayer" ("Comments"). For an opposite reading of this *hadith*, see Shakir, "Female."

82. Mahmood, *Politics*, 87–88. Likewise, Mernissi quotes Ibn Rushd: "Opinion is very divided on the ability of women to be imam for a congregation of men [that is, to lead the prayers]; some even question her ability to lead the prayers for a congregation of women. . . . Shafi'i authorizes her to lead the prayers of women; Malik forbids it; as for Abu Tawr and Tabari, they allow her to be imam in both cases. Nevertheless, the consensus of the majority [of religious authorities] is to forbid women to be imam for a congregation of men" (*Forgotten*, 33; see also Safi, *Shattering*). Emerick, *Islam*, 142; Khattab, *Muslim*, 4; al-Munajjid ("Women") exemplify the general agreement that a woman may act as the leader in prayer if *only* women are gathered, standing in the middle of the first row of women, as one of them. If there are men present, a man must lead, with the leader (imam) alone in the first row.

these spaces, female preachers have expanded the potential for women to occupy positions of religious leadership among women."[83] The move to mosque gatherings rather than in private homes enabled a greater range of religious activities, as well as promoting a sense of community of faith rather than family.

In discussion with expatriates, Anisah Huda could quote historical examples of women who had advised Muhammad, women who had transmitted *ahadith*, and women like Umm al-Darda who had taught congregations including the Caliph in the mosque: with examples of women now writing books and teaching mixed classes in universities, and a woman in a "very rural area where there was no sheikh," who had men attend her lectures. She told us that the qualifications to be a sheikh were that "they needed to study the Qur'an and the *shari'ah*," but entrance should be more stringent. Gender was not included in her description. However, I did not hear her publicly, specifically espouse religious leadership for women across genders, although she endorsed the possibilities in non-religious domains.

Anisah Huda could contemplate the possibility of women in leadership; but her public teaching and practice was more conservative. In the community in which she lived and taught, cultural conventions restricted the range of practical interpretation of religious traditions, despite what she taught about the time of Muhammad and the immediately succeeding centuries. Reinforcing cultural restrictions, requirements of purity regulated the practices of *salah*, fasting for Ramadan or at other times, and reciting the Qur'an, and thus the shape of possibilities for women's leadership in the mosque community.

Conclusion

A shift in allegiance from extended kin family to mosque community is embodied in a different set of performative practices which are culturally-shaped according to the specific community of allegiance and the mimetic ideal. Kinship values are redefined within a new *telos*, with *ikhlaq* (Islamic virtues) rather than kin honor as the primary frame. Buergener describes such a shift for Zaynab, a Syrian woman who persevered in going to religious lessons which entailed returning after dark, despite strong criticism from her family and neighborhood community that such behavior brought shame on them. However, though attending and learning in those lessons,

---

83. Le Renard, *From*, 116; see also Jaschok and Shui, *History*, 28–29, Davidson, *Women's*.

she acquired honor through leadership in the religious community to which she belonged.[84]

Allegiance to the mosque community encompasses appropriate concealment of body and voice: however the anonymity of community membership enabled public production of some of the women's voices. The mosque program shapes the meaning and practice of *salah* within the mosque as well as at home, and women observe *Eid*s and Ramadan within the mosque community, beyond extended family and domestic space. Time, place, and practice find powerful community expression in *laylat al-qadr*.

Anisah Huda teaches women in the mosque program to interpret the differential impact of Islamic purity requirements in terms of God's mercy rather than inherent female deficiency. Mosque teaching both enables more detailed understanding of purity restrictions and more possibilities in negotiating them. And women's place in the mosque gives space for women's leadership. While the cultural context restricts the practice or even promotion of female leadership in mixed-gender contexts, the women are aware of historical and contemporary examples of women teaching and even leading mixed prayer.

Community allegiance and loyalty to the exemplar leader engender particular performative practices, ways of inhabiting historical and cultural space and time, that both reflect and shape community values. All of our ways of being and doing are imitative and thus culturally formed, and also formative of community members. Religious practices are part of these ways of becoming according to particular community allegiance. Together these performative practices, ways of being, form the women into members of the mosque community. The next chapter discusses community practices around religious texts.

---

84. Buergener, *Becoming*, 100–101.

8

Texts, Practices, and Meanings

Anisah Huda tells the women that the heart is less effective if it's not *bayt al-Qur'an* (home of the Qur'an), "so, sisters, God willing, we'll memorize all the verses."

Introduction

THE MOVE IN ALLEGIANCE from kin community to mosque sorority is evident in the practices that signal community membership and that are imitative of the ideal leader. Ways of relating to the Qur'an and other primary religious texts constitute a dimension of performative practices that is of primary significance for scripture-based religions. In this chapter I discuss the way women engage with the Qur'an, *tafsir* (interpretation) and *ahadith* (traditions). A shift in allegiance is signaled by moving from a focus on the physical form of the Qur'an and its function in healing and protection, to internalizing the Qur'an through memorization and production (*tajwid*), with the prestige it brings in this life and promises for the next. The mosque community emphasizes knowledge ('*ilm*), embracing both religious and scientific knowledge, drawing on traditional and contemporary interpretation (*tafsir*) for understanding. If *tajwid* offers uniformity of recitation across different language groups in the *ummah*, choice of *tafsir* locates the women within particular communities of interpretation. Qur'anic texts and *ahadith* are reread for their application to women's daily lives and duties.

Physical Presence

The physical manifestation of the Qur'an dominates life in the Muslim world. It appears in written shape: in books placed carefully on stands in places of household honor, or wound, labyrinth-like, around the circumference of mosque walls and minarets, or embossed in intricate calligraphic swirls in picture frames. In aural form it can be heard wafting sinuously over the air from minarets five times a day, or broadcast from radios, TV sets, and cassette players in shop fronts, or murmured by people at prayer or as they pace, pulsing prayer beads through their fingers. Muslims believe that the Qur'an is the word of God, revealed to Muhammad over about two decades through the angel Jibril, and regard it as the "final link in the chain of revealed scriptures,"[1] even as Muhammad is accounted the final "seal" of the prophets.

Padwick's description, discussing the use of the Qur'an in Muslim devotions, evokes the associated sense of the sacred: "So the book lives on among its people, stuff of their daily lives, taking for them the place of a sacrament. For to them these are not mere letters or mere words. They are the twigs of the burning bush, aflame with God."[2]

Within the Muslim community there are a diversity of ways of approaching the Qur'an. It may be viewed primarily as a source of protection and healing, understood literally as authoritative for all time, or interpreted within the cultural and historical context in which it was written down.[3] Across that diversity, the Qur'an retains its place as embodied and authoritative revelation.[4]

Qur'an in Homes

In Muslim houses throughout the Middle East, a copy of the Qur'an usually takes pride of place in the reception area. Sometimes it lies in an ornate box, more often on a *kursi* (Qur'anic stand), honored as the physical form of the preexistent original kept in heaven as a "tablet preserved" (*al-Baruj* 85:22)

1. Haneef, *What*, 18.

2. Padwick, *Devotions*, 119. Stowasser also: "Muslims experience the Qur'an as God's living presence" (*Gender*, 32). Guessoum's description of its practical outworking is familiar: "In their daily lives, Muslims treat the Qur'an as a sacred book and object, both in the text it contains and as a package. Among the many examples one could cite in this regard are that the Qur'an is always supposed to be placed on top of a pile of books, it must never be put on the ground, no Muslim would carry even fragments of it into a bathroom, and one is supposed to touch a Qur'an only after having performed ablutions" (*Qur'an*, 412).

3. Duderija notes the "plethora of communities of interpretation" and "divergent scripture interpretational models" that exist (*Constructing*, 1, 2).

4. Thus El Fadl, at the beginning of his book on authority in interpreting the Qur'an, is concerned to assure the reader of his belief "in the authenticity of the Qur'an as God's uncorrupted and immutable Word" (*Speaking*, 6).

with God. On a visit to Anisah Huda's house, there were three copies of the Qur'an placed carefully on the middle table in the sitting area, the central one sitting on a *kursi*.

Women in their kinship communities encountered the Qur'an in material form, whether written or read aloud, as efficacious source of *barakah* (power or protection). A friend told me that reading a portion of the Qur'an each day would ensure that no harm or *hasad* (envy) would enter her home. It was common for people to read the Qur'an to bring blessing on the reciter(s) or the house in which it took place, or with intercessory intent for someone else in need. Women would describe how they had written names of the prophets (bringers of the books) on a piece of paper and immersed it in water (to drink for internal healing) or in oil (to anoint an afflicted part), or recited specific Qur'anic verses into their hand-palms held together, which were then wiped on the required part of the body. Other discussions explained which Qur'anic verses or other religious invocations should be said when (morning or evening, during what month) and how many times, for proper efficaciousness in healing or protection.

These practices are not new. Old metal bowls, silver, brass, and copper, (more often found now in museums or antique/artifact shops) had been engraved with Qur'anic verses, so that someone drinking from them might be healed or kept safe in childbirth. The abundance of similar examples[5] are well summed up in Padwick's description of "the overwhelming sense in Muslim devotions of the holy power of the Qur'an, a power which is felt to be a spiritual protection. . . . hence the innumerable uses of Qur'anic texts in charms, and the output of separate *surahs* printed in minute form to be carried on the person for protection."[6] It is this same sense of power associated with the material embodiment of the Qur'an that finds common expression in practices today.

Qur'an in Hearts

Copies of the Qur'an were present in the mosque, whether piled up in shelves at the back, or open in front of some of the women to whatever passage Anisah Huda was teaching on in her Tuesday lectures. The *khitmah* (sealing, or complete recitation) of the Qur'an took place each Ramadan, throughout the evening *tarawih* prayers; and Anisah Huda referred to its recital at funerals. The use of text as a source of *barakah* or power appeared occasionally, as in the recipe in *Mahjubah*, a magazine distributed at the

---

5. See "Practices of Life and Faith" in chapter 6: see also Doumato, *Getting*.
6. Padwick, *Devotions*, 113–14.

mosque (see chapter 6), and Anisah Huda's mention of people reading *surah 6 al-'ana'am* multiple times for healing. The effective power of the Qur'an in *barakah* was not disputed; however, the focus in the mosque program was far more on the Qur'an as memorized and recited. It was prominent in aural form, being recited by women having their memorization and *tajwid* heard, whispered during group *salah*, and the murmured rendition of the *Fatihah* (first chapter of the Qur'an) punctuated many of the mosque activities. It was not enough for women in the mosque program to have copies of the Qur'an in their homes: Anisah Huda encouraged them to internalize it through memorization, to make their hearts "the home of the Qur'an."

Upon entering the women's section of the mosque for a lecture or *dhikr* session, it was common to see women pacing backwards and forwards with the Qur'an,[7] or seated in pairs, one holding a Qur'an and following it while the other recited. Qur'anic memorization is increasing among women and girls: in the back streets of Syrian cities and towns on a Friday or Saturday there were often groups of young girls, some garbed in headscarf just for this session, waiting to enter or emerging from classes at the local mosque on memorizing the Qur'an. From only four or five girls in her religious classes in her youth who had memorized the Qur'an, Anisah Huda commented that there were thousands now. She suggested that women (not in paid employment) had more space for Qur'anic memorization than men. However, it was not restricted to home-based women: many of the young women at the mosque and some of the older women were in professional work, still carrying responsibility for home duties, and also memorizing, or teaching memorization of, the Qur'an.

To be able to hear/train others in Qur'an recitation, the hearer must herself have memorized the Qur'an and *tajwid* and received an *ijazah* (license)[8] through a certified chain of instructors (which can include women, although this does not extend into public recitation in Syria). There were now a number of women in the Garden Mosque program who were qualified instructors, and Anisah Huda had herself been teaching since she was seventeen. She described the process:

> When I want to learn the Qur'an, I come to the supervisor to memorize it and we agree together about it. . . . Maybe I

---

7. Walking to and fro is a common way of combining body movement with repetition to aid retention—students employ it in homes, on flat roof-tops, or in fields, with their text books at exam times.

8. Ebtisam explained that the reciter is passed when she can recite the whole Qur'an in *tajwid* twice. Then she has to pass exams cumulatively in order to receive the *ijazah*: an exam in each section alone, then in each five sections, then in each ten sections, then in each fifteen sections, and finally an exam in the whole Qur'an.

memorize a *surah* from the beginning or from the middle; more often we follow an order, from the beginning to the end, or from the end to the beginning. The final *surah* is small, which makes it easier while one's getting used to memorizing.[9]

The mosque program held ceremonies to honor those who had memorized part or all of the Qur'an. One of these parties was my first encounter with Anisah Huda and the women's program. At one such celebration, the women's chorus sang:

> Raise your voices and congratulate her, she memorized the entire Qur'an.
>
> Raise your voices and applaud.
>
> What you will get is more valuable than the world's treasures,
>
> In heaven you will be crowned,
>
> Make a procession and congratulate her, and crown her with honor,
>
> Raise your voices with cheers and applause.[10]

Anisah Huda told the women that the heart is less effective if it's not *bayt al-Qur'an* (home of the Qur'an). A person's status or reward in paradise was said to be directly related to how much of the Qur'an they had memorized: "If he memorized it all, he would gain the highest standing, if he memorized half, a medium rank, if he memorized a small portion, then he would be of small status." Benefit could also be gained in this world: those who had memorized would receive a small gift as encouragement from the directors of the program, according to the resources they had at the time. Memorizing the Qur'an led to honor in the mosque community as well as in the next life.

Right Recitation—*tajwid*

Memorizing the whole Qur'an was a feat to be celebrated, whether in heaven or on earth. But recitation was also accompanied by careful reproduction of detailed rules of pronunciation, *tajwid*.[11] Anisah Huda commented:

---

9. Kahteran suggests a circular method of learning the final page of each section, then the penultimate, and so on to the conclusion of each section in turn (*Hafiz*, 233).

10. Meltzer and Nix, *Light*.

11. *Tajwid* refers to the rules governing Qur'anic recitation. It "preserves the nature of a revelation whose meaning is expressed as much by its sound as by its content and

Some say *tajwid* should come before memorization, and some say there's no reason why memorization and *tajwid* shouldn't go together. Some say memorization first and then *tajwid*. I am afraid when the girls memorize, that the *tajwid* is so hard they won't want to memorize, so I tell them, memorize it like you memorize anything, and then when we complete the memorizing, the *tajwid* will be easy, God willing. But if someone came and said that she wanted to learn the *tajwid*, I say, "Yes," there's no problem with this. The important thing is that you memorize, because the purpose is to memorize and to understand the Qur'an.

Welch comments, "For Muslims the Kur'an is much more than scripture or sacred literature in the usual Western sense. Its primary significance for the vast majority through the centuries has been in its oral form."[12] The foremost encounter of Muslims with the Qur'an is in its aural dimension rather than semantic. The emotional impact of hearing the Qur'an recited was cited as proof of its divine origins. A male speaker during the *tarawih* evening prayers at the mosque described reciting the Qur'an with non-Muslims listening who thought he was singing and were very touched by the sound, "as if they were listening to God's voice." He concluded, "If you want to know about Islam, recite/read the Qur'an in Arabic."[13] So too Cragg notes

---

expression, and guards it from distortion by a comprehensive set of regulations which govern many of the parameters of the sound production, such as duration of syllable, vocal timbre, and pronunciation." Nelson goes on to quote Muhaysin: "The intent of *tajwiid* is the recitation of the Qur'an *as God Most High sent it down*, . . . knowledge of it is a collective duty" (Nelson, *Art*, 14, 15, italics added; al-Habash, *Qur'an*, 47). See Fathi, "Introduction," for a useful beginning summary, and appendix 2 for the description of a *tajwid* lesson.

12. *Al-Kuran*, 425. The early Arabic orthography lacked both vowel and inflection endings, and many of the consonants were also unpointed, with the same form used for three or four different sounds. So its reading was dependent on the memorized recited text, in order to know how to interpret the unpointed script. Hence the memorized/recited form of the Qur'an has traditionally had priority over the written and the written text became a mnemonic for the recited text. Even as recently as the last century, recitative tradition rather than early manuscript evidence was the primary basis for preparing the Cairo edition of the Qur'an (1342/1923-4), now generally accepted as standard (Graham and Kermani, *Recitation*, 116, 117). Kahteran renders *hafiz* (memorizer) as "guardian, custodian" ("Hafiz," 231). Also Khan: "The accuracy of the written or printed text needs to be attested by at least two persons of good repute who can recite it from memory, and not the other way about" (Khan, *Qur'an*, xii).

13. Zaka Ullah, an Indian Muslim leader, told his Christian friend, "You will never understand this power and warmth of religion among us until you can feel in your own heart the poetry and music of the *Qur'an al-Sharif*. There was never music in the world before like that" (quoted in Cragg and Speight, *Islam*, 11). See also Nelson's poignant description of people's emotional response to a Qur'an recital in Cairo (*Art*,

that "the Qur'an is for recital rather than mere perusal, so that its sequences, strophes and accents have this in view rather than a studied logic. . . . In Jalal al-Din Rumi's metaphor, the Qur'an, like a Damascus brocade, has an under and an upper side and must be read accordingly."[14] Pursuing Rumi's image, rules for *tajwid* set the warp for the damask weave. They ensure a recitation which is common throughout the wider imaginary community of the *ummah*, whatever the reciter's language of origin.

There were special sessions at the Garden Mosque on the protocols of *tajwid*. Amira gave lessons each Saturday morning, followed by hearing individual women recite; she suggested that much of the benefit is not just in learning the rules, but hearing the women recite and her correcting them, where the rules of *tajwid* function as an aid to help the student remember what she has heard.[15] It should be remembered that all these women already spoke and read and wrote in Arabic. While some *tajwid* recalls formal (*fushah*) Arabic grammar, other rules are specific to recitation of the Qur'an, including length, pause, connections, and mode of articulation of some phonemes. Amira taught with reference to a book by Dr Muhammad al-Habash, *How to Memorise the Qur'an?* (*kayf tahfadh al-Qur'an?*). The divisions of the book suggest the significance of *tajwid*: the first section, "How did the Qur'an come to us?" is a third of the book; section two on the rules of *tajwid*, "How do we read the Qur'an?" covers more than half; and the final section, "How do we memorize the Noble Qur'an?" is less than a fifth of the total pages.

Reciting the Qur'an entails taking on a distinct way of configuring speech organs. Everyday written (formal) Arabic has different syntactic-phonetic rules and a contrastive lexicon to spoken dialects[16] but Qur'anic recitation is not like reading a newspaper or textbook. In *tajwid*, the reciters are using language in a formation that is distinctly that of the mosque and neither of the home nor of civic institutions.[17] Correct recitation was taught

---

xii). Women told me popular tales of people who had become Muslims purely through hearing the Qur'an recited, with no comprehension of its meaning.

14. Cragg, *Muhammad*, 7.

15. Nelson, *Art*, 15.

16. "Nobody's mother tongue," formal or *fushah* Arabic is generally spoken of by Arabs as "proper" Arabic and spoken varieties are referred to as "slang." On a linguistic basis of mutual intelligibility, they could be called different languages: comprehension of formal Arabic by "native" Arabic speakers is closely linked to the amount of formal education they have received.

17. Kahteran suggests that *tajwid* relates to three features: the articulation of the phonemes; rules guiding pausal and initial forms; and phonetic modification due to the surrounding phonemes ("Tajwid," 637). Some phonetic features concern length (*mad*—duration) and rhythm (*waqaf* and *ibtada'*—pause and beginning). The manner

as a religious responsibility, part of pious formation. Graham and Kermani warn that "chanting the Qur'an is potentially an actualization of the revelatory act itself, and thus how the Qur'an is vocally rendered not only matters, but matters ultimately.... It is in its oral recitation that the Qur'an is most clearly experienced as divine."[18]

Anisah Huda admonished *tajwid* teachers she was supervising: "They should read better than this.... If she has memorized ten sections with mistakes, it's not accepted by God and it's not right before people." Another mosque teacher told her student, "We recite with *tajwid* so that our understanding of the Qur'an is clearer and we obey the rulings of God (may He be exalted). We should obey God in all the details of our lives. This is piety." Correct articulation was a matter of religious obedience, as the path to divine and human approval.

Qur'an classes were also an entry to the wider program of participation in the mosque community. Anisah Huda told the girls, "We don't just want you to memorize Qur'an. Hopefully this course will leave you with more knowledge about God, the mosque, and your sisters in faith." An overnight excursion to a swimming pool complex, for pupils who were attending a mosque summer program on the Qur'an, together with their teachers, was a chance for Anisah Huda to powerfully model piety personally to the young mosque program teachers as she led them in *qiyam al-layl* prayers at 2:00 a.m., and also to train them in their role:

> The children are with us one day each week, and they're living their regular lives every other day. How can we make our teaching fixed in their minds and lives, and influence their lives and development, if our teachings aren't very advanced and very distinctive? Yes, they're young, but they won't forget, even when they're grown-up. Put in your minds, I am here to serve these kids, and give them a love for the mosque, the Qur'an, and Islam. You have a mission. Stick to it.[19]

Norton and Toohey note that language and learning are not static or isolated activities, but rather social practices "in which experiences are

---

of articulation includes some standard linguistic categories (*takrif*—trilled/flapped "r" and *safir*—fricative). Others are existing categories that are extended to cover more phonemes than in standard Arabic (*tafkhim*—backing and pharyngealization), or given more emphasis which results in a different tenor of pronunciation (*ghunah*—nasalization). Then there are those particular ways of articulation that have no parallel in standard Arabic (*qalqalah*—agitation), or the addition of a schwa after syllable-final /q/, /d/, /T/, /b/, and /j/, which gives a vibrating effect with a stronger tone (Nelson, *Art*, 21–31).

18. Graham, *Recitation*, 118, 119.
19. Meltzer and Nix, *Light*.

organized and identities negotiated."[20] The summer classes for girls to learn the Qur'an did not just involve memorization, correct recitation, or even individual formation, but becoming part of the immediate mosque sorority and wider *ummah*.

While Anisah Huda herself had memorized the Qur'an as a schoolgirl "because of the recompense, and closeness to God," she described it as also making her lessons "stronger," as she was able to refer to more verses as evidence for her teaching. Memorizing and re-reading ("Muslims should read/recite every day, even if it's only one page"[21]) would be a constant reminder to follow it. She herself found the best times to read were after the pre-dawn prayer and in the night, reading one page or up to forty according to the time available. "And the best times for reciting the Qur'an are at night and at daybreak, these are times of clarity and spaciousness when there's no disturbance or someone talking to you or someone taking you away from reading; you recite and you take your time and reflect on it and think about it." These are the reflections of a busy teacher! But the best times for reciting the Qur'an are not just about quiet space, but correspond also to the times when God is most likely to hear and answer prayers, the times of sunrise and sunset, of the boundary between day and night. "The closest a person comes to God is his words, and the way a person speaks to his Lord is when he reads the noble Qur'an." For Anisah Huda and the women reciting the Qur'an, God was most present to them in his words in the Qur'an, which in turn became their speech back to him.

Beyond Recitation to Interpretation

Being native speakers of Arabic didn't automatically confer on the women the right way to recite the Qur'an; neither did it offer easy access to the meaning of scriptures in the language of a society fourteen centuries ago. Mernissi describes being taught the Qur'an as a child, but being discouraged from any attempt to understand the verses she was writing and memorizing.[22] Like Mernissi's teacher, some argue that correct recitation of the Qur'an is sufficient by itself. Kahteran writes that the best recitation is when language, reason, and heart work together for proper pronunciation, understanding,

---

20. Norton and Toohey, *Identity*, 432.

21. Kahteran quotes his own *muhaffiz* (teacher) on the importance of daily reciting: "The Qur'an is like a bird—if you let it go, it loses no time in flying out of your hand" ("Hafiz," 233–234).

22. Mernissi, *Harem*, 102–3.

and obedience. Nevertheless, he finds recitation a good work in its own right:

> The utterance of the words of the Qur'an (*tilawat al-Qur'an*) is a good deed (*thawab*), regardless of whether their exoteric and esoteric meaning is understood or not, while the significance and value of the act derive from the conviction, knowledge and recognition that the Qur'an is a revelation from the Lord of the Worlds.[23]

However, while accepting the emphasis on correct form, Anisah Huda was also concerned for understanding (again suggesting a lower position on the grid axis—see appendix 1):

> A person needs to know *tajwid*. But if he memorized the Qur'an and doesn't know *tajwid*, he's not penalized. But if he memorized the Qur'an and didn't know the meaning, this is culpable—he needs to understand what he reads. More important than *tajwid* is to understand what he reads. But if he *yajawwad wa yingham* [recites it musically] without understanding what he is reciting, this is of no use.

Learning *tajwid* follows rules that are constant across the Muslim *ummah*. Learning the meaning of the Qur'an places the reader within a particular community of interpretation. In the mosque program, this began through memorizing a classic commentator on the Qur'an: the concise commentary of Ibn Kathir (1301–1373).[24] The women were encouraged to enter competitions on memorizing his commentary. There were regular announcements of the competition, with details of which part of the Qur'an and commentary they were to memorize, followed by regular tests in reciting the *tafsir* for the different sections of the Qur'an. Then those who did well had their names read out and received prizes.

Contemporary Commentators

However, the women weren't restricted to the set text. They could also use the library and read the different commentators there, and make up their own minds. Zeinab, the young woman who oversaw the library told me that she liked to read the Egyptian al-Sha'arawi's (1911–1998) *tafsir* (another

---

23. Kahteran, "Tajwid," 636. Also Murat and Chittick comment that "The Arabic form of the Koran is in many ways more important than the text's meaning" (cited in Guessoum, "Qur'an").

24. An early literalist commentator, favored by Islamists.

young woman also borrowed al-Sha'arawi while I was with Zeinab), and she showed me the books of *tafsir* that had been written to date by Dr Muhammad al-Habash. "Ultimately it's his ideas," she told me, "I might think differently." This reflected Anisah Huda's advice to the women: "We read many books in the mosque. If we read it, it doesn't mean we agree with everything that is said. To not read a book because you disagree with something in it is *ta'asab* [bigoted]. . . . The *tafsir* books were written a thousand years ago. The *tafsir* books need change." Many of the women also listened to popular Qur'anic teachers via satellite and cassette tapes. Ibn Kathir's standard commentary was to be a beginning but not a boundary for the women's understanding of the Qur'an and how it was interpreted. Contemporary (generally conservative) commentators also shaped the women's reading and understanding.

Tafsir Modeled—Mimesis

In the mosque program the women saw *tafsir* modeled by their female teachers. In the Tuesday morning lectures, Anisah Huda taught gradually through the chapters of the Qur'an, reflecting on their meaning with reference to contemporary issues, from domestic matters in women's daily lives to affairs of the international Muslim *ummah*. She had begun *al-Zumar* 39 in the first Tuesday lecture I attended in mid-January. During the month of *rabia' al-'awwal* the program was interrupted to focus on Muhammad and his qualities; and Ramadan might also divert attention from text to the meaning of fasting and worship. In early October, the group had commenced *al-Ghafir* 40, and moved from *al-Ghafir* to *al- Fussilat* 41 in the third week of March the following year. A lecture might cover two verses or ten. The verses were not announced by number (the beginning chapter and verse was given sometimes when the lecture commenced) or read aloud, but provided the stimulus or context for Anisah Huda's teaching, sometimes highlighting particular phrases. Often *ahadith* or other stories were narrated.

Al-Zumar 39:9 was announced at the start of one lecture:

> Is one who is obedient to Allah, prostrating himself or standing during the hours of the night, fearing the Hereafter and hoping for the mercy of his Lord? Say: "Are those who know equal to those who know not?" It is only men of understanding who will remember.[25]

---

25. Al-Hilali and Khan, *Translation*, 900.

My notes from some of Anisah Huda's comments include:

> The hypocrites don't remember God except in front of people. Those who remember God do so also in times of pressure. Neither pressure nor grace changes them. The servant of grace draws closer to him everyday. Always reverence, standing for worship always with God. The responsibility for worship is greater at night than during the day. In the day there are pressures, work, business, concerns of the house. At night there are twelve hours. There are different kinds of worship: there is the service of the home and children, teaching the children, caring for their food and cleaning.

To show that "worship gives strength to people," she cited the example of an old person who "rises early and sleeps early, and is strong, can stand up with family and work." Here the traditional emphasis on reverence and rising to worship at night (*qiyaam al-layl*) is taught in the specific context of women's lives of professional work and family responsibilities.

The second part of the verse prompted discourse on the importance of *ʿilm:* "True religion and true learning lead to each other.... From darkness to light, from ignorance to learning. One period in learning is better than a year in the mosque. Learning is the best of worship." And Anisah Huda encouraged the women to visit "ignorant Muslims. Ignorance leads to disbelief. (We need) connectedness and faith and learning." So the women should ring, ask after, visit one another: "We love the mosque, sisters of the mosque; ... sisters in God." They are the ones who will support us in difficulty, testify to us in heaven. So ask after, greet, visit the other person, because "our sisters are the believers, whether we like them or not, whether they are rich or poor." Anisah Huda uses this Qur'anic verse to encourage the women in learning as "the best of worship" and in allegiance to the mosque community.

While she uses *ahadith*, her *tafsir* is *bil-raʿy* (personal opinion, individual initiative, and expression),[26] followed by many contemporary commentators, in contrast to *Ibn Kathir*, whom the women had to memorize, who followed *tafsir bil- maʾthur* (by traditions).[27] Anisah Huda's explanation goes beyond general teaching on the importance of choosing worship over

26. However, see Engineer's discussion of "*biʾal-rai*," which he understands as deviant, and different to "understanding the Qur'an in the light of one's own experience and consciousness" (*Rights*, 3–4).

27. Stowasser, *Gender*, 32; Barlas, *Believing*, 38. However, Anisah Huda's teaching remained within the "traditional," "linear-atomistic" *tafsir* criticized by Wadud (*Rereading*, 2) and Barlas (*Believing*, 8), who both pursue the thematic interpretation advocated by Rahman (*Major*).

other "frivolous or self-indulgent activities,"[28] to explain it with reference to the situation and daily lives of her listeners. She teaches the text interacting with the personal, communal and international challenges the women faced, demonstrating with examples both from the *ahadith* and daily life. Her teaching places her within Gaffney's category of "Preacher as Scholar."[29]

In modeling this community of interpretation, Anisah Huda draws on conservative commentators. She uses the text for daily application to the everyday/everynight lives of her hearers. In this mosque program, the women are not passive recipients of teaching. Rather, they are encouraged to access a range of commentators and choose from their comments. With the other teachers in the program, Anisah Huda is a cogent exemplar of a woman doing *tafsir*, encouraging the women to use their minds and not accept uncritically what they hear or read, applying the teaching to the details of women's own lives, and, most significantly for her audience, as a woman taking and teaching the text of the Qur'an.

---

28. See al-Ghazali on this verse (*Thematic*, 5).

29. Gaffney, *Prophet's*, 38. Compare her discussion on this verse with *Ibn Kathir*, as follows:

(*Is one who is obedient to Allah, Ana'a Al-Layl prostrating and standing*) meaning, one who is humble and fears Allah when he prostrates and stands (in prayer). It was reported that Ibn Mas`ud, may Allah be pleased with him, said: "The obedient one is one who obeys Allah and His Messenger." 'Ibn `Abbas, may Allah be pleased with him, Al-Hasan, As-Suddi and Ibn Zayd said, "Ana'a Al-Layl means in the depths of the night. (*Fearing the Hereafter and hoping for the mercy of his Lord*) means, in his worship he feels both fear and hope. Both are essential in worship, and fear should be stronger during one's lifetime. Allah says: (*fearing the Hereafter and hoping for the mercy of his Lord.*)" At the time of death, hope is uppermost, as Imam `Abd bin Humayd recorded in his Musnad from Anas, may Allah be pleased with him, who said, "The Messenger of Allah entered upon a man who was dying, and said to him, 'How do you feel?' He said, `I am both afraid and hopeful.' The Messenger of Allah said: (These do not co-exist in a person's heart at times such as this, but Allah will give him what he hopes for and protect him from that which he fears.)" This was recorded by At- Tirmidhi, An-Nasa'i in Al-Yawm wal-Laylah, and Ibn Majah from the Ahadith of Yasar bin Hatim from Ja`far bin Sulayman. At-Tirmidhi said, "Gharib." Imam Ahmad recorded that Tamim Ad-Dari, may Allah be pleased with him, said that the Messenger of Allah said: (Whoever recites one hundred Ayat in one night, it will be recorded as if he prayed all night.) This was also recorded by An-Nasa'i in Al- Yawm wal-Laylah. (Say: "*Are those who know equal to those who know not*") means, is this one equal with the one who sets up rivals to Allah to mislead (men) from His path. (It *is only men of understanding who will remember*) means, the only one who will understand the difference between them is the one who has understanding. And Allah knows best. (Ibn Kathir, "Az-Zumar")

The Importance of ʿilm

A constant theme in Anisah Huda's teaching was the importance of ʿilm (knowledge). The first word of revelation from God is believed to be the command to 'iqra' (recite/read),[30] from which verb the word qur'an itself derives.[31] Both Anisah Huda, and educationalist Hanan Laham,[32] who addressed the women at the opening of the mosque women's library, took this to mean "read" in the sense of "learn, study," giving divine warrant to the imperative for women to learn.[33] When I asked Anisah Huda why they had the women's library (the first of its kind in a Damascene mosque), she explained that there were 200 verses in the Qur'an on ʿilm.[34]

Anisah Huda told the women, "We made this year in the mosque especially for al-ʿilm." But it was more than the flavor of the year—ʿilm was the dominant motif in Anisah Huda's teaching, part of or surpassing ritual worship. She often repeated that "an hour of learning (or thinking) is better than a year in the mosque (or worship)" and also, "Muhammad said that learning is better than worship. Learning is worship—it's not just piety and fasting. In Islam everything is worship. Learning is better than worship, better than fasting." So too "'aqal [the mind] is as important as din [religion]. Muslims through the community are good at practicing their religion, less good at using their minds—both are important." Even though dhikr was an important part of preparation for the lecture: "If you need ʿilm, take the

---

30. Compare the semantics with Robert Alter's explanation of "murmurs" in Psalm 1:2, where the verb "means to make a low muttering sound, which is what one does with a text in a culture where there is no silent reading" (Book, L871).

31. Al-ʿalaq 96:1. Welch (Al-Kuran) supports the suggestion that the word qur'an originated in the Qur'an as an Arabic masdar form from qara'a (the verb which gives the imperative "iqra"), to represent the Syriac "qerhana" (scripture reading, lesson), for example, as used in Christian liturgy of the sixth century. Other titles for the Qur'an from within the Qur'an itself include: al-furqaan (the evidence), al-kitaab (the book), al-tanziil (that which descended), al-mashaf (collection of leaves or pages) (al-Habash, Qur'an, 9–11).

32. At 68 years, she was active in encouraging a non-violent response to the regime in Syria as unrest broke out and extended from the beginning of 2011 (Malas, "Opposition;" Pressenza, "Non violence").

33. I did not hear al-Hajj 20:114, "wa-qul rabb zidni ʿilman" (and say, Lord, increase me in knowledge) cited in lectures, even though it is regularly used in encouraging people to learn and gain basic literacy in Egypt, and appears commonly on Islamic websites to advocate learning.

34. Akhtar notes that, "in the Qur'an the word ʿalim has occurred in 140 places, while al-ʿilm is in 27. In all, the total number of verses in which ʿilm or its derivatives and associated words are used is 704" (Akhtar, "Islamic").

time you spend in *dhikr* to learn.³⁵ Learning is the best part of worship. Saying *salah ʿala al-nabi'* [blessings on the Prophet] five thousand times doesn't lead to forgiveness and closeness to God." This focus on knowledge and learning has historical and more contemporary origins within Islam.

Islam predates itself with the *jahiliyyah* (the time of ignorance). Right guidance, or knowledge, is the difference between those who have received God's grace and those who are under his wrath (*al-Fatihah* 1:6–7). Akhtar affirms that "'*ilm* is Islam ... It may be said that Islam is the path of 'knowledge.'"³⁶ Hence epistemology, the communal understanding of *ʿilm*, is of central significance within Islam. The widening of *ʿilm* to include non-religious sciences emerged from the work of Egyptians Muhammad Abduh (1849–1905) and his follower Rahid Rida (1865–1930). They promulgated the use of social and physical sciences in understanding the Qur'an. Hamdy cites Iqbal's description of "the colonized response of Muslim world, seeking modern science and technology to gain "economic, military, and political power."³⁷ Hence, in

> the Muslim reformers' desire to free Islam from European subordination through the acquisition of modern science ... almost all the reformers translated modern "science" into the Arabic world *ʿilm*, which in Islamic epistemology represents all-encompassing knowledge toward which humans must strive, but which remains only absolute with God the Divine.³⁸

The emphasis on *ʿilm* in the mosque program found its place within the *daʿwa* concern to promulgate the preeminence of Islam in response to other (particularly) Western worldviews.

---

35. The combined emphasis on *dhikr* and *ʿilm* is present also in the third principle of the Jamaat Tabligh: *ʿilm* and *dhikr*, knowledge and remembrance of Allah. The others are: 1. *kalima*, the *shahaddah*; 2. *salat*, performance of the five daily prayers; 4. *ikhlas al-niyya*, the purity of intention and sincerity as most pleasing Allah; 5. *ikram al-Muslimin*—respect and honor fellow-believers; 6. *tafriʿ al-waqt*—time for self-reformation, and proselytization missions (Makol-Abdul, Rahimah and Abdul-Rahman, "Religious," 709).

36. Akhtar, "Islamic."

37. The focus on learning and logic across contemporary Islam suggests the mediaeval Muʿtazilite emphasis on rationalism. This rational resurgence is particularly notable in (post) modernist writers such as Duderija, who describes how "progressive Muslims" take a neo-Muʿtazilite position when they "do not subscribe to the notion of a legalistic Divine Will in which human beings are trapped," nor to "the notion of 'uncreatedness of the Qur'an,' ... but maintain that the 'createdness of the Qur'an' 'defreezes,' to use Abu Zayd's term, its meaning" (*Constructing*, 141).

38. Hamdy, *Science*, 361.

TEXTS, PRACTICES, AND MEANINGS 157

Tafsir 'ilmi

While the women were exhorted to learn, religious teaching in the mosque incorporated an uncritical view of social and physical sciences. Anisah Huda's commentary on *al-Zumar* 39:5 used *tafsir 'ilmi* (scientific interpretation) to indicate the divine origins of the Qur'an:

> *yukawwir al-layl 'ala-al-nahar wa yukawwir al-nahar 'ala al-layl.*[39] *Al-takwir* is the same as *al-laff*. So the night and day go round the earth as if round a head. What is the number of years the Qur'an has been on earth? Fourteen and a half centuries—1426 years. All that time, God has kept the world turning. So God showed that the world was round in the time when the Qur'an was revealed. In 1957, through a telescope and pictures people saw stars, and knew that the world was round—it shows that the Qur'an is not from Mohammed. He didn't read, he was a son of the desert, he was illiterate and so was his tribe—so whence could all this knowledge have come if not from God? The sun and moon and earth spin, don't overtake each other—each one has its own time. Where did the prophet get this knowledge from? All the details of creation are in the Qur'an and the *tafsir*.

And on verse six: "This is evidence that the Qur'an is from God: we have our torso, and within that the womb, and within that the fetus. This was only discovered in the twentieth century. But they are all mentioned in the noble Qur'an."

Geussoum summarizes *tafsir 'ilmi*[40] as two streams: "(1) the 'scientific exegesis' school," which uses modern scientific knowledge to better understand passages of the Qur'an: and "(2) the school of the 'scientific miraculousness of the Qur'an' (*i'jaz*)," which claims that many verses of the Qur'an express "scientific truths that were discovered only recently," showing the miraculous and divine origin of the Qur'an. Both Mir and Geussoum reject

39. "He makes the night to go in the day and makes the day to go in the night" (Al-Hilali and Khan, *Interpretation*, 899).

40. Mir (*Scientific*) notes the recent move to develop *tafsir 'ilmi* as a discipline on a par with other forms of *tafsir* (such as *riwa'i* [reported], *kalami* [theological], *fiqhi* [legal], *nahwi* [grammatical] and *adabi* [stylistic]); although some justify it through claiming its antecedents in the writing of al-Ghazali (d. 1111), al-Razi (d. 1209) and al-Suyuti (d. 1505). Proponents refer to *Al-'ana'am* 6:38: "We have neglected nothing in the Book," as justification for seeking to find the origins of all knowledge in the Qur'an. It finds expression in English-language publications including Ibrahim's *A Brief Illustrated Guide to Understanding Islam*, and Naik's booklet, *Qu'ran and Modern Science*, disseminated by mosques and Islamic bookstores in the West; see also earlier writers such as Bucaille (*Bible*). Geussoum (*Qur'an, Religious*) offers a synopsis of Arabic discussions.

the plausibility of the latter (used above by Anisah Huda), but both approve the impulse, suggesting the former, together with the doctrine of multiple meanings in the Qur'an, may be the basis for a new understanding of some Qur'anic verses in the light of scientific discoveries.[41]

Learning and Life in Religion

In the women's mosque community both religious and academic knowledge were seen as desirable and interconnected. In the primary kinship communities of some of the families who sent their daughters to the mosque program, parents preferred their daughters to stay at school only until they got married (usually upper secondary). However, Anisah Huda encouraged the girls and women who attended her classes to stay on at school, to keep learning. A number of the young women were also studying *shari'ah* law at university or Islamic institutes. Many of the teachers in the program worked professionally as teachers or in other areas. Anisah Huda sometimes had young women give summaries during her lectures of books they had read on history and science in relationship to Islam. There was active promotion of science as grounded primarily in Islam. "The first experts of science, chemistry, mathematics, medicine, were Muslims. . . . Muhammad opened countries to learning and mercy," and contrasted with the "Christian time," when "there was no science." The women's program included lessons on "all the scientific discoveries made within Islam, who discovered what, a scientific history, and also how the discoveries related to the Qur'an." Anisah Huda frequently invoked the wonder of the natural world as motivation to worship God. Scientific knowledge was subsumed within the interpretive framework of the dominance of Islam.

Learning also encompassed practical life issues. In her own lectures Anisah Huda made constant reference to everyday affairs, and she organized special lectures at other times by medical doctors, or on marriage, and how to answer children's questions. Along with *'ilm*, practical duties figured as importantly in connection to ritual piety:

> If you fill all your time with worship, there is no time for good deeds. If we pray this or that *surah* forty times or this litany or another a thousand times, if you spend lots of time multiplying prayers, there's no time to help your mother or your mother-in-law. Visiting one another is better than sitting. Work is worship. Cleaning the house is worship. Cooperating and working for unity is better than reading the Qur'an a thousand times.

41. Guessoum, *Religious*, 419.

While the reformers'[42] separation between *'ibadat* (doctrines, beliefs, and rituals) and *mu'amalat* (human relations, political, social, and cultural issues) might be useful in reinterpreting the Qur'an and *ahadith* for a changing world, for Anisah Huda and the women she taught, they formed a unity of pious practice that shaped every part of life. In this program, as in the women's piety movement in Egypt and the Gulf, social reform is seen as deriving from and achieved by individual reform.[43] The focus on *'ilm* in the women's program was in the context of an emphasis on personal piety which reinforced the place of domestic and family duties, but within a primary framework of pious practice rather than kinship loyalty.

The Qur'an and the Community

The emphasis on *'ilm* was also within a non-critical acceptance of traditional teaching on the beginnings of the Qur'an and the Muslim *ummah*, reflecting the community from which the women came.

Anisah Huda taught the account of the Qur'an's beginnings, "on leaves and all kinds of material. By a hundred years after the Prophet's death, the Sunnah were written, and the Qur'an gathered. In the time of Uthman, one of the four copies was kept. The Qur'an was first *juma'* (gathered), *nusaq* (ordered), and *wuza'* (distributed).[44]

---

42. Muhammad Abduh (Haddad, *Islam,* 3-4) and Ahmed Khan (Rippin, *Muslims,* 221).

43. Mahmood, *Politics,* 34-35; *Rehearsed,* 829; Krause, *Women,* 93. Thus Dr Magda in Egypt describes teaching in mosques and having a shop for healthy and wholegrain products as both part of her *da'wa* work for God (Maher, *Veiled*).

44. Islam asserts both that the Qur'an came in the language and historical and geographical context of seventh-century Arabia, and that it originates from the eternally existent *'umm al-kitab* (Mother of the Book) (*al-'imran* 3:7; *al-Ra'ad* 13:39; *al-Zukhruf* 43:4), whence it passed to Muhammad via the angel Jibril over a period of about two decades. Muslim traditions teach that Muhammad didn't leave a compiled written text, but it was first gathered together by Zayd in the time of Abu Bakr, "whether written on palm branches or thin stones or preserved in the hearts of men." Uthman is generally held responsible for the authoritative collection, with its distribution, and the suppression of alternative forms. Welch suggests an earlier compilation, pointing to the report that Zayd "used to write down the revelations for the Prophet," and to alternative stories of other Caliphs being responsible for the official collection (Welch, *Al-Kuran,* 404-5; see also Bell and Watt, *Introduction,* 32, 37; Emerick, *Islam,* 17-21; Rippin, *Muslims,* 34-35; Leehmuis, *Palm Leaves,* 145-46). Neuwirth also suggests a date earlier than Uthman, as it would have been difficult to implement effective unification of the texts after dispersion through the great conquests (*Structural,* 99).

The orthodox tradition requires an accepted account of how the Qur'an went from the "Preserved Tablet" in heaven, through oral revelation via Muhammad, to its present written form. Muslim tradition includes two interacting paths of discussing Qur'anic

The immutability of the Qur'an was taught as a contrast to Christianity, reflecting both the dispute with fundamental Christian doctrine that is intrinsic to the Qur'an,[45] and a general awareness of inter-religious polemic. Anisah Huda taught the women,

> We've no doubt, among Muslims or non-Muslims, that the Qur'an doesn't change, from Mecca to the ends of the earth, to Western countries, it's the same book, no letter changed. No other book is like that. The gospels—there are a number of them, different to each other. . . . There are more than one gospel—four gospels—people believe this. The Qur'an doesn't have this problem.
>
> Ten of the Friends agreed on the verses and fixed the Qur'an. You don't find a Qur'an anywhere in the world that is different from any other *mashaf,* they are the same to every dot.[46]

---

origin and unchangeability: the oral tradition from Muhammad, and the written text, deriving in its current form from the time of Uthman. So Rippin notes that "within thirty years of the death of Muhammad, it is understood that the Qur'an existed in its fixed, if skeletal form; theologically, it is held that the form that the text was in at this point was an image of the 'heavenly tablet,' suggesting that its structure and content were precisely that which God desired for it" (*Muslims,* 35).

For a summary of more recent and controversial suggestions about the formation of the Qur'an, see Motzki's article (59-75): "Alternative accounts of the Qur'an's formation." Wansbrough suggests that "the entire process of canonization will thus be seen as a protracted one of community formation" (*Quranic,* 51). Ibn Warraq typically goes further: "There is no such thing as *the* Koran. There is no, and there never has been, a *textus receptus ne varietur* of the holy book of the Muslims," and he uses Muslim sources to verify his claim (*Which,* 23–79).

45. *Al-Baqarah* 2:75 and *al-Nisa'* 4:46 are commonly used to support the claim that the books of Judeo-Christianity have been corrupted. The Qur'anic teaching of itself as successor and seal to *Torah, Zabbur,* and *Injil,* faces the issue of conflict between it and the other three accounts—hence the emphasis on the supposed corruption of the latter and unchangeability of the former. Other verses are used to oppose a trinity taught as God, Mary, and Jesus; and the divinity of Christ (e.g., *al-Nisa'* 4:71, *al-Ma'idah* 5:72-75, 116-117; *al-An'am* 6:1; *al-Jinn* 72:3).

46. Within the accepted textual tradition, Ibn–Mujahid (d. 324/936) concluded that there were seven *'ahruf* (different "readings" of the Qur'an), based on a tradition that Muhammad had been taught seven recitations (in al-Bukhari, *Fada'il al-Kur'an,* Book 4; Muslim, *Salat al-musafirin,* Hadith 270-74; cited in Welch, *Al-Kuran,* also Bell and Watt, *Introduction,* 48–50). Saeed discusses possible meanings of the *'ahruf* (*Interpreting,* 69–76). Kahteran describes these seven readings as "the different linguistic, lexical, phonetic, morphological and syntactical forms permitted when reciting the Qur'an" deriving from "the fact that the linguistic system of the Qur'an incorporates the most familiar Arabic dialects and vernacular forms in use at the time of the Revelation," (*Hafiz,* 233; *Tajwid,* 638; Graham and Kermani, "Recitation," 117, 118). Al-Habash includes ten readings (*Qur'an,* 33–40). *Al-Muyissah Fii al-Qur'an al-'arba' 'asharah* gives fourteen readings, as its name suggests. These readings are recognized by Muslims,

Those who want to undermine Islam by any way study night and day to find points of weakness.

"People of the Book" were presented as co-religionists but also polemic rivals, in a debate where the traditions of Muhammad were given authority as the ultimate proof of veracity. In this *da'wa* community, the women were being encouraged and equipped to engage with both Muslims and non-Muslims on issues of faith. Anisah Huda alluded to both inter- and intra-religious historical controversies when she referred in a lecture to "the debate about the Messiah as word of God and the Qur'an, the debate about whether it is created or not."

In a context where widespread education for women is still relatively recent, Anisah Huda emphasized that Muhammad was illiterate,[47] as further evidence of the divine origins of the Qur'an, and also its inimitability (*i'ajaz*).[48] Associated with the latter, Anisah Huda argued for the Qur'an being in pure Arabic, without any borrowed words:

> The *surah* begins with *ha mim*—they are ordinary Arab letters,[49] not foreign or Hebrew, so that people could hear that they un-

---

but not regarded as affecting the basic unchangeableness of the Qur'an. It was unclear whether Anisah Huda's "no letter changed," "same to every dot" was rhetorical, or suggested a lack of awareness of the extent of the "linguistic, lexical, phonetic, morphological and syntactical" variations among the readings. For further discussion of the other textual traditions in the first four centuries AH, particularly those attributed to Ibn Mas'ud (Kufa), Ubayy (Syria), and Abu Musa (Basra), see Welch, *Al-Kuran*, 406–408; Bell and Watt, *Introduction*, 44–47; Wild, *Reading*, 34.

47. From the use of the word *ummiy* (unlettered) to describe Muhammad (*Al-Ma'idah* 7:157–58: also *Al-'ankabut* 29:48). However, archaeological evidence shows writing present in Arabia for centuries before Muhammad's time. It is unlikely that, as a merchant in a commercial society, Muhammad and the people of Mecca did not know anything of writing. Bell and Watt (*Introduction*, 30–36) and Cragg (*Event*, 56–62; *Muhammad*, 85–86) argue that the term *ummiy* refers to him belonging to a people without a written scripture. Also Khalifa, who sees the miraculous nature of the Qur'an as mathematical not literary, insists: "Prophet Muhammad was the first to write down the Quran revealed to him. He also had other scribes helping him in the writing. He had to be *a literate man*" (Khalifa, "Writing," and "Appendix 28").

48. The inimitability of the Qur'an is based on the following verses, which are said to have come as a reply to Muhammad's detractors at the time: *Al-Tuur* 52:34; *Yunus* 10:38–39; *Huud* 11:13–16; *Al-Qasas* 28:49; *Al-Baqarah* 2:23; *Al-'isra'* 17:88. And it became dogma with al-Rummani (Rippin, *Islam*, 39). It is also used to argue against translation of the Qur'an, because "if one were able to make a literal translation of the Qur'an, a translation that manifested all the subtleties of the original text, then the miracle of the Qur'an would be equaled," defying the Qur'anic edict in *surah* 17:22. Leemhuis concludes, "It could not be done and thus it should not be done" ("Palm leaves," 155).

49. *Al-Fussilat* 41. The letters at the beginning of a number of the *surahs* have

derstood it. So the Qur'an is all Arabic. If the Arabs themselves don't understand and explain the Qur'an which is Arabic language, how can non-Arabs? The reason is that people have become distant from the Arabic language.[50]

Thus Muhammad's illiteracy, with the dogma of the eternal, perfect, and inimitable nature of the Qur'an, become evidence of its divine source; and the miraculous essence of the Qur'an in turn is used to prove Muhammad's prophetic standing. The emphasis on the Arabic origins and expression of the Qur'an reinforces both the place of Muhammad as unique prophet for Arabs,[51] and the privileged place of the Arabs within the *ummah*. Anisah Huda responded to the testimony of a Chinese woman who had come to Damascus to learn Arabic, "Holy Damascus, noble Damascus. The message came in our language, the language of the Qur'an." Commenting on *al-Zumar* 39:28, Anisah Huda asked the women:

> How do foreigners read the Qur'an? They can hear the sound but without understanding. We are Arab and there are words in the Qur'an we don't understand without interpretation—the Qur'an is in our language—how can we ask from foreigners to understand the vocabulary, study all the Arabic language. It's not impossible, but it's not easy. We are responsible.

---

perplexed both Muslim and non-Muslim scholars for fourteen centuries. Different theories have been proposed, but no one has come up with a satisfactory explanation for them. They are important in the internal order of the Qur'an, in that *suras* with the same introductory letters are grouped together, rather than strictly according to length (so this *surah* is part of a group from 40–46). Some have linked them to the introductory formula in the *suras*. Welch notes that they introduce the rhyming scheme of the *surah* they begin (*Al-Kuran*, 412–414; see also Bell and Watt, *Introduction*, 61–65, 206–210).

50. Anisah Huda follows al-Shafi'i's position that the Qur'an is pure Arabic (*Al-Nahl* 16:103; *Al-Shu'ura'* 26:195) without any loan words from other languages, as part of the dogma of the eternity and perfection of the Qur'an. However, other Muslim scholars such as Ibn 'Abbas, Abu 'Ubayd, and later al-Suyuti and 'Abd-ar-Rahman ath-Tha'alibi, have argued for the presence of foreign loan words that had been incorporated into Arabic and Arabicized, and so were still in "a clear Arabic tongue" (Welch, *Al-Kuran*, 419; Bell and Watt, *Introduction*, 82–85; Motzki, "Alternative," 68). This is supported by one of the early "linguistic *tafsir*," "*Tafsir Ghaib al-Qur'an al-majid*" ("The *tafsir* of the foreign words of the noble Qur'an") by Zayd b. 'Ali (d. 121/738) (Demircan and Rifat, *Tafsir*, 629). Carter (*Foreign*) lists and categorizes both the extensive suggested borrowings and opinions about them.

51. For the latter, see *al-Sajdah* 32:3; *YaSin* 36:6; *Saba'* 34:44. This understanding of Muhammad's particular relationship with the Arab people is held in tension with the teaching of the universality of his message.

Recitation is linked again with understanding, and the intrinsic privilege of being part of the defining Arab community within the wider *ummah* is used to call the women to live out their *da'wa*.

Meaning and Application

For application of the Qur'an to contemporary life, the women's mosque community drew on the doctrine of multiple meanings within the text, and of *ijtihad*. Teaching *al-Zumar* 39:21, Anisah Huda explained,

> In a verse, we ask is it this meaning or this meaning? Maybe it is all the meanings. The precious Qur'an has many secrets. It's not that a verse or a word has one meaning and the rest are wrong. Some day, a new interpretation will emerge, widen our understanding. The Qur'an all the time offers new meaning. So how can the Islamic *shari'ah* go with all times and places? Because it renews. New scientific discoveries show new meanings. Now we have the car and then the aeroplane and then the rocket. If the meaning of the Qur'an was fixed, there would be no place for these inventions—it would only mean the horse.

After talking about different kinds of earth, the need for good works and attitudes, overcoming life pressures and problems, being oppressed by others, she commented, "Three meanings from the verse: maybe you yourself if you reflect will find more meaning and benefit from it." Then she exemplified her own comment with a further interpretation/application of morality, before moving on to the following verse.

The hermeneutic understanding of multiple interpretations for the Qur'an is supported by verses such as Al-'Imran 3:7. It is cited to demonstrate both the inspiration of the Qur'an and its relevance to every time and situation. Saeed links this hermeneutic to Ghulam Ahmed Pervez (1903–1985), whereas Guessoum suggests that it has been generally shared by Muslim writers going back to the time of Ibn-Rushd (1126–1198) and beyond.[52] The unchangeability of the text is taken to support its divine nature, in allowing variant readings in different contexts.[53]

Anisah Huda acknowledged that some Muslims believed that the time of *ijtihad* (reinterpretation through personal effort) in understanding the

---

52. Saeed, *Interpreting*, 21; Guessoum, "Qur'an."

53. In this context, Saeed also mentions the hermeneutic which distinguishes between cultural contextual rulings in the Qur'an, and the underlying universal principles behind them (*Interpreting*, 21). See also Rahman (*Major*) and Wadud (*Qur'an, Inside*). Barlas (*Believing*) seems to move between the two.

Qur'an was closed, but she taught its continuing application.⁵⁴ It was an *'amal al-'aqal* (matter of the mind). Contrary to those who taught that there was no longer anyone who could fulfill the requirements to be a *mujtahid*, Anisah Huda listed the conditions as needing "to know the Qur'an, the *ahadith*, to have good Arabic language, and to show proper behavior in their lives." According to these conditions, some of the women in the mosque community could be eligible to engage in *ijtihad*. One of the women attending the program explained to me:

> If there are two women in another country and there is no indication of the direction of prayer, one woman might say, "This is the direction," and pray that way, and the other woman suggest another direction and pray that way. In that case they would both be right because they are using their minds. *idha ma fiy dalil, kul wahid mujtahid* [If there is no evidence, everyone is a *mujtahid*].

And there was the possibility of personal choice of interpretations. Anisah Huda explained to me that people were free to agree with a given *ijtihad* or not, even as they were free to take from any of the four different schools of interpretation, and they could choose different schools for different times or subjects. Those who were unlearned could choose arbitrarily; however those who were educated needed to have understanding guiding their choice. Her position accords with Saeed's description of those who

> see it as the right of all Muslims to approach the Qur'an at a personal level and to try to make sense of it according to each person's ability. . . . These Contextualists argue that the emphasis on individual and personal interpretation and on reflective study is not foreign to the Qur'an, and that, in many verses, the Qur'an calls on individuals to contemplate and think over its verses, . . . aiming at some understanding of God's word is not a sin,⁵⁵

---

54. While some consider "the door of *ijtihad* is closed" because no one could fulfill the qualifications required today of a *mujtahid*, "a certain degree of *ijtihad* is inevitable and has always gone on" (Glassé, *Encyclopaedia*, 238, 479; Saeed, *Interpreting*, 154). The "re-opening of the door" of *ijtihad* was advocated by eighteenth- and nineteenth-century reformers such as Waliullah (Saeed, *Interpreting*, 10), Ahmed Khan (Rippin, *Islam*, 221), and Muhammad Abdu (Haddad, "Islam," 3–4). Latterly, El Fadl criticizes the contemporary "virtual flood in self-designated so-called experts indulging in *ijtihad-talk* and simultaneously spewing a plethora of ill-informed *fatwas*" ("Foreword," xiii). More recently, Femin Ijtihad has been founded "to analyze possibilities for women's rights within the Islamic legal framework, and training activists and lawyers" (Feminijtihad, "Strategic").

55. Saeed, *Interpreting*, 22. He adduces *al-Nisa'* 4:82, *al-Mu'minuun* 23:68, *Sad* 38:29 and *Muhammad* 47:24.

TEXTS, PRACTICES, AND MEANINGS 165

and also with Mahmood's description emphasizing "the importance of individual choice and the right of the Muslim to exercise this choice."[56] This approach offered hermeneutic possibilities in dealing with texts traditionally cited in relation to women.

On Troubling Texts

How did the members of the program deal with some of the more controversial Qur'anic texts and *ahadith* in relation to women?

> Men are the *quwwamun* [protectors and maintainers] of women, because Allah has made one of them to excel the other, and because they spend from their means. Therefore the righteous women are devoutly obedient, and guard in the husband's absence what Allah orders them to guard. As to those women on whose part you see ill-conduct, admonish them, refuse to share their beds, beat them; but if they obey you, seek not against them means. Surely Allah is ever high, most great. (An-Nisa' 4:34)[57]

An-Nisa' 4:34 is the subject of much contemporary debate from Muslim writers, particularly in regard to the spousal injunctions in the second half of the verse. Discussing the term "*quwwamun*,"[58] Anisah Huda interpreted it in singular locational terms: "the man is the protector/authority over the *house*" (*al-rajul quwwam 'ala al-bayt*), rather than in plural gendered terms according to the Qur'anic text—"men are protectors/in authority over *women*" (*qawwamun 'ala al-nisa'*).

> This means that he is responsible for the house, fixing things, children's study, the needs. It's best [seen] in action and not in the self. I wish men knew the meaning of *quwwam*—the right of the women for the man to be responsible for the house, [to provide] the woman's income. It was once thought that women are *min an-najasah* [[originating] from uncleanness][59]—this isn't in Islam.

---

56. Mahmood, *Politics*, 85, 99ff.

57. Al-Hilali and Khan, *Qur'an*, 170.

58. The word *quwwamun* is variously translated as "protectors and maintainers" (al-Hilali and Khan, Yusuf Ali), "authority" (Dawood), "overseers" (Malik), "in charge of" (Pickthall). Wehr's dictionary suggests "manager, director, superintendent, caretaker, keeper, custodian, guardian" (*Dictionary*, 800). See Wadud, *Qur'an*, 71–74 for further discussion of this term.

59. See chapter 7, note 357.

Anisah Huda interprets the verse in terms of role responsibilities, in behavioral rather than ontological terms of men versus women, and challenges popular linking of women with uncleanness (see chapter 7). However, she doesn't mention the ways to deal with women "on whose part you see ill-conduct," and I heard no discussion of this part of the verse on any other occasion within the mosque community. This is in contrast to the wider contemporary discussion around that verse.[60] It may have been too controversial in that social and cultural context.[61] Thus the women in the program operate within the permitted cultural space, but seek a re-reading that is more balanced, within the framework of gender complementarianism.

To help the women think further about Qur'anic interpretation, Anisah Huda would ask her students sometimes "about why woman was half of man with regard to witness and inheritance, and leave them for a period of a week or ten days to think about it, and then I would discuss it with them." In considering *al-Baqarah* 2:282 (the verse on witness) with expatriate women, she suggested different possibilities: that women didn't pay much attention in matters of money and were easily scared in violent crime, so it applied (only) to felonies of money and violence. Or else "now when women had the opportunity to study and be equal to men, their witness was of equal value: this was Islam." She described other situations when a woman's witness equaled that of a man, citing these examples:

> One woman is sufficient to testify to a birth. If a woman breastfeeds a child, she stands in a mother relationship to it which will guide future marriage decisions (the child of the wet nurse has a sibling relation to the breastfed child, and is not eligible as marriage partner). The witness of one woman that she has seen the other breastfeeding the child is enough.[62] In examining a girl's virginity, the witness of one woman is enough. The witness of four people, whether men or women, is necessary to prove adul-

---

60. Discussions include: Hashmi, *Women*, ch. 2; *Comparative Islamic Studies*, 2/2, 2006 has an issue with four articles dedicated to this verse; Mahmoud, *To Beat*; Ali, *Religious*; Ammar, *Wife*, 537–50; Scott, *Contextual*, 60–85; Dunn and Kellison, *Intersection*, 11–36; Duderija, *Case Study*, 1–30. Having tried to read this verse "with different methods for two decades," Wadud finally "cannot condone permission for a man to 'scourge' or apply *any kind* of strike to a woman" and concludes at this point that "we acknowledge that we intervene with the text" (*Gender*, 200, 204; original emphasis).

61. See for example the vehement rejection by clerics of laws against domestic violence in Lebanon in 2013, on the basis of this verse (Aziz, "Islamic").

62. Note that there is some disagreement about whether the breastfeeding should take place once, three or five times before the child becomes *mahram* to the woman's children. The evidence of the woman who breastfed may also be taken as evidence (al-Munajjid, "Her Children," and "Ruling").

tery.⁶³ In sighting the new moon for the beginning and end of Ramadan (times of community transition in the religious year), the word of one man or one woman is sufficient.⁶⁴

Contrary evidence from the *hadith* was also used to support different reasons for restricted application of the verse to women now.

When I asked Anisah Huda about the oft-quoted *hadith* that the majority of the inhabitants of hell were women, she explained that its textual context referred to women who cursed frequently and were ungrateful to their husbands: women who didn't have those characteristics didn't need to worry. She continued on to the phrase "deficient in intelligence and religion," and said that some didn't accept it as a valid *hadith*, which was her understanding.⁶⁵ Or else there were three possible interpretations: that the Prophet was referring to a particular group of women in a particular context; that he was saying that women had incomplete mind and religion, but were still smarter than men; that while men and women both had both mind and affection, you could say that men were lacking with regard to affection, as they were more guided by the mind. Conversely women were lacking with regard to the mind as they were guided more by affection. She instanced the effort and labor of having and raising children, and said that if as women we were guided only by our minds, we wouldn't have children.

---

63. For adultery, most Muslim writers require four *male* witnesses. Iranian law (Qisas Bill 1982, Article 91) requires four men, or three men and two women, and so on. However, Asghar Ali Engineer cites Imam Shafi`i that "in matters connected with women such as childbirth" women can bear witness without the testimony of a man being required. Ibn Taymiyyah also agreed that "if in a place of bathing only women are present and something punishable by *hadd* (rape, adultery, etc.) takes place then the case will be decided on grounds of women's testimony alone" (*Rights*, 79).

64. Hanafi, Hanbali, and some Shafi`i concur: Malikis and most Shafi`i (and also Sistani) refuse the evidence of a woman with regard to citing the new moon (Esin-Home, "Testimony"; Al-Sistani, "Moon Sighting").

65. Narrated Abu Said Al-Khudri: Once Allah's Apostle went out to the *Musalla* [to offer the prayer] of `Id-al-Adha or Al-Fitr prayer. Then he passed by the women and said, "O women! Give alms, as I have seen that the majority of the dwellers of Hell-fire were you [women]." They asked, "Why is it so, O Allah's Apostle?" He replied, "You curse frequently and are ungrateful to your husbands. I have not seen anyone more deficient in intelligence and religion than you. A cautious sensible man could be led astray by some of you." The women asked, "O Allah's Apostle! What is deficient in our intelligence and religion?" He said, "Is not the evidence of two women equal to the witness of one man?" They replied in the affirmative. He said, "This is the deficiency in her intelligence. Isn't it true that a woman can neither pray nor fast during her menses?" The women replied in the affirmative. He said, "This is the deficiency in her religion." (al-Bukhari: Book #6, Hadith #301, and Book #24, Hadith #541. Sahih Muslim, Book #001, Hadith #0142.)

"Deficient in religion," she explained as being from God, not a matter of our choice (as it related to menstrual abstention from pious practices). "*If* that *hadith* was true," it meant that God had lightened the religious load on us when we were carrying so many other loads in our work with children, house, other responsibilities; so our monthly period absolved us from having to carry out the religious duties also. But why would the Prophet make women leaders and teachers and then describe woman as "deficient in intelligence and religion"? Here she cited the example of Umm Salama advising Muhammad to perform the peace treaty at Mecca as an example to his men.[66] These discussions were with expatriates; this common *hadith* was not addressed in the public lectures I attended.

While this widely cited interpretation of God's mercy on women who were physically burdened is drawn from a traditional deficiency model of women,[67] here it is not given in the context of women's innate weakness as "crooked" and "deficient." Anisah Huda goes further to challenge application of the *hadith* by suggesting its restricted relevance today, and by using another that contradicts and thereby questions the usual reading.

Barlas argues that "even though there are only about six misogynistic *Ahadith* accepted as *Sahih* (reliable) out of a collection of 70,000, it is these six that men trot out when they want to argue against sexual equality, while perversely ignoring dozens of positive *Ahadith*."[68] Anisah Huda preferred to draw on the "positive *Ahadith*," such as the woman confronting and correcting Umar (second *khalif*),[69] or Umm Hani giving protection in the face

---

66. Al-Bukhari, Book #50, Ahadith #891.

67. "There is no argument that the woman's work is inside providing for the comfort and happiness of the family and managing the house and keeping it in order . . . If the woman competes and participates with the man in his work while she is exhausted by menstruation, pregnancy, childbirth, and raising the children, given the fact of her natural incapacity, she would have transgressed her condition and deviated from her nature. Then the family system would be undermined and its bond would disintegrate and there would be no love and mercy between them. . . . Woman was created crooked, lacking in intelligence and religion" (in Haddad, *Islam*, 9, from Muhammad Atiya Khamis. *Al-Shari'ah al-Islamiyah wa al-Harakah al-Nisa'iya*. Cairo: Dar al-I'tisam, 1987:56).

68. *Believing*, 46.

69. My search did not find this in *al-Bukhari, Muslim, Abudawud,* or *Malik's Muwatta*. Nahim (*Division*, 131) quotes the story and suggests a number of commentators, including Suyuti and Ibn Kathir, as references. Islam's *Women*, "Marriage," describes it as "a weak ahadith which has no validity." Most websites mention Umar restricting dowry amounts, with no mention of a woman's challenge.

of Muhammad's sentence of judgment on a man.[70] The expansiveness of the corpus of *ahadith* inevitably tends to its selective use on any subject.[71]

Although Anisah Huda made extensive use of *ahadith* in her teaching, I did not hear her discuss their source or compare their strength or authenticity. She would sometimes make significant use of weak *ahadith*. Mahmood cites "the principle that if the argument in which the weak *hadith* is located inspires virtuous conduct, then its use is justified,"[72] as support for using dubious *ahadith*. The first step in disputing a *hadith* is to check the veracity of its *isnad,* chain of transmitters. Mernissi, questioning the validity of the *hadith* about women rulers,[73] does so by querying its transmitter, Abu Bakra. She describes the process, "Going through the religious literature is no small task. . . . the vastness of the task and the rather limited reading time is enough to discourage most researchers," which may explain why it was not in evidence at the Garden Mosque.[74]

Although Anisah Huda suggested that some *ahadith* were not valid, she did not herself challenge *hadith* transmission. "Those who say they can't guarantee the *ahadith* don't know anything of the study of the *ahadith,* those who studied night and day to see the details of the chain (*musalsal*)." To support the rigor of the *isnad* she quoted the example of a transmitter who was discounted, because he didn't care for his horse, and thereby showed himself untrustworthy. She preferred to seek different readings from the context that could offer a variant meaning or restrict its application, or to

70. Narrated Abu Murra (the freed slave of Um Hani): Um Hani, the daughter of Abi Talib said, "I went to Allah's Apostle in the year of the conquest of Mecca and found him taking a bath and his daughter Fatima was screening him. I greeted him. He asked, 'Who is she?' I replied, 'I am Um Hani bint Abi Talib.' He said, 'Welcome! O Um Hani.' When he finished his bath he stood up and prayed eight Rak`at while wearing a single garment wrapped round his body and when he finished I said, 'O Allah's Apostle! My brother has told me that he will kill a person whom I gave shelter and that person is so and so the son of Hubaira.' The Prophet said, 'We shelter the person whom you have sheltered.'" Um Hani added, "And that was before noon (Duha)" (al-Bukhari, Book #8, Ahadith #353, also Book #73, Ahadith #179).

71. So too the stories of Muhammad in the mosque program presented him as forbearing, forgiving, compassionate, rather than the more war-like figure of *Sirat* Ibn Ishaq. Traditions quoted included further instances of a long-suffering Muhammad, in the context of widespread outrage among Muslims worldwide over cartoons of Muhammad.

72. Mahmood, *Politics,* 97, note 26.

73. Narrated Abu Bakra: During the battle of Al-Jamal, Allah benefited me with a Word (I heard from the Prophet). When the Prophet heard the news that the people of Persia had made the daughter of Khosrau their Queen (ruler), he said, "Never will succeed such a nation as makes a woman their ruler." (al-Bukhari, Book #88, Ahadith #219)

74. Mernissi, *Feminist,* 113, 114.

point to other traditions of Muhammad that seemed to contradict it. She told the women,

> If you see a *hadith* that is against logic or mind or the Qur'an or religion, it's not *sunnah*. Or something that is not against these things, but you don't understand the purpose or reason ... The *ahadith* were for specific situations at the Prophet's time—they're not all appropriate now. ... The problem is not in the *ahadith* but in people's understanding.

The teaching in the mosque program was shaped and punctuated by *ahadith*, choosing ones that opened possibilities for women's involvement in the faith community, without obvious regard to their status as *sahih* (sound) or *da'if* (weak). The mosque program promoted the authority of the *ahadith*, while at the same time participants in the program were exhorted to find ways of interpretation that went beyond traditional deficiency views of women.

Similarly Anisah Huda argued for the authority of *shari'ah*, as it was "for every time and place," and "the basis of our lives," able to "solve the problems of the world." She and many of the young women she taught advocated a wider application and proper use of *shari'ah* as the solution to social needs. Some of the young women were studying *shari'ah* at Damascus University, or at the *al-Fatah* Mosque, where the *al-Azhar* (Egyptian) course could be taken. Anisah Huda denoted *shari'ah* as the validation for controversial positions such as sending her daughter abroad to study and encouraging two women to take paid work in the face of their father's opposition.

Esposito, noting the sacrosanct status of family law in many Muslim societies, comments on its gendered origins: "Islamic law is the product of divine law (sharia) as understood (*fiqh*), interpreted, and applied by male religious scholars in the past and preserved in legal texts and manuals."[75] Within the mosque program I saw no evidence of critique of how jurisprudence was applied to contemporary society, in contrast to groups such as Sisters In Islam and Femin Ijtihad.[76] Anisah Huda endorsed the logic and rigor of the traditional texts, while encouraging the women to find a reading that was less restrictive. The Qur'an is not just a source of power, but through *tafsir*, of guidance for the affairs of daily and community life; and the women are invited to participate in its interpretation, with the *hadith*, but within the constraints of wider community conventions.

---

75. Esposito, *Women*, xii; see also Engineer, *Rights*, 6–15.
76. Hooker, *History*, 355.

Conclusion

Moving from an emphasis on the physical form of the Qur'an as a source of *barakah*, within the Garden Mosque community, women's primary focus on the Qur'an was as memorized, recited, and interpreted. Correct articulation, *tajwid*, was a pious duty. Rather than being subject to texts without question, the women were given a range of interpretive possibilities, within the bounds of an uncritical approach to the preeminence and sources of their faith.

Anisah Huda modeled an approach to Qur'an and *ahadith* that did not question the form but sought a reading that was more in line with contemporary understandings. Qur'anic verses and controversial *ahadith* were reinterpreted for a less misogynistic reading of God's mercy. Apart from a comment on cultural accretions, there is no suggestion of critiquing the community within which the *ahadith* were developed. This contrasts with some recent writers in the West, such as Barlas: "the state also influenced the development of the *Tafsir, Ahadith,* and *Shariʿah* along conservative and patriarchal lines."[77]

Abugideiri describes the shift in exegesis from (Arabic and Urdu) texts since the late eighteenth century that "conceptualize woman as a relational being, with the ontological category of Mother serving as the single most defining referent," to recent scholars including Engineer, Jawad, Stowasser, El Fadl, who "scrutinize the canonical sources of Islamic exegesis to elucidate the contextual factors that have contributed to modern patriarchal readings" and the reconstructive writers (often American Muslim academics) who "opt for a fresh reading of the Qur'an, and consequently a different understanding of women, namely as an independent viceregent [*khalifa*]," with a shift in understanding woman's nature "from relational to independent viceregent."[78]

Anisah Huda affirms the model of mother, but points beyond it to the place of women as *khalifat al-nabi*. The *barakah* of the Qur'an offers women access to power to negotiate life's challenges, and going beyond form to access the meaning and application of the Qur'an should offer women power for pious reformation in their personal lives, leading to social transformation. Remaining firmly within conservative lines of adherence to *ahadith*, Anisah Huda nevertheless goes beyond unquestioning submission to texts, seeking more choice for women through alternative interpretation, but not questioning cultural patriarchal norms. The teaching in the Garden Mosque

---

77. Barlas, *Believing*, 46; Wadud, *Qur'an*, 2.
78. Abugideiri, *Qur'an*, 249, 253–54.

does not challenge the transmitted texts nor the sheikhs who teach and implement them. The challenge is in women being able to be in the mosque, to read and to teach the texts, and to learn their application to their lives for themselves.

9

Dhikr

In Islam, as in any other faith, a stranger desiring not to remain a stranger could best feel the pulsing life of religion through a study of the devotions actually in use.[1]

Introduction

I HAVE DISCUSSED THE women's mosque program as an alternative community of allegiance to traditional kinship networks. This shift of allegiance finds expression in imaginary and local alternate community, ideal leadership, particular performative practices (with a focus on gendered ways of being), and practices around the memorization, recitation, and interpretation of texts. In this chapter I look at words of worship: the practice of *dhikr* (remembrance or recollection of God) as it has developed historically, leading to a discussion of how it is practiced within the women's program at the Garden Mosque. The *dhikr* phrases chosen for use in the mosque program may offer us a window on the way in which this community contemplates God, and considers itself in relation to God.

'Udhkur Allah (be mindful of God) is written all around the Middle East, whether graffitied on walls, embossed in mosque decorations, or as roadside signs.

Dhikr is part of devotion throughout much of the Muslim world, central to Sufi worship. In many schools it is associated with vigorous movement and chanting, and in popular thinking with the spinning *darawish* of the Mevlevi tradition. Not part of the five pillars of Islam, it is regarded with suspicion by Salafi Muslims. An internet writer complains:

---

1. Padwick, *Devotions*, xi.

"Salafis" accuse us of deviation and heresy because we sit and recite *dhikr*—loud or silently—together: the *kalima al-tayyiba*, and *astaghfirullah*, and the *Fatiha* and other *Suras*, and *salawat* on the Prophet, and *la ilaha illallah*, and Allah's beautiful Names. Some of them object because it is loud and they claim it should be silent; others object because it is silent and they claim it should be loud; others object because it is in a group and it should be individual; others because they claim our emphasis on *dhikr* is excessive and we should raise funds or study or hold conferences or make jihad instead; others object because some people are affected by the *dhikr* so as to sway or move this way or that instead of sitting still, so they want everyone to sit absolutely still; others because we sometimes perform *dhikr* in dim surroundings rather than in a glaring light; others yet object to reciting the name ALLAH by itself and claim it is an innovation, so that we should only say: YA Allah. Finally, they also accuse us of innovation and misguidance because we use *dhikr*-beads which we carry in our hands.[2]

The proponents of *dhikr* cite the Qur'an for justification. Muhammad himself meditated in a cave, and Qur'anic verses make reference to the coming of Gabriel (*An-Najm* 53:1–18; *At-Takwir* 81:19–25) and Muhammad's night journey. (*Al-Kahf* 17:1) Other verses suggest a mystical apprehension of God (*Al-Baqarah* 2:115, 186; *Al-Taubah* 9:123; *Al-'Ankabut* 29:20; *Qaf* 50:16), especially the famous verse of light. (*Al-Nur* 24:35) The word *dhikr* appears often in the Qur'an such as *Al-Ma'idah* 5:91; *Al-Jum'ah* 62:9; *Al-A'la* 87:15, and more particularly *Al-Baqarah* 2:200; *Al-'imran* 3:41; *Al-A'araf* 7:205; *Al-Muzzammil* 72:17. The most quoted verse is *Al-Baqarah* 2:152 "So remember Me, I will remember you" (*fa-adhkuruni 'adhkurkum*). Dhikr is not one of the essential pillars of devotion, but "a glorious appendix to the prayers of the five hours."[3]

Development of Sufism

Advocates of Sufism look back to Al-Hasan of Basra (642–728 AD).[4] An early Muslim leader, he knew many of the Companions of Muhammad, and was highly regarded for his asceticism and pure life. Loose gatherings for religious discussion, spiritual exercise (*halaqa*), and to do *dhikr*, were record-

2. As-Sunnah Foundation, "Dhikr."
3. Padwick, *Devotions*, 9.
4. Aydinli cites his legacy to suggest that Mu'tazilism and Sufism originated from the same source (*Ascetic*, 174).

ed as early as the first half of the third/ninth century. Adherents emphasized purity, abstinence, and piety, which it was claimed would lead people to communion with God. Love of God and for God was emphasized, with a focus on *tawhid* (oneness with God), gained through a *Tariqa* (pathway), together with *tawakkul*—reliance on God. Mansur al-Hallaj (858–922) of Persia was an early Sufi whose trance utterance, "I am the Truth," (*'ana al-haqq*) led to his trial, imprisonment, and execution for blasphemy.

The third/ninth and fourth/tenth centuries saw a growing emphasis on inner knowledge (gnosis) (*ma'rifa*) as opposed to *'ilm*, formal knowledge. Inner knowledge was privileged, with no checks and balances, and a different content and character to intellectual knowledge. Inner life was described in terms of stages of spiritual development (*maqamat*), and states (*ahwal*) through which the mystic passes, leading to absorption/annihilation (*fana'*) in Allah. Belief in saints and miracles developed more in the fifth/eleventh centuries, while the sixth–seventh/twelfth–thirteenth centuries saw the beginning of the Sufi brotherhoods.

Abu Hamid al-Ghazali (1058–1111), preeminent teacher of Islam, claimed Sufism as a legitimate expression of Islam, through his book *The Revivication of the Religious Sciences* (*'ihya' 'ulum al-din*). An Islamic teacher at Baghdad, he left there to become a wandering darwish before he returned to teaching in Baghdad and Damascus. Rahman writes of al-Ghazali:

> His purpose was to live through the verities of the Faith and to test those verities through the Sufi experientialist method. ... The test confirmed his faith, and he concluded (1) that it was only through the "life of the heart" that faith could really be acquired and (2) that Sufism has no cognitive content or object but the verities of the Faith.[5]

More controversial was Ibn al-'Arabi (d. 638/1240). Born in Spain, he died and was buried in Damascus. He taught that intuitive knowledge (*kashf*) was the highest and only sure form of cognition. Ibn al-'Arabi was influenced by women teachers, and is notable for the amorous imagery with which he describes love for God in his poetry. He taught that Adam was really the first female, for Eve was born from his inside, an act repeated by the second Adam, Mary, in generating Jesus.[6]

The twelfth and thirteenth centuries witnessed the development and growth of Sufi brotherhoods. These were characterized by the use of *dhikr*, or *wird* (litanies), and prayer beads, along with music, dancing, and body movement to contribute to an ecstatic state. Saints' tombs and relics became

---

5. Rahman, *Islam*, 144.
6. Rahman, *Islam*, 146; Schimmel, *My Soul*, 45–47.

venerated and places of pilgrimage. Entry to the Sufi order was through initiation ceremonies, and the leader was the transmitter of *barakah*. The leader (*shaykh, pir/murshid* in Persia, India or *muqaddam* in North Africa) had total authority over the disciple. "Thou shalt be in the hands of thy Shaykh like a dead body in the hands of its cleanser." The Naqshabandi order teaches that "the seeker must submit to the will of the *shaikh* and to [sic] obey him in all his orders and advice."[7] Leadership was passed on through (often family) lines of descent, which, as embodied chains of transmission of *barakah*, had a place within Sufism akin to the importance of *isnad* in verifying *hadith* .

Sufism was the contextualizing edge of Islam, with a tendency to compromise with local forms, enabling the spread of Islam more quickly in India, Central Asia, Turkey, and Africa. It offered the devotee communion with God. It also (especially for non-educated classes) offered a pattern of social life in socio-religious cults, which afforded some security against uncertainty, and changes in state authorities.

Women in Sufism

Women have always been part of Sufism. The most well-known female Sufi is Rabia of Bosra (717–801AD).[8] She was an outstanding, but not isolated example. Abu ʿAbd al-Rahman al-Sulami (d. 412/1021) wrote *Dhikr al-niswa al-mutaʿabbidat al-Sufiyyat* which includes 231 entries on women, not including Muhammad's family.[9] In Syria Sufi women mentioned include Halima (mid-ninth century), a descendant of Muhammad. She taught Rabia bint Ismail of Syria (d. ca. 850),[10] to whom the following verse is attributed:

> A Beloved unlike all others:
>
> He alone has touched my heart.
>
> And although absent from sight and touch,
>
> He is ever present in my heart.[11]

---

7. Rahman, *Islam*, 154.

8. See Smith's biography, *Rabi-a*.

9. Khadija, Fatima, and Aisha are cited as part of the female heritage of Sufism (Schimmel, *Soul*, 7, 11, 18).

10. Dehlvi, "Women Sufis."

11. Schimmel, *Soul*, 38.

Other notable Sufi women in Syria included Umm Harun, Bayda bint Mufaddal, Thawbiya bint Buhlul, Lubaba al-Mu'addiba, and Fatima of Damascus.[12]

Women functioned as formal directors in the early period. Unayda (early fourth/tenth) is reported to have had 500 male and female students. They also had less formal roles as mentors and preachers. Rumi (1207–1273) mentions Sufi women holding meetings in their homes to which he was invited, and Helminski notes:

> There have often been Mevlevi shaykhas who have guided both women and men. Mevlana (Rumi) himself had many female disciples, and women were also encouraged to participate in sema, the musical whirling ceremony of the Mevlevis. (Women usually had their own semas, but sometimes performed semas together with men.)[13]

Ibn al-'Arabi, who was convinced that women could reach the highest ranks in the hierarchy of the saints, chose women as fourteen of the fifteen individuals to whom he gave the *khirqa*, the patched frock of the dervishes.[14] As the more structured Sufi brotherhoods took shape, women were usually connected through their husbands or brothers. Only occasionally did they have a more formal teaching role. "There were however, in many of the orders, coordinated women's circles that were led and continue to be led by women. Occasionally a woman might also be appointed to stand as teacher and exemplar for both women and men within a particular community."[15] As well as Sufi orders, women's institutions known as *ribat* developed as refuges with Sufi links. Sabra describes them:

> Usually founded by a prominent female patron, the *ribaat* functioned as a home for single women, usually widows or divorcees. What makes it of particular interest is that not only the patrons and beneficiaries but also the administrators, or *shaykhas*, were women. The *shaykha* was charged with the responsibility of leading the women in the *ribaat* in prayer and *dhikr*, and with giving them lessons in Islamic law. ... Although some of the women who lived in these institutions were impoverished, others came from elite families and chose to live out their final years in pious poverty.[16]

12. Helminski, *Women*; Nurbakhsh, *Sufi*; Schimmel, *Soul*.
13. Helminski, *Women*, xxiv; Silvers, *Representations*, 541–43.
14. Schimmel, *Soul*, 47.
15. Helminski, *Women*, 73.
16. Sabra, *Poverty*, 491; see also Schimmel, *Soul*, 48–9; Ahmed, *Women and Gender*,

Silver concludes:

> A path of great piety was open to women who ardently aspired to it ... from all levels of society and regions in both periods traveling, praying publicly, and secluding themselves in mosques for long periods, visiting with men in all manner of fathering places, and strolling with them in the streets.... average Muslim women, scholars, and Sufis alike had greater freedom of movement than is assumed now ... Nevertheless, the reports indicate that the women who enjoyed these freedoms were either exceptional women or average women in exceptional circumstances.... If Ibn al-Jawzi's entries are representative, then women made up nearly a quarter of participants on this path.[17]

Mahmood makes no mention of *dhikr* in her descriptions of the women's mosque movement in Cairo, despite the existence of Sufi orders and also religious singers in Egypt.[18] Use of *wird* (litany) in morning and evening devotional practice is deeply embedded across the Muslim world in Orthodox Islam,[19] including among those with no connection to Sufi orders. While Syria has a rich tradition of Sufism, attested by the proliferation of shrines for those who know to look for them, use of *dhikr* in the mosque is not necessarily seen as a Sufi practice. So Shannon comments that in Aleppo, "many participants ... understand *dhikr* to be an orthodox Sunni practice, and not something associated primarily with Sufism."[20]

Dhikr in the Garden Mosque

> Women are sitting in silent concentration. It is quiet, just the sound of lips moving with the beads, and someone's periodic murmur. A few of the women are rocking, some passing the prayer beads through their fingers. There is a little movement as women adjust their position. One woman takes off her coat. The outside noises of cars, voices, come in from the road. Inside the women are quiet, still, concentrating. The girl beside me is crying. She swallows, continues to pass the prayer beads through

---

110.

17. Silvers, *Representations*, 541.

18. Mahmood, "Rehearsed," *Politics*; Helminski, *Women*, 224–25.

19. Padwick, *Devotions*, xii. For example, *al-Ma'thurat* is a collection of *adhkar* (pl. of *dhikr*) and *ad'iya* (pl. of *du'a*) from the Qur'an and *ahadith* compiled into a *wird* by Hasan Al-Banna (1906–1949), founder of the Muslim Brotherhood in Egypt.

20. Shannon, *Aesthetics*, 381.

her fingers. A low voice begins to recite something, and others join in quietly for a little while. Then there is silence again, with only the muted sound of voices whispering to themselves, lips moving. A woman in the front row begins to sing quietly, a song of worship. *A'ariftak ya rabb bi-qalbi wa-fikri* (I knew you, O Lord, in my heart and my thoughts.) She sings this a few times, and some other phrases. It is quiet, beautiful. Others sit quietly, some moving their lips, some rocking their bodies a little.

When I mentioned Sufism in a conversation, Anisah Huda was careful to say that not all Sufism is a proper representation of Islam. However, her family had links with a prominent mosque and Muslim leader of the Naqshbandi group, also characterized by its emphasis on *sunna* and *'ilm*.[21] A young woman giving her testimony at one of the mosque gatherings described herself as from a Sufi background. She had enjoyed the Sufi *dhikrs* "but the feeling never lasted." She came to this mosque, happened to arrive at a *dhikr* the first time, and then also found the lectures meeting the gap she felt. Her comments support a perceived distance between the practice of the Garden Mosque and Sufism, together with a close link between *dhikr* and *'ilm* of the lectures.

Dhikr is a regular part of meetings at the Garden Mosque, and always takes place before a lecture. The communal mosque practice of *dhikr*, with its rich heritage, deepens the women's awareness of themselves as part of a community that is geographically and historically wider than family networks. This *dhikr* is not characterized by vigorous action: the women sit quietly, the only movement that of prayer beads between the fingers of some of the supplicants, with invocatory phrases and sometimes songs interspersed with periods of silence. Here is not the privileging of esoteric inner knowledge over rational understanding that characterizes much of Sufism—rather knowledge or learning of the mind is exalted. The women are taught that "an hour of learning [*'ilm*] is better than a year of *dhikr*."

However, *dhikr* is an essential part of preparation before the *'ilm* (lecture). Anisah Huda placed a high importance on this time of "spiritual preparation" for the lecture, to help people put aside the distractions and pressures of home or work and be able to concentrate on the teaching which followed. Anisah Huda told the women: "The lesson without the *dhikr* is about a quarter of its usefulness. The *dhikr* is the spiritual preparation and gives us concentration, so we don't miss half the lecture."

In this way *dhikr* is used to underline the importance of *'ilm*. The lecture time is too important to just walk into, arriving preoccupied with other

---

21. "There is no sufism without Ilm" (Sunni Forum, "Criteria").

matters. *Dhikr* is needed to form or prepare the mind in order to be able to learn. Resorting as she often did to an agricultural metaphor, Anisah Huda describes how *dhikr* "prepares the ground of the heart as we prepare the ground by plowing before we sow the seed." That's why "I guard it, I won't give a lesson unless there's been *dhikr* . . . even ten or five minutes, to recollect your heart to God." *Dhikr* is seen as an essential part of formation of body and mind so as to benefit from ʿ*ilm*.

The benefit is perceived to extend into daily life. Recollection in *dhikr* encompasses both God and self. Invoking God's forgiveness is tied to awareness of one's sins. "People take account of themselves and ask forgiveness for sins—so someone who does *dhikr* regularly will be less likely to sin." Even though Anisah Huda prioritizes ʿ*ilm* as more important, *dhikr* is so significant in formation and awareness that she is prepared to describe it as *fard* (necessary): "*Dhikr* is necessary; although its time is not specified, but it is said *udhkuru Allah dhikran kathiran* [Remember Allah with much remembrance]. For *salah* is five times, *Hajj* once in a lifetime, fasting once a year, only *dhikr* is frequent, so *dhikr* is very important in our lives." *Dhikr* occurs at the mosque before lectures, and also at other specific *dhikr* sessions. I didn't see Anisah Huda at any of the dedicated *dhikr* sessions at the mosque, but she emphasized the importance of *dhikr* at home for the individual as well: "It is required for each person to do *dhikr* at home on their own, each day, morning and evening." Thus participation in the mosque program reshapes the women's practice of piety in domestic space.

With the emphasis on knowledge comes a focus on formation of and through the mind, beyond the formation through "disciplinary acts" of the body noted by Mahmood.[22] Anisah Huda recommends ritual ablutions before *dhikr*. She associates this with the recitation of Qur'anic verses as part of *dhikr*, but it highlights the place given to *dhikr*—usually ritual purity is only associated with required practices of *salah*, fasting, pilgrimage, and reading the Qur'an—the restrictions of purity and dress are not typically applied to *dhikr*.

Dhikr Content

In this section I review the text of the *dhikr* times that I attended: what words and phrases were used, and what do they suggest about their users' view of God?

The content of *dhikr* at the mosque varied, however invocatory phrases, times of silence, songs, Qur'anic verses, invoking Muhammad and *duʿaʾ*

---

22. Mahmood, *Politics*, 126.

(petition) were regular elements. While *du'a'* often refers to specific petitions, many of the invocations were said with intercessory intention: the boundary between *dhikr* and *du'a'* is fluid.

Taking Refuge

The time of *dhikr* most commonly began with:

> I take refuge in God, the Hearing, the Knowing, from the accursed devil.
>
> *'a'udhu billahi al-sami'i al-'alim min al-shaytan al-rajim.*

followed by

> In the Name of God the Compassionate the Merciful.
>
> *B'ism Allah al-rahman al-rahim.*

IN SALAH

In this the *du'a'* echoes the formal *salah* which follows the beginning *Takbir* and *du'a'*:

> God is greatest. Praise to you, O God, and all praises are due to You and Your name be blessed and your majesty exalted, and there is no god but You.
>
> *Allahu akbar. Subhanak allahum bihamdak wa tubarak ismak wa-ta'ala wa jaddak wala illahu ghayrak.*[23]

immediately with taking refuge:

> *'a'udh billahi min al-shaytan al-rajim. Bism Allah al-rahman al-rahim.*
>
> I take refuge in God from the accursed devil. In the name of God, the Compassionate, the Merciful.

and then reciting the *Fatihah*.

The "taking refuge" is only said once at the start of the time of *salah* and not repeated in succeeding *raka'*. It has Qur'anic authority from *Al-Nahl* 16:98 ("and when you recite the Qur'an seek refuge with God from

---

23. This *du'a'* can be used, or there are some other phrases attributed to Muhammad, which may be used instead (Saqib, *Guide*, 29).

Satan the accursed.") The same phrase begins *Al-Falaq* 113:1 and *Al-Nas* 114:1, the last two and oft-quoted *surahs* of the Qur'an.[24] It occurs frequently in the books of recommended *du'a'* invocations.[25] Padwick describes it as the "cry of frightened humanity ... in a demon-haunted world, in a world ... where the evil eye is to be feared as well as the attacks of less uncanny human enemies," and notes its connection with the words used for charms and amulets (*ma'adhat*).

Danger Without and Within

"Taking refuge" is thus found in the heart of both the formal prayer-rite and *dhikr*, as well as the exclamation of the ordinary person in the street who has a fright. Here is the link between the formal practices of faith which offer hope for the afterlife, and informal practices that offer a way to manipulate the forces directing the present life. Between God and his follower lie a host of threatening forces. Padwick links this protective invocation together with the use of *b'ism Allah al-Rahman al-Rahim* (in the name of God the Compassionate the Merciful) to the old practice of "saining": "the use of the sign of the Cross to control or purify what is suspect of evil influence, and to bless and sanctify the common acts of life."[26] Some of the perils from which the worshipper seeks refuge in God include: "the evil of the whisperer who withdraws ... the evil of today and the days after it, laziness and old age, the punishment of hellfire and the grave" and similarly, "the grave and its torture ... the evil of my soul and the evil of the devil and his helpers ... the evil of the created world." Other times to take refuge are at the conclusion of *salah* (as well as its beginning), going into the mosque, in the evening, before going to sleep.[27]

Closely linked to the sense of danger without is the worshippers' sense of boding evil within themselves. So a common *du'a'* in the mosque was:

---

24. See also *Al-Mu'minun* 23:97, 98.

25. Al-Qahtani, *Devotions, Fortress*; al-Husaynaan, *1,000*; see also Padwick, *Devotions*, 83, 97.

26. This is still seen in both Muslim and Christian use in the Middle East, invoking respectively the name of God the Compassionate the Merciful, or the Cross, at the top of any exam paper, or before doing any mundane job such as putting a cake in the oven, starting to cut a piece of material for sewing, or killing a bird or animal to be eaten.

27. Al-Qahtani, *Devotions*; Al-Husaynaan, *1,000*. Padwick adds the sudden rising of the wind and the marriage night (see *Tobit* in the Deuterocanonical books for a parallel in the Jewish tradition), to these examples (*Devotions*, 87).

> I take refuge in You from the evil I have done, and I come to You in Your grace to me, and I come to you in my sin, so forgive me, for there is no one who forgives sins except You.
>
> *a'udh bik min shirr ma sana'at, 'abu' lak bi-na'matak 'alayya wa-'abu' bidhanbi faghfir li f'inahu la yaghfir al-dhanub 'ila 'anta.*

The consciousness of the worshipper's need of forgiveness was a constant theme in the mosque *dhikr*, and the most frequent use of refuge-taking, in contrast to the Qur'an, where most of the references are seeking refuge from external danger of the Devil or people (*Al-'imran* 3:36; *Al-A'araf* 7:200; *Yusuf* 12:23; *Maryam* 19:18; *Al-Mu'minun* 23:97–98; *Ghafir* 40:27, 56; *Fussilat* 41:36; *Ad-Dukhan* 44:20)[28] Even in taking refuge from the devil at the beginning of *dhikr*, the *b'ism Allah* was closely followed with *istaghfir Allah*. God is both the one who gives refuge from evil and who forgives the doer of misdeeds.

The light of His face also offers protection, as in:

> I take refuge in the light of Your face, which brought light to the darkness.
>
> *a'udh bi-nur wijhika aladhi 'ashraqt lahu al-dhulmat.*

Similarly, in discussing the final *du'a'* of the prayer-rite, Padwick cites this poignant example, reminiscent in its longing of St Patrick's "breastplate" prayer of protection for his Celtic followers against all the natural and supernatural forces of their world:

> O God appoint for me light in my heart and light in my tomb and light before me and light behind me; light on my right hand and light on my left; light above me and light below me; light in my sight and light in my perception; light in my countenance and light in my flesh; light in my blood and light in my bones. Increase to me light, and give me light, and appoint for me light, and give me more light, give me more light, give me more light![29]

The shift in emphasis from external danger to internal evil suggests a shift in social space to a less differentiated society, down the grid axis (chapter 5; appendix 1), where expression of faith is more internalized.

---

28. With the exception of *Hud* 11:47, where Noah seeks forgiveness for questioning God.

29. Padwick, *Devotions*, 212, quoted from a prayer-book: *Dala'ilu 'l-khairat ma'a 'l-ahzab*. Al-Qahtani's popular *Fortress of the Muslim* includes an extended version of this prayer (32).

The Compassionate, the Merciful

"In the Name of God, the Compassionate, the Merciful," as noted above, is often used at the beginning of *dhikr* after taking refuge. It sometimes is also used near the conclusion of a session, apparently in a dedicatory sense. As suggested in the previous section, this invocation also has a protective function that links it with taking refuge. It also frequently appears in written form in buildings and on public vehicles, with the same protective role.

This description of God reappears in the *dhikr* in a common invocation which affirms God's character of mercy vis-a-vis the worshipper:

> There is no god but You, praise You. I was among the wrongdoers, and You are the most Merciful of the merciful.
>
> *la ilahu ila 'inta subhanak 'iniy kunt min al-dhalimin wa inta 'arham al-rahimin.*

Forgiveness

Although the doctrine of innate sinfulness is foreign to Islam, God's mercy is his most repeated attribute. In line with this, the *dhikr* prayers are deeply imbued with the worshippers' sense of needing God's forgiveness. Phrases such as the following abound:

> Forgive, great God, from every sin I have done.
>
> *istaghfir Allah al-'athim min kul dhanb qad fa'alt*
>
> Lord, I am drowning in my sins; beautiful is your pardon.
>
> *Rabbu 'iniy ghariq bi-dhanubiy jamil 'afuk.*
>
> Forgive, great God, whom there is no god but Him, the Living, the Maintainer, and I repent/turn to Him.
>
> *istaghfir Allah al-'athim aladhi la illahu 'ila huwa al-hayy al-qayum wa-atub 'ilayhi.*

as cited above, the repeated:

> There is no god but You, may You be praised. I was among the wrongdoers[30] and You are the most Merciful of the merciful.

---

30. Saqib (*Guide*, 42) translates it, "I was among the cruel (by ignoring my duty to you); Ebtisam glossed it as "I was among those who wrong themselves."

la illahu ila 'inta subhanak 'iniy kunt min al-dhalimin wa 'inta 'arham al-rahimin.

or just the oft-murmured

God, forgive.

istaghfir Allah.

God is invoked as the One who forgives sins and errors (*Allahum ya ghafir al-dhanub wa-al-khatayat*) even as He heals illnesses (*Ya Shafiy al-'amrad*).

IN SALAH

As with the preceding elements of *dhikr*, seeking God's forgiveness is also drawn from *du'a'* within the *salah* prayer-rite, based on *hadith* recounting Muhammad's example in praying *salah*. As the Muslim returns to a kneeling position from prostration, s/he prays: "Lord forgive me and have mercy on me" (*rabb ighfirliy wa-irhamniy*).[31]

> O God, forgive me, and have mercy on me, and keep me on the right path, and keep me healthy, and provide for me, and complete my shortcomings, and exalt me.
>
> *Allahum ighfirliy wa-irhammniy wa-ahdiniy wa-a'afniy wa-irzaqniy wa-ijbirniy wa-irfa'aniy.*[32]

In *dhikr*, refuge is taken from the evil (*shirr*) the worshipper has done. Forgiveness is most commonly sought for *dhanb/dhanub* (pl.). Padwick notes that this word "expresses not sin but a sin, a single, articulated act of transgression."[33] It is the word used in the most common Arabic form of the Lord's Prayer.

God also forgives *khatayyat* which has the sense of errors or mistakes (*Al-Nisa'* 4:92), or faults (*Al-Shu'ara'* 26:82).[34] This is the word most often used by Arab Christians to describe sin, both as specific acts, and also as a state of humanity.

---

31. Mujahid, *Prayer*, 212, quoted from a prayer-book: *Dala'ilu 'l-khairat ma'a 'l-ahzab*.

32. Saqib, *Guid*, 38–39.

33. Padwick, *Devotions*, 191.

34. Abraham is shown in this reference as a prophet who may make mistakes, but according to the Islamic understanding of prophethood, cannot sin.

And God's mercy is sought for the *dhalimin*, those who oppress or wrong themselves (*Al-Aʿraf* 7:23—Adam and Eve; *Al-Naml* 27:44—the Queen of Sheba before Solomon).[35]

While there is overlap with Christian terminology, the understanding from these *dhikr* is of sin being specific acts that primarily harm the sinner. Here there is no mention of sin against God, or of others hurt by sin, no notion of an inherent state of sinfulness, nor of the necessity for the one seeking God's mercy to translate forgiveness received into forgiveness of others.

A number of the *dhikr* quote *al-ʿimran* 3:135: "none can forgive sins but God" (*man yaghfir al-dhanub ʿila Allah*). The basis for the worshipper seeking God's forgiveness, then, is in God's own nature, as most Merciful of the merciful. Razi describes God as under no obligation to act mercifully, but he does so because of his favor and generosity, from a *hadith*: "When God completed creating the cosmos He wrote down in a book right above his throne: 'Verily, My mercy predominates My wrath.'"[36] This idea of a God more inclined to mercy than punishment is reinforced by an assessment of good deeds as weightier than bad ones, whether double (*Al-Nisa'* 4:40) or (at least) ten times more (*Al-Baqara* 2:261, *Al-Anaʿam* 6:61); and the *hadith* "When someone excels in their religion, then their good deeds will be awarded ten times to seven hundred times for each good deed whereas a bad deed will be recorded as it is."[37] Women from the mosque program would quote from the second part of this *hadith*:

> Whoever comes with one good deed, there are in store for him ten like it and even more, and whoever comes with one evil deed, it is only for it that he will be called into account. I even forgive him [as I like].
>
> Whoever draws close to Me by the span of a palm I draw close to him by the cubit. Whoever draws close to Me by the cubit I draw close to him by the space covered by two hands. Whoever walks towards Me I rush towards him. Whoever meets Me in the state that his sins fill the earth, but not associating

---

35. Padwick suggests *shirk* and *kufr* as the worst sins for Muslims. "If for the men of the Chinese civilization the essential sin was that which broke the due proportions of the rightly adjusted life; if for an African, ... the essential sin was that which broke the unity of the tribe; if for Israel of old the essential sin was unfaithfulness to Jehovah's covenant; for Islam, ... the essential sin is unfaithfulness to that revelation of the Divine Unity which it is Islam's business to proclaim with passionate intensity" (*Devotions*, 175–76).

36. Cited in Moucarry, *Search*, 27, 36. Also in Muslim's hadith collection, (Book #037, Hadith #6626, #6627, #6628).

37. Al-Bukhari, (Book #2, Hadith #40; Book #76, Hadith #498; Book #93, Hadith #592).

anything with Me, I would meet him with the same vastness of pardon.[38]

I heard this *hadith* also from women in other mosque programs, even in other countries; however, I did not encounter it from women whose faith is expressed primarily in family contexts. This suggests the possibility that the mosque teaching may offer a more hopeful view of God's mercy to his follower.

As God's tendency is to forgive, humanity's tendency is to sin, because they are created weak by God (*Al-Nisa'* 4:28). On the one hand, God's sovereignty excludes any necessity to forgive. On the other hand, it is easy for an omnipotent God to forgive: because he has not been sinned against (for sin hurts the sinner rather than God), there is no cost involved for him. In this understanding of the transaction between forgiver and the forgiven, there is no obligation to forgive, and neither any cost.

Moucarry suggests a focus on God's justice as the basis for forgiveness for Mu'tazilite thinkers, drawing on *Al-Nisa'* 4:31 and *Al-Zalzalah* 99:6–8; on his mercy for Sufis (as represented by Ibn al-'Arabi), with *Al-Zamar* 39:53 as a foundation verse; and on the sovereignty of the Almighty as representative of Sunni Islam (with *Al-Nisa'* 4:48 and *Al-Baqarah* 2:284 as key texts).[39] While the focus on *'ilm* in mosque lectures suggests an impulse towards contemporary Mu'tazilitism: and the *dhikr* hints at underlying Sufi influence, the *dhikr* prayers indicate that for these women God's sovereignty is the basis on which they seek his forgiveness. God can forgive who he wills—but he has sovereignly chosen not to forgive those who commit *shirk*.

If God's sovereignty is the basis for his forgiveness, it is accessed by the worshipper best through adherence to right ritual. The following *du'a'* was often used in the mosque:

> O God! You are my Lord. There is no god except You.
>
> You have created me and I am Your servant.
>
> I am faithful to Your covenant and Your promise as much as I can.
>
> I seek refuge with You from the evil I have done.
>
> I acknowledge before You the blessings (grace) You have bestowed upon me.

---

38. Al- Muslim, (Book #035, Hadith #6473, 6496, 6499; and Book #037, Hadith #6610)

39. Moucarry cites John 3:16 as the fundamental Christian understanding of Love as God's basis for forgiveness (*Search*, 317).

I confess my sin to You.

So please forgive me—for no-one forgives sin except You.

Allahum 'inta rabbiy la ilahu 'ila 'inta

Khalaqtaniy wa-'ana 'abuduka wa-'ana 'ala 'ahadak wa-wa'adak ma astata'at

'a'audh bik min shirr ma sana'at

'abu' lak bi-na'amatak 'alayya wa-'abu' bi-dhanbiy

fa-'aghfir liy fa-'innahu la yaghfir aldhanub 'ila 'inta.

Each citation of this prayer notes:[40] "Whoever recites this with conviction in the evening and dies during that night, shall enter Paradise; and whoever recites it with conviction in the morning and dies during that day, shall enter Paradise."[41]

God is sovereign and will bestow forgiveness (and other blessings, such as protection, healing, and provision of needs) as he wills. On the recipient's side, they place themselves in position to receive forgiveness through the use of prescribed phrases (ideally in Arabic) at prescribed times. Sometimes intent is specified, as in this *du'a'*; at other times a number of recitations is required, whether three or thirty-three or some other multiple. Intent of the heart is not absent in this understanding of prayer, but more fundamental are the required formulae of language and time.

Qur'an

In salah

Recitation of the *Fatihah* and other Qur'anic passages is foundational to Muslim *salah* (*Al-Isra'* 17:78). Padwick describes the *Fatihah* as "the very heart of the prayer-rite, and possibly that round which the rest was built."[42]

---

40. Moucarry, *Search*, 50. Padwick does not mention it; Cragg includes only the last line as part of "Prayers of the Naqshabandi Order" (*Alive*, 92). However, it is cited in both Al-Qahtani's collections (*Fortress*, 78–79; *Devotions* 28–29) and in Al-Husaynaan (*1,000*, 95–96) suggesting more widespread contemporary use.

41. With minor variations in translation. All source it in Bukhari and others' collections: Moucarry has the most extensive list, including: al-Bukhari, Book #75, Hadith #318; Abu Dawud, Book #36, Hadith #5052; and he also lists it in Tirmidhi's and Nasa'i's collections.

42. Padwick, *Devotions*, 108. The opening chapter of the Qur'an, the *Fatihah* is the only one which is in the form of a prayer rather than a sermon or lecture (Gibb and

Recited in each *raka'*, it is repeated at least seventeen times each day by the conscientious Muslim through the five daily prayer-rites. It is also part of transactions in daily life, such as weddings, funerals, and sealing contracts.[43] If the *Shahadah* records the entry of a new-born child or adult convert into Islam, and reminds the community that it is time to gather for prayer, the *Fatihah* is the constant refrain of liturgical life and expression of communal identity for Muslims.

Similarly the *Fatihah* (or sometimes other Qur'anic passages) were used to begin or conclude sessions of *dhikr*.[44] The leader would say, "the *Fatihah*" or "the noble (*shirif*) *Fatihah*" and also frequently "the noble *Ikhlas*,"[45] and the women would murmur the passage silently to themselves. Other short passages were quoted, such as, "Have we not opened your breast for you?" (*'alam nashrah lak sadrak?*) (*Al-Sharh* 94:1), "Oh Ever-Living Sustainer" (*ya hayyu ya qayyum*) (*Al-Baqarah* 2:255). So with Shannon's description of the *dhikr* in Aleppo, it:

> always begins with a recitation of passages from the Qur'an, often an entire sura, in the melodious tajwid style.... Recitation of the Qur'an itself is generally preceded by a prayer to ward off Satan, and then the fatiha ("the opener"), the opening chapter of the Qur'an, starts the recitation.[46]

The memorization or recitation of the Qur'an undergirded the whole program. Each time I entered the upstairs women's area of the mosque, when there was no formal program underway in the main section, I would find women sitting in pairs, one reciting while the other more qualified woman listened and corrected her as needed. There were regular classes on how to read and correctly pronounce the Qur'an according to the rules of *tajwid*, "the system of rules regulating the correct oral rendering of the Qur'an."[47] (See previous chapter.) There was no evidence of women drawing

---

Kramers, *Encylopaedia*, 100, 101; Cragg, *Event*, 74). The Qur'anic verse mentioning the seven repeated verses (*Al-Hijr* 15:87) is said to refer to the *Fatihah*. Al-Hilali and Khan (*Interpretations*, 1) cite Sahih Al-Bukhari, Bo#ok 6, *Hadith* # 1: see also al-Banna (*Al-Ma'thurat*, 83). Prayer-booklet authors assert the value of the *Fatihah* as "two thirds of the Qur'an," outweighing the rest of the Qur'an "seven times," and gathering together "all the meanings of the Qur'an" (Padwick, *Devotions*, 108–9).

43. Graham and Kermani, *Recitation*, 124; Lane, *Manners*.

44. This is similar to the use of the Lord's prayer in the Coptic *'Agbiya* prayers of the hours, and other forms of Christian liturgical prayer.

45. *Al-Ikhlas*, surah 112 in the Qur'an.

46. Shannon, *Aesthetics*, 385. Also Kazuhiro, *Combining*, 162.

47. Nelson notes, "Muslims interpret the Qur'anic verse 'Recite the Qur'an with tartil' (74:4) as meaning 'Recite the Qur'an according to the rules of tajwid'" (*Art*, 14).

on knowledge of the Arabic melodic system for the more complex *mujawwad* recitation. This accords with Nelson's analysis of public Qur'anic recitation in Egypt, "a recitation tradition which is exclusively male." Some women professional reciters, who were also singers (most notably Umm Kalthum), had been broadcast in Egypt in the 1930s and 1940s. However, women reciters are no longer broadcast in Egypt as public figures because "a woman's voice makes one think of things other than Allah."[48] Outside the Middle East, particularly in Indonesia and Malaysia, women reciters do become public figures. The mosque program offered a context for women to recite and within the wider community their ability (even without public performance) still gained them recognition and honor.

Invocatory Phrases

Much of the *dhikr* was invocatory phrases, chanted once or a number of times. The name of God was most frequent, usually *Allah* or sometimes *Ya Allah*. The most frequently heard invocation, after "*Allah*" was the first half of the *shahadah* (creed): "There is no god but You, may You be praised"[49] (*la illahu 'ila 'inta subhanak*), often chanted for several repetitions. There are numerous traditions describing the efficacy of the affirmation of God's uniqueness, for protection and forgiveness. It was most often paired with a reflection on the worshipper's unworthiness and God's mercy:

> There is no god but You, praise You: I was among the wrongdoers,[50] and you are the most Merciful of the merciful.
>
> *la illahu 'ila 'inta subhanak: 'iniy kunt min al-dhalamin wa-'inta 'arham al-rahamin.*

Here the creedal place of Muhammad is displaced by the worshipper.[51] God is praised as he reveals his attribute of mercy to the worshipper who

---

One woman at the mosque told me she took ten years to memorize the Qur'an—the first three or four years to memorize it, and the rest to say it with *tajwid*.

48. Nelson, *Art*, 102, 202–3; see also Rasumussen, *Women*.

49. This foundational affirmation of the unity of God, "There is no god but God" (*la illahu 'ila Allah*), with echoes of the shema' of Judaism (Deuteronomy 6:4–5), affirmed again by the Messiah (Luke 10:27) finds its closest form in the Qur'an in *Al-Baqarah* 2:255 (the throne verse), *Al-Naml* 27:26, *Al-Qasas* 28:88: *la illahu 'ila huwa*.

50. Sin is offensive because of its impact on the sinner rather than in relation to God. See also Padwick, *Devotions*, 192.

51. It is interesting that this displacement occurs in *dhikr*, which is where the adoration of Muhammad reaches its peak.

has wronged her/himself. Again, comparing God's omnipotence with the worshipper's weakness:

> God, You are my Lord, there is no God but You.
>
> You created me, and I am your slave: and I am not sufficient for your covenant and promise.
>
> *Allah 'inta rabbiy la illahu 'ila 'inta*
>
> *Khalaqtaniy wa-'ana 'abuduka wa-'ana 'ala 'ahadak wa-wa'adak ma istata'at.*

Praiseworthy

In *dhikr*, God's praiseworthiness is closely associated with his uniqueness. Again this echoes the *salah* prayer-rite, where the most frequent *du'a'* used after the *takbir* is:

> May you be praised, O God, and all praises are due to you, may your name be blessed and your majesty exalted; there is no god but You.
>
> *subhanak Allahum wa-bihamdak wa-tubarak ismak wa-ta'ala jadak wa-la 'illahu ghayrak.*

with "Praise my great Lord" (*subhan rabbiy al-'athim*) which is repeated at least three times (or any greater odd number) in bowing, and "Praise my exalted Lord" (*subhan rabbiy al-'ala*) similarly repeated in prostrating.

In addition to the "there is no god but You, may You be praised" (*la illahu 'ila 'inta subhanak*), discussed above, other praise couplets affirmed the theme of God's otherness, in an elaborated form of the common speech exclamation "*God be praised*" (*subhan Allah*).

> Praise God the great, Praise God in extolling Him.
>
> *subhan Allah al-'athim subhan Allah wa-bi-hamdiy.*
>
> Praise the Eternal of eternity, Praise the only One.
>
> *subhan al-'abad al-'abadiy subhan al-wahid al-'ahad.*

These couplets were chanted briskly and repetitively: or else in a more extended reflection:

> Praise the only One, there is no god but God.

> Praise the First without beginning, Praise the End without ending.
>
> There is no god but God. You are the One, there is no god but God.
>
> *subhan al-wahid al-'ahad la 'illahu 'ila Allah.*
>
> *subhan al-'awal bila badayyah, subhan al-'akhir bila nahayyah.*
>
> *la illahu 'ila Allah. 'inta al-wahid la 'illahu 'ila Allah.*

The recitation of God's otherness is closely associated in the *hadith* with benefits for the reciter in the next life. If the *tasbih* "*subhan Allah*" is said thirty-three times, along with the *takbir* "*Allahu akbar*" and *tamhid* "*al-hamdu lillah*," each recitation is counted as an act of charity and earns the reciter a tree planted for them in paradise for each repetition.[52]

Benefits are similarly accrued with reciting "Praise God in extolling Him" *(subhan Allah wa-bihamdihi)* 100 times.[53]

Other frequent phrases included:

> O Living and Eternal One, in your mercy we ask for help.
>
> *Ya hayyu ya qayyum birahmatika nistaghith*
>
> God is sufficient for us, and He is the best Disposer of affairs.[54]
>
> *hasabna Allah wa-na'am al-wakil.*

These phrases were usually repeated up to ten or twenty times at a brisk pace.

There was regular recitation of God's characteristics (not in a set order), each mentioned once. In order of the frequency with which I recorded them from the sessions I attended, these included:

> "O God, Reliever of troubles" (Allahum ya kashif al-muhimat)
>
> "O God, Healer of the sick" (Allahum ya shafiy al-'amrad)
>
> "O God, Companion of those who remember *(dhikr)* [You]" (Allahum ya jaliys al-dhakirin). Occasionally this was rendered

---

52. Al-Husaynan, *1,000*, 80–87, 138–39.

53. "Whoever recites this one hundred times in the morning and in the evening, will not be surpassed on the Day of Resurrection by anyone having done better than this except for someone who had recited it more." (Al-Bukhari: Book #4, Hadith #2071, cited by Al-Qahtani, *Devotions*, 43, 54). See also Al-Qahtani, *Fortress*, 88, 90, 178; and Padwick adds further examples (*Devotions*, 72–73).

54. From *Al-'imran* 3:173.

as: "O God, Companion of the men and women who remember" (Allahum ya jaliys al-dhakirin wa al-dhakirat)

"O God, Bestower of gifts" (Allahum ya basit al-'arzaq)

"O God, Answerer of petitions" (Allahum ya majiyb al-da'uwat)

"O God, Defender of the gates" (Allahum ya dafa' al-babat)

"O God, Defeater of enemies" (Allahum ya makiym al-'a'da')[55]

"O God, Forgiver of wrongs and sins" (Allahum ya ghafir al-dhanub wa-al-khatayyat)

"O God, Hearer of [our] voices" (Allahum ya sama' al-'aswat)

Sometimes the women sitting in the *dhikr* sessions would write down the words of the songs and *dhikr* chants. Anisah Huda told the women on one occasion, "There are fifteen pages of *dhikr*; the ones who haven't memorized it can take the pages and photocopy them—each year learn more." Thus the mosque *dhikr* shaped the women's perception of God and his focal characteristics. The attributes of God that were invoked were those that brought benefit to the worshippers, such as Healer, Giver, Defender, and Forgiver. This may be an understanding of the effectiveness of the spoken word.[56] The God who is Companion to the people who remember him, will act towards them according to the attributes with which he is remembered or recited.

If the worshipper does their part in prescribed religious duties and behavior, then they can invoke God's assistance in the crises or daily trials of life. Mahmood describes this attitude in use of the metaphor of "trading with God," explained by an al-Azhar sheikh citing *Al-Nisa* 4:40:

> We are awarded ten merits [*hasanat*] for every good deed we perform with sincerity of intent, but only one sin [*sayyi'a*] is written against us for every bad deed we do. It is a testimony to His munificence that if we perform even ordinary tasks, but do them with the intent of pleasing Him, it will accrue us rewards with Him.[57]

---

55. These two suggest the frequent occurrence of war in the region.

56. The word spoken or written. Daily life in the Middle East is imbued with a sense of the sacredness of the name of God (even a piece of paper with the name of God on it cannot be thrown away), and power of the sacred word for healing and blessing; this understanding goes back to the earliest days of Islam (Zadeh, *Touching*, 464ff.).

57. Mahmood, *Politics*, 96.

In the *dhikr* invocations we see God as transcendent, other, unknowable—and God through his attributes vis-a-vis the worshipper. Offering a contrasting perspective to the Psalms, praise-book of both Judaism and Christianity, here there is no mention of God himself or even his attributes, as revealed in his creation or his word. Does such an understanding of God's transcendent unknowableness circumscribe his creatures' worship, beyond acknowledgement of God's inapprehensibility, to only the statement of his capacity in relation to their needs?

In Praise of Muhammad

Saying the *shahadah* (creed), "There is no god but God and Muhammad is the messenger of God" (*la illahu 'ila Allah wa Muhammad rasul Allah*), is first of the five practices or pillars of Islam. It is both entry into Islam (whispered in the ear of the new-born child, recited by the new convert) and exit (the last statement before death). Padwick suggests that the upright stones at each end of the Muslim's grave represent the two limbs of the creed.[58] These two parts are conjoined within Islam, with the second half the point of departure between Muslims and adherents of the other monotheistic faiths. As noted above, in the *dhikr* it was the first half, affirmation of God's unity, which occurred most frequently on its own, or commonly with an affirmation of the reciter's need of mercy. The second phrase, affirming the Muslim understanding of Muhammad's role, was occasionally included (usually once after a number of recitations of the first part).

However, praise of Muhammad was not lacking within the *dhikr*, particularly songs at feasts or during *Rabiya' al-'awwal*, the month when Muhammad's birth is commemorated. When the Danish cartoons featuring Muhammad came out, there were more choruses in his praise in the mosque, and Enas recited a poem that she had written praising him. And Muhammad was the constant example for people's behavior, both explicitly during the teaching sessions, and implicitly in the practice of *dhikr* and *du'a'*. Most *dhikr* sessions included asking God's blessing upon him:

> Prayers and peace be with you, O Lord, O Messenger of God.
>
> *al-salah wa-al-salam 'alayk ya sayydiy ya rasul Allah*

or variations such as:

> Prayers and peace with our Lord Muhammad and on his family and friends.

58. Padwick, *Devotions*, 132.

> al-salawat wa-al-salam ma' sayyidna Muhammad wa-'ala 'ahlahi wa-'ashabahi

or invoking God more directly:

> O God, blessing on Muhammad. O Lord, prayers/blessings and peace be on him.
>
> *Allahum saliy 'ala Muhammad ya rabbiy saliy 'alayhi wa-salam*

And of course a common take-up from the *salah* rite is the Abrahamic prayer, as in this example:

> O God, prayers for Muhammad and on the family of Muhammad as You prayed for Abraham and the family of Abraham—You are praiseworthy and glorious.
>
> O Lord, blessings on Muhammad and the family of Muhammad, as You blessed Abraham and the family of Abraham—You are praiseworthy and glorious.
>
> *Allahum saliy 'ala Muhammad wa-'ala al Muhammad kama salayt 'ala Ibrahim wa-'ala al Ibrahim 'inak hamid majid*
>
> *Allahum barak 'ala Muhammad wa-'ala al Muhammad kama barakt 'ala Ibrahim wa-'ala al Ibrahim 'inak hamid majid*

Padwick describes at least a third of the manuals on which she built her book as variations on this prayer, reflecting both Muslims' regard for Muhammad, and the belief that the one who calls down blessing on Muhammad will himself be blessed by God. This was made specific in the mosque *dhikr*:

> And make us from the people of your Beloved, Muhammad, God's prayers and peace be on him.
>
> *wa-ja'alna min 'ummat habibak Muhammad salah Allah 'alayihi wa-sallam*

Its benefits for the Muslim include forgiveness of sins, relief from the terrors of the tomb and of judgment, a reward of glory, and communion with Muhammad.[59]

This example shows how comprehensive is blessing on Muhammad:

> O Lord, blessing on our Lord Muhammad in the first
>
> O Lord blessing on our Lord Muhammad in the last

---

59. Padwick, *Devotions*, 152–55, 159–163.

O lord, blessing on our Lord Muhammad in the fullness of the highest until the day of judgment.

Ya rabb salay ʿala sayyidna Muhammad fiy al-ʿawalin

Ya rabb salay ʿala sayyidna Muhammad fiy al-ʾakharin

Ya rabb salay ʿala sayyidna Muhammad fiy al-milaʾ al-ʾaʿala ʿila yawm al-diyn.

Other repeated titles ascribed to Muhammad included "Beloved of God" *(habib Allah)*, "our great Advocate with God" *(wasilna al-ʿathama ila Allah)*, "Advocate of deeds to God" *(wasil al-ʿamal ʿila Allah)*. And those mentioning his name sought his intercession: "O Muhammad, we come to you, intercede for us with your Lord" *(ya Muhammad ʿinna nitwasal bik, ishfaʿ lana ʿind rabbak)*. Another *dhikr*, while seeking blessing on Muhammad, his family, and friends, described him as "Healer of hearts and their Remedy, and Eternal Tenderness and Gratification and Light of those who see and their deeds" *(Allahum salah ʿala sayyidna Muhammad tib al-qalub wa-duʿaʾha wa-ʿafiyyah al-ʿabdan wa-shaqaʾiha wa-nur al-ʾabsar wa-saniyaʾiha wa ʿala alahi wa-sahibihi wa-sallam.)*

These prayers lead inevitably to the question of whether this expression of Islam ascribes divine characteristics to its prophet. Does the constant mention of faith in God alongside Muhammad risk *shirk*? How far does Muslim longing for a tangible expression of an unknowable God take them in devotion to Muhammad?

Duʿaʾ

The women have been involved in *dhikr*. Now there is a slight shifting of position of women, leaning forward slightly, hands together, palms up. Anisah Huda leads in the *duʿaʾ*. There are about five minutes of petition for Muslims throughout the world, for our sisters in Iraq, in Palestine. She asks God to heal us, our land, our society. Don't cut us off from your service. God, purify us from our sins and trespasses. The women join in with "*Amin*" after each petition. Anisah Huda finishes by saying, "The *Fatihah*," and the women murmur it quietly with her. At the end a number of them wipe their faces with their hands.

In the mosque program, *duʿaʾ* comes at the conclusion of the time of *dhikr*.[60] It is characterized by a change in position, hands extended palm-up

---

60. In the same way that it completes the time of *salah* for the individual worshipper.

rather than occupied with prayer beads. Anisah Huda described the place of *dhikr* and *du'a'*: "The *dhikr* must be completed (sealed) with *du'a'*—the person has asked forgiveness from God, and is clean and pure from inside, and God willing, the petition will more likely be answered."

In *salah* the actions, words, and actual language of prayer are specified, together with the order, time, and number of performances at each occasion (both required and recommended), for the *salah* to be valid. *Dhikr* is less prescribed than *salah*. *Anisah Huda explained*:

> In *salah* there are specific words of the Qur'an when standing, praise, in kneeling and prostrating and when sitting before the peace, the blessed greetings—but in *dhikr*, if you add or subtract something—there's nothing specific required in *dhikr* for the person to do. . . . But I can pray while I'm walking or working, or at the end of *dhikr*—there's no special time.

While in *dhikr* and *du'a'* there is freedom for individual expression, specific use of certain (Arabic) phrases in particular contexts is recommended. *Dhikr* invocations, as with other pious practices,[61] can be performed with intercessory intent. Popular prayer books in non-Arabic language will usually include the Arabic form, both written in Arabic script[62] and often also transliterated, for the non-Arabic speaker's use.[63] Even here Arabic remains the standard and best language, whatever the language of the petitioner.

The distinction between *dhikr* and *du'a'* is not clear-cut. Ebtisam wrote in answer to a question on my notes:

> There is no[t] much difference because Zikr [sic] itself is *du'a'* as during Zikr we ask for forgiveness, for interests of both lives. But in *du'a'* we ask God for certain needs, like saving the Palestinians and Iraqis.

In mosque use, the *du'a'* prayers were usually general prayers asking for God's forgiveness, or for blessing on Muhammad. Sometimes more specific mention was made of "our sisters in Palestine," or asking God to "give relief to Muslims in Iraq, and in Afghanistan." Group *du'a'* in the mosque program involved the women in more awareness of the wider *ummah* and its needs. Anisah Huda's description of her own petitions at home was more personal, using mostly general phrases for specific contexts; "According to

---

61. Such as "sealing" the Qur'an with intent for a particular person or need, going on the *Hajj* with efficatory intent for another person.

62. Al-Husaynaan, *1,000*, Al-Banna, *Al-Ma'thurat*,

63. For example, Al-Qahtani, *Devotions, Fortress*.

the need at the time. When I'm in distress or war I prefer the petition, 'O Lord, relieve me, O God have mercy on us.' For example, when I'm starting to learn about something, I say, 'My Lord, increase my knowledge, O God, open to me the gates of learning,'" or more personally, "When my daughter is studying my most frequent prayer is, 'O God make her one of the top or best in the class.'"

The du'a' supplications express the petitioner's desires for God's intervention in the happenings of the world. Du'a' can take place anywhere, on any occasion, and anyone can do it. Women at the mosque would often ask me to petition for them, or say, "Supplicate for me, and I supplicate for you." However, certain situations make the supplication more efficacious. When I visited Anisah Huda soon after her husband and daughter had returned from making the lesser pilgrimage to Mecca, she offered us water from the spring of Zamzam, served in small golden cups, and instructed us to say a petition when we drank, because God would answer it. The Night of Vigil in Ramadan is also a time when petitions are answered.[64]

Emotions

I attended other group sessions of du'a' independent of dhikr, such as the conclusion of a group recitation of the Qur'an, or the suhur prayers in the early morning hours during Ramadan. There the preferred leader of du'a' was the person with the most affective or evocative voice, to elicit emotion and tears in those responding. A particular sheikh in a mid-city mosque was popular, and at 2:00–3:00 a.m. in Ramadan his mosque was tightly packed with 500–700 women in the upper section and more men below, crying "Amin" after each du'a' with rising emotional intensity. There was less overt display of emotion at the Garden Mosque, but dhikr sessions usually included a few women crying quietly, or sniffing as they murmured, Ya rabb (O Lord) in a choked voice.[65]

When I asked Anisah Huda about tears in prayer, she quoted a hadith that God will not punish (with Hell) someone who weeps tears of reverence.[66]

---

64. On both those occasions Anisah Huda encouraged me to intercede "because your petitions will be answered"; and she also referred to them in an interview as efficacious times.

65. Television footage of people circumambulating the ka'abah during the time of Pilgrimage commonly show large numbers of men and women weeping.

66. The following hadith is the only one I could discover for her quote, but it has almost the opposite import:

Narrated 'Abdullah bin 'Umar: Sad bin 'Ubada became sick and the Prophet along with 'Abdur Rahman bin 'Auf, Sad bin Abi Waqqas and 'Abdullah bin Masud visited

Tears could come when someone was "feeling oppressed and reflected on his sin and he weeps," or "when someone recollects the greatness of God and his own weakness and recollects the mercy of God and his own sins and rebelliousness, and suffers because of his sin and his smallness before his Lord, he weeps." She cautioned that it could be real or pretense—only God knew the heart.[67] While they are well aware of the possibility of "putting-on" emotions, there remains an expectation that spontaneous tears can be a normal part of worship, and this emotional expression is facilitated by the corporate context of the mosque program.

The relatively small amount written in books and articles on Islam about *du'a'* belies the multitude of booklets and oral instruction about what to say when, and the place of *du'a'* in Muslim popular piety. Not only at the end of *salah* or *dhikr* sessions, its use extends into every context in daily life. It is not so often specific as it is situational. God is not called so much to intervene in daily life as to protect the worshipper through it. There are invocations or *du'a'* for every situation, from the mundane to the poignant—walking out of one's home or into a mosque, in or out of the toilet, getting in a car, doing *salah*, before and after eating, at a child's funeral, when hearing a dog bark, when afraid, when you see the first dates of a season. And while the words of *du'a'* can be the informal expression of the worshipper's heart, often they are phrases used in *dhikr*, said with intent. The set phrases frequently have particular efficacy or protection associated with them:

> "Whoever recites this three times in the evening, will be protected from insect stings."

> "Whoever recites this with conviction in the evening and dies during that night, shall enter Paradise; and whoever recites it

---

him to enquire about his health. When he came to him, he found him surrounded by his household and he asked, "Has he died?" They said, "No, O Allah's Apostle." The Prophet wept and when the people saw the weeping of Allah's Apostle (PBUH) they all wept. He said, "Will you listen? Allah does not punish for shedding tears, nor for the grief of the heart but he punishes or bestows His Mercy because of this." He pointed to his tongue and added, "The deceased is punished for the wailing of his relatives over him." 'Umar used to beat with a stick and throw stones and put dust over the faces (of those who used to wail over the dead). (Book #23, Hadith #391)

67. Middle Eastern Christianity also describes tears in prayer. Matthew the Poor's book on prayer includes a chapter on tears and the gift of mourning. However, the Desert Fathers he cites likewise caution against outward show. So St. John Climacus comments caustically that: "The man who takes pride in his tears and who secretly condemns those who do not weep is rather like the man who asks the king for a weapon against the enemy—and then uses it to commit suicide" (*Orthodox*, 227). For the Desert Fathers, tears may express awareness of sin, or of God's benevolence. In no sense are they redemptive.

with conviction in the morning and dies during that day, shall enter Paradise."

"Allah will spare whoever says this four times in the morning or in the evening from the fire of Hell."

"Whoever recites this one hundred times a day will have the reward of freeing ten slaves. One hundred Hasanah will be written for him and one hundred misdeeds will be washed away. He will be shielded from Satan until the evening. No one will be able to present anything better than this except for someone who has recited more than this."[68]

The place of repetition, as with the emphasis on specific (Arabic) language, indicates an understanding of the effectiveness of prayer based at least in part on the worshipper's performance (when it is said and how often), rather than situated solely in the beneficence of God. Numbers of times of repetition are specified in *salah*, *dhikr*, and *duʿaʾ*. The importance of specific tally in repetition is attested to by the common presence of prayer beads for counting, and by the counters that are making an increasing appearance in popular use.

When I asked her about multiple repetitions, Anisah Huda challenged popular use as not being properly grounded in the example of Muhammad; "People say that if someone is sick, they read the chapter *al-ʾanʿam* twenty-one times—this didn't come from the Prophet. The Prophet said God doesn't forgive more than seventy times in a day."[69] However, she still affirms the use of numbers and repetition to add weight to personal piety:

> For example, so that I don't cut it short, I can say, "O God" a hundred times, another time, "Forgive," a hundred times, another occasion, "Blessing on the Prophet," one time "There is no god but God," and I keep those repetitions so I don't forget the *dhikr*—that's one thing: but one person can't enforce a number on someone else. It's for each person to determine.

Use of prayer beads, or counting on finger joints (both in multiples of eleven), involved the women in repetitious movement during the *dhikr*. While short of more exuberant or convulsive body movement practiced in some Sufi contexts, this gave a rhythmic physical dimension to *dhikr*. In this context Shannon notes that:

---

68. Al-Qahtani, *Fortress; Devotions*, 50, 52, 53, 59.
69. Padwick refers specific numbers directly to traditions about Muhammad (*Devotions*, 71).

What Mauss (1979) termed "techniques of the body" are ways in which ideologies and beliefs are embedded in specific repertoires of aesthetic; i.e. sensate practices. Moreover, aesthetic practices are the primary means through which ideologies, whether sacred or profane, are cultivated in the bodies of actors as participants in communities of practice.[70]

Another physical dimension was the practice of many of the women of wiping their faces with the palms of their hands after completing the time of *dhikr* and *du'a'*. Anisah Huda explained, "Wiping the face is for blessing (*barakah*) ... of course this is for healing," while cautioning that the petitioner shouldn't abandon medicine and doctors. This also reflects an understanding of the efficacy of spoken sacred word, which flows out in *barakah* or healing power.

As with *dhikr*, Anisah Huda saw *du'a'* as having a role in forming the petitioner's inner attitude to God:

> When I petition God and am confident about the response and the answer is fulfilled, this brings a person closer to God and gives him confidence and hope that when he prays a second, third or fourth time, even if the prayer isn't fulfilled quickly, I know that God will fulfill it, but at the appropriate time, which may not be now.

Silence

Dhikr may be verbal: "recollection with the tongue (*dhikr jali*)" or (*lisani*); or silent: "recollection in the heart (*dhikr kafi*)" or (*qalbi*). Silent *dhikr* is sometimes described as superior (seventy times better, citing a *hadith* from 'Aishah) to verbal *dhikr*.[71] It is particularly, although not exclusively, linked with the Naqshabandi order.[72] Padwick mentions *Al-Ra'd* 13:28 repeatedly quoted in prayer manuals as the basis for silent *dhikr* and prayers for inner peace.[73]

In the Garden Mosque, *dhikr* sessions were characterized by periods of quiet, particularly when Anisah Huda was leading it, interposed with invocatory phrases. Other leaders made more use of extensive songs.

---

70. Shannon, *Aesthetics*, 382.
71. Geels, *Note*, 229–230; Hadad, "On Dhikr."
72. Naqshbandi, "Dhikr."
73. Padwick, *Devotions*, 122.

Songs

Mahmood makes no mention of songs in her descriptions of the women's mosque movement in Cairo. Discussing Sufi practice, Helminski describes the *munshidin* of Egypt. "The *shaykh* or *shaykha* would be the main instructor and the one who would generally compose the lyrics and the rhythm of the chants or songs to be sung." She cites "one of the well-known munshidiin of Egypt," a woman named Sabra, who sings at *mawalid*.[74] In the Garden Mosque, there were two kinds of songs beyond the normal *dhikr* invocatory chants.

Tarnim

One was extended songs by the leader of the *dhikr*, sometimes with women joining in the chorus. These were more often from leaders other than Anisah Huda. Ebtisam described these as "*tarnim*,[75] like *dhikr*." These were times when leaders could show their skill in singing, and some of the listeners would be weeping quietly as they murmured "*Ya rabb, Ya rabb,*" (O Lord, O Lord).[76] These songs were characterized by more extended passages and less repetition, focusing on the worshipper's individual response to God. An excerpt (with Ebtisam's translation) includes:

> I pray, whispering, praying. I rise in the night before dawn.
>
> I pray, whispering, praying, with tears. Whatever I face in this life,
>
> The small problems—I am busy with you, apart from what my eyes see.
>
> Bitterness becomes sweet if You are satisfied.
>
> Who is for me apart from You? And who apart from You sees and teaches my heart?
>
> All creatures are shadows.
>
> I cry to you, O Lord, I cry to you, O Lord. Forgive my small sins in your generosity.
>
> Make my good thoughts intercessions.

74. Helminski, *Women*, 224–5; also Waugh, *Ritual*, 94–5.
75. This word is commonly used for hymns by Arab Christians.
76. See earlier discussion of emotion in *du'a'*. Waugh (*Ritual*) describes the place of the Egyptian *munshidin* in facilitating the listeners' emotive response.

Hearer and Knower of all my situation, Answerer of all questions

Let your favor change my situation

There is no strength but by You. Be gentle and have mercy on my situation.

Forgive my small sins and pardon.

Life is pure if you are satisfied, from every fear of destination.

So take away from me all of life's crises

O Hearer and Knower of all my situation, O Answerer of all questions.[77]

أدعو وهمس دعائي أقوم بالليل والأسحار ساجية

أدعو وهمس دعائي بالدموع مهما لقيت من الدني

وعارضها فأنت لي شغل عما يرى جسدي

تحلو مرارة عيش في رضاك

من لي سواك ومن سواك يرى قلبي ويعلمه

كل الخلائق ظل

أدعوك يا رب أدعوك يا رب اغفر ذلتي كرماً

واجعل شفيع دعائي حسن معتقدي

يا سامع وعالماً بكل حالي يا مجيب السائلين سؤل السؤال

عسى يغير فضلك حالي

لا قوة إلا بحولك ألطف بحولك وارحم حالي

أصفح عن ذلاتي واعف

الحياة برضاك تسفو من كل خوف في مآل

فاصرف عني كل بلواها

يا سامعاً وعالماً بكل حالي يا مجيب السائلين سؤل السؤال

---

77. For this extended example, I have not transcribed the Arabic, but only included the translation.

Anashid

Another form of singing was songs accompanied by a drum and led by a group of young women sitting demurely at the front on chairs, usually on days of special remembrance or feasts. One of the women would beat a frame drum,[78] while the others led in a lively chant, often one of the invocations that were part of normal *dhikr* sessions. Ebtisam described these as *anashid*,[79] and they were featured also on the CD recording of women from the mosque program.

Whether *tarnim* or *anashid*, the choruses were often sung briskly with a strong rhythm. On my first visit to this mosque for the opening of the women's library, I noticed the similarity to tunes I had heard in Coptic Orthodox worship. More generally, the importance of alliteration and of rhythm and rhyme in the *dhikr* was evident in examples such as:

> A'udh bi-Allah as-sami' al-'alim min al-Shaytan ir-rajim. B'ism Allah al-rahman al-rahim.

and

> Allahum ya muhawal al-hawl fa-hawal halna ila halin.

At gatherings on feast days, Anisah Huda would encourage women to give their testimony. One young woman spoke of how she had come from a singing/dancing background and her path to regular involvement in the mosque and Anisah Huda asked her to sing a religious song to the group. Women at the mosque were aware of the discussion around women's voices being 'awrah and took care that individual voices were not distinguishable outside the space of their gathering. However, the mosque program offered a place where those with musical gifts could use them. Rather than their voices being 'awrah and contrary to pious practice, they could gain recognition here for their good voices, and use them to express their longing for God (although in appropriately muted form). Hegland and Ghadialli similarly describe women cantors in Pakistan and India receiving recognition through leadership roles in women's gatherings.[80]

---

78. *Dhikr* music is generally sung *a capella* except for a drum (reflecting the ambiguous attitude within Islam to music and musical instruments). Some orders such as the Chisti include other instruments.

79. This word is sometimes used by Arab Christians for choruses.

80. Hegland, *Shi'a*; Ghadialli, *Hajari*.

Conclusion

Women have been involved in the history of Sufism generally and in Damascus in particular. While the Garden Mosque does not define itself as Sufi, practice of *dhikr* is a significant part of worship practice in the women's program. Elements of *dhikr* reflect the *salah* rite.

Because the words of *dhikr* are not mandated, the women's choice of words may offer us a perspective on their understanding of God in relation to his worshippers. Common components in the women's *dhikr* include: taking refuge, seeking forgiveness, passages from the Qur'an, invocatory phrases, praise of Muhammad, *duʿaʾ*, and the use of both silence and songs. While some of the terms are common to Muslim and Christian prayer, there may be different understandings of their meaning or implications. God is invoked as protector from present evil (external and internal), only Forgiver, and supplicated for assistance in the common trials of life. Praise of God and eulogization of Muhammad both find their place in *dhikr*. Both silence and songs enhance the time of *dhikr*. Right language, right words, and repetition, are all significant in ensuring the effectiveness of *dhikr* for the worshippers' present and future life. In mosque *dhikr* as well as in formal lectures, women learn more about God and ways of addressing him in order to access his divine characteristics towards the worshipper. By being able to use their voices in the public space afforded by the women's mosque program, they gain recognition as singers as well as memorizers and reciters of sacred text.

This analysis of the women's *dhikr* prayers concludes our examination of the women's program in the Garden Mosque. Their understanding of life and faith, God and community, is shaped within their allegiance to the mosque community. This shift of communal allegiance and identity has been explored in the facets of imaginary and local community, the mimetic ideal, particular performative practices that find gendered redefinition in the mosque community, use and interpretation of texts, and words of worship. The final chapter draws these aspects together.

10

Conclusion

IN THE WORLD OF people and cultures, every situation has both unique and common aspects. The detailed exploration of a particular women's mosque program may help illuminate aspects of similar programs in other contexts, as well as deepen our understanding of the women's mosque movement as a wider phenomenon within contemporary Islam. In telling the story of this mosque, its program, and the women who attend it, I have sought to include detail and description rich enough to enable comparison and contrast with other settings. At the same time, in using their own words as far as possible, and through a high level of participant feedback on field notes taken, I have tried to present the women's own voices and understanding of the program and their involvement in it, in the context of wider discussions in Islam.

Questions arising from observations in the mosque have invited the use of different conceptual frameworks to interpret the various dimensions of the program and women's involvement.[1] Thus the cultural theory of Grid and Group opened up a way to explain the shape of community dynamics and response. The combination of Girard's and Taussig's separate work on mimesis gave an integrated basis to understand how leadership functioned at both ideal and local levels. Concurrently, this ethnographic case-study is written in the context of wider conversations about Muslim women and the women's mosque movement. Noting Asad's and Mahmood's influential writings on the conscious use of pious disciplines in self-formation, in this study I have proposed "performative practices" as a heuristic category, which can incorporate both conscious practice and also the communal dimensions of pious exercises in formation.

The existence of women scholars in Islam is not new. As transmitters, teachers, and learners, their place within Islam from its earliest days has been located in the context of wider political developments and directions.

1. Heath and Street, *Ethnography*, 33–34, 50–51.

Hence the expanding women's mosque movement is situated in the history of women in Islam as well as within more contemporary developments in emancipatory trends (post-colonial and gender), education, and media. So too the discussion of a specific place and group of women engaging in particular pious activities is grounded in patterns of use of space and time, shaped both by religion and gender, as well as by cultural, national, and international currents.

Growth in the Women's Mosque Movement

The growth in women's piety movements can be seen as a response to the same needs for divine empowerment in their everyday life responsibilities that have sometimes taken women into more fringe areas of religious ritual, whether sanctioned or otherwise. However, now increased access to learning and to mosque and textual space are enabling women to define and practice empowerment in new ways. These ways include women gaining more admittance to traditional means of blessing such as reciting (sealing) the whole Qur'an, to which lack of religious education limited their access in the past. They also include newer paths such as the redefinition of textual meanings to empower women within the situation in which they find themselves. These new ways exist alongside more customary means of mediating power for women in their personal lives and family roles. In attending the mosque, the women are accessing both moral/religious authority for their actions, and also the power of blessing for the needs of their everyday life roles.

The promotion of women's place as in the home (as well as the expansion of middle classes) gives women more leisure time for involvement with text and mosque, contributing to their growth in religious engagement. In restricted social environments, women have always used religious occasions in the home, such as Qur'anic recitations or *dhikr* to gain blessing and enjoy the religiously-sanctioned opportunity to gather and talk together over a glass of tea or a meal. The shift of allegiance seen here is part of a wider expansion in conservative Islamic practices and use of texts. Increasingly, homes and special gatherings are being used as sites for *daʿwa*, encouraging women to conform their lives and dress to what are taught as prescribed Islamic norms. A birthday party becomes a place to urge the claims of *hijab* on all the young women attending. Mosque classes train women how to conduct themselves and how to give appropriate teaching at extended gatherings such as weddings or births. At the same time we see the women renegotiating their place and re-reading some of the restrictive texts, within the bounds of their cultural context.

The women's mosque movement can be understood in terms of shifting allegiance from kinship community to the wider Muslim *ummah,* as it finds local realization within the mosque sorority. This change of allegiance is strong enough to challenge certain traditional norms of kinship loyalty, cultural compliance, and obedience to government authorities. This is evident in women's testimonies about their involvement in the mosque program, which often mention tensions with the requirements of their families of origin and of marriage. The mosque and its community becomes a place for the women to celebrate feasts and fasts hitherto primarily observed among extended family gatherings. And the program teaches the women how to use family and community events as sites of *da'wa* to their relatives and friends. However, changing allegiance does not constitute a challenge to women's traditional role within the family; instead their role is reinterpreted in terms of Islamic virtue. Women demonstrate their adherence to Islam through exemplary performance of domestic duties, upheld as (women's) proper worship in its own right, as well as through pious practices.

Loyalty to, and identity, with the international Muslim *ummah* is strengthened by increasing media access both to international Islamic teachers and also global news of events that contribute to a sense of attack upon Islam and on other Muslim communities. Allegiance to the wider Muslim community finds concrete realization in the local mosque community. The local mosque community is positioned here in opposition not just to kinship allegiances, but also to restrictive government policies.

Muslims regard Muhammad as the ideal model for the Muslim community. The good Muslim is one who faithfully follows his example and precepts, seeking mimetic access to Muhammad's power and blessing for this life as well as the next. "Orthodox" Islam is placed in a continuum with many of the practices of "folk" Islam when seen as ways of connecting to or copying Muhammad. As allegiance to the imaginary community is best expressed through its local manifestation within the mosque, so too the shape of loyalty to Muhammad as ideal Muslim finds form in the example of local leaders, who mediate mimetic desire through embodying community virtues. Within the kin community, the mother is the female ideal. In the mosque community, the *da'iya* is described in relation to the prophetic role, and as successor (*khalifah*) to the Messenger. Through following her model, women in the program gain a role and influence beyond that described in purely maternal mode, to responsibility and influence characterized in prophetic terms within the Muslim community.

Community belonging is embodied in particular performative practices, ways of being and doing. In shifting allegiance to the mosque community, Islamic virtues rather than family honor become the determining frame for behavior. This enables the redefinition of gendered performative practices, such as in (women's) use of time and space around the observance of *salah* and of feasts and fasts. Modes of dress pertaining to concealment of the female form (as well as the female voice) are part of inculcation into the mosque program. At the same time, the anonymity of membership in the mosque community gives opportunity for the public production of some women's voices in religious songs, and women's space in the mosque opens up more possibilities for female leadership.

Requirements of ritual purity and cultural conservatism constrain the advocacy of women's leadership within the mosque program, although some of the women are aware of historical and contemporary examples of female teachers and leaders within Islam. However, through the program and its female leaders, women are enabled to find more detailed answers to their questions about ritual purity and thence more possibilities of negotiating the rulings in relation to pious practices.

The community of allegiance also shapes performative practices around use of authoritative texts. Going beyond a focus on the power of the material text, in the mosque program the women learn to memorize the Qur'an and to recite it with *tajwid*, as an act of pious obedience. As well as internalization of the Qur'an through memorization and correct articulation, Anisah Huda taught and modeled the significance of interpretation. Her lectures and the establishment of a women's mosque library gave the women access to traditional and contemporary conservative commentators. An emphasis on knowledge (*'ilm*), presented in religious terms, also included both educational and practical knowledge. Science was taught as originating in the Qur'an and emerging principally from Islamic civilization and teachers. An uncritical approach to the origins and authority of the Qur'an and *ahadith* was allied with a sometimes sympathetic, more often antipathetic, approach to other "peoples of the Book," and the women were taught to exercise *da'wa* through responding to challenges to Islam. Teaching in the mosque program modeled interpretive practices which were flexible within bounds of textual authority and cultural requirements: this was the basis for suggesting ways to reinterpret some of the more controversial Qur'anic texts and *ahadith* on women's position in the Muslim community.

While discussion of *dhikr* has not found much place within other writings on the women's mosque movement, it was a significant part of this program. It united the women in communal prayer as an essential preliminary to learning, as well as being performed at other times together in the mosque or alone in homes. An analysis of *dhikr* sessions and of invocations used at the mosque found them closely linked to elements within the *salah* ritual, as well as to the *du'a'* phrases that are deeply embedded in daily life for many Muslims. Common *dhikr* ingredients included taking refuge in God, seeking his forgiveness, Qur'anic phrases, invocations to God and praise for Muhammad, *du'a'*, silence, and songs. Neither *dhikr* nor *du'a'* are circumscribed by cycles or conditions of purity, and so are open to participation for women who experience restricted access to more central religious ritual. Emotional demonstration and the non-scripted nature of *dhikr* intersected with the efficacy of preferred phrases and recommended repetition in this activity of shared apprehension of God in relation to faith community.

Shifting Allegiances

The women's mosque movement takes its place within the context of growing Islamism. This ethnographic study has described it in terms of shifting allegiances between kinship networks and the mosque sorority. What are the conditions that facilitate communal allegiance? I suggest the shape of five of the contributing factors that have been discussed in this book.

First is the existence of a wider imaginary community of belonging, that also finds material presence in a local community. Relationships of mutual care within the immediate community may be conceived in family terms, and the community and its space of meeting become an alternate place to mark significant celebrations. And the local community gains legitimacy and attractiveness from its link with the wider imaginary community.

The second factor is the presence of a mimetic ideal who mediates desire for community members. The role of this influence needs to be more fully recognized in shaping community aspirations and allegiances. Ideal leadership of the imaginary community finds accessible realization within leadership in the local community, in someone who concretely embodies the values of the new community. She demonstrates ways of being and doing that are honored in the new community of allegiance. Hence she offers community members the possibility of realizing desire through mimesis, accessing power to negotiate the challenges of this life and the next.

Third are the performative practices that show community membership. These performative practices, ways of being and doing, of dressing and speaking, walking or reading, take and reinterpret the practices of the community of first allegiance, and in reinterpreting them according to a new ideal, transcend them. Recognizable but different, the performative practices of the new community of allegiance enable the women to challenge the values and practices of their community of origin. New performative practices allow women ways to redefine themselves and acquire authority according to the values and mimetic ideal of the new community.

Particular performative practices in relation to the community's authoritative texts constitute the fourth factor. Community membership is realized in ways of reading and interpreting (sacred) text. These textual practices may be conservative (recognizable in terms of the values of the community of origin), offer power (such as through memorization and correct recitation), and are both authoritative and also accessible ways of reading that relate to the women's own lives, issues, questions, and daily concerns.

The fifth factor I have discussed in allegiance to a community of faith is ways of prayer. In *salah* and *dhikr*, the mimetic ideal is both taught and also manifested in the communal context, so that prayer is not fitted into the spare spaces in life, but rather life is built around prayer. Forms of prayer (such as *dhikr* and *duʿaʾ*) may be appropriated at any time by community members, outside restrictions of ritual purity. In *dhikr*, community members articulate and thereby seek to access characteristics of God in regard to the pray-er, such as healing, protection, and forgiveness.

Faith is lived out in physical bodies, in space and time and community. The new community of allegiance is a living demonstration in ways that fulfill, rather than contradict, those of the community of origin, thus enabling participants in the new community to challenge previous norms on the basis of a new embodied ideal.

In the *daʿwa* movement within Islam, women are taking up both physical (public and mosque) and textual space in new ways. This book contributes to the understanding of this movement by making use of ethnographic case study to describe the *daʿwa* movement more fully within a particular local context. In doing so, it offers an integrated understanding of community, leadership, and pious practices inside a mosque community. The primary ethnographic categories of time and space have provided a descriptive framework for the women's practices within the mosque program. In asking how the women viewed their community (of family and of faith) and themselves within it, I have suggested Grid–Group theory as an analytic tool for understanding the local community expression of imaginary community, as well as to explicate both local community response and wider international reactions to what are perceived as attacks on Muhammad, Prophet of Islam. The synthesis of Taussig's and Girard's writings on mimesis was used to bridge the problem of the etic perception of the orthodox/folk divide in Muslim practices and to suggest a new understanding of the role and function of leadership. The same chapter notes the role of the *daʿiyya* as offering a new mimetic ideal to Muslim women that finds radical new shape in prophetic terms, as "successor of the Messengers." In discussing the shape of women's participation in the mosque program, I have proposed the use of "performative practices" as an interpretive device to describe the women's conscious and communal exercise of pious ritual. And the analysis of the women's use of authoritative writings, placed within wider discussions of their use, illustrated how they read them with reference to their own lives and issues, and also how cultural constraints shaped their engagement with gendered texts. The account of the place of *dhikr* in the program offers a dimension that is not generally found in discussions of women's mosque movements.

I have suggested that we can understand the growing women's mosque movement as a process of competing allegiances between kin and mosque community. This shifting loyalty implicates ways of being and doing in space and time, of relating to text, to others, and to God, which are modeled and given shape within the local community and in its ideal leaders.

Caught in Time

> Communities may tolerate or even enjoy the ethnographer's presence, but they know, as does the ethnographer, that the latter is a visitor rather than a citizen. As the Songhay people of Niger like to say: "The stranger is like the puddle. S/he may be here in the morning, but will be gone by afternoon." As ethnographer/strangers we move on and lose direct contact with those we have tried to understand. Meanwhile, our others continue to live in their communities. Their lives twist and turn in the flow of local and global history.[2]

During my time in the mosque program and subsequent return visits, evidence sometimes surfaced of underlying tensions between the mosque community and the restrictive apparatus of state security. Since then, regional and local economic factors have combined to explode the country into a savage civil war, further inflamed by outside contributions and incoming fighters.

The area in which the Garden Mosque is situated was the scene of protests in the city early on, and clashes have occurred around the street and even the building in which Anisah Huda lived. I hear that she is now in another country in the region; many others have joined the overwhelming flood of internally and externally-displaced people.

2. Stoller, *Presence*, 199.

Issues of community loyalty and allegiance in this society of complex interplay between family, ethnic, religious, and economic affiliations, have taken on tragic significance in Syria today. And allegiances to wider imaginary communities have brought fighters from many different nationalities to join the conflict. But the situation is not restricted to Syria, grave as it is. Bano's study of the women's program in the Red Mosque in Pakistan demonstrates the strength of women's personal and communal loyalty even in the face of family, government, and military opposition, and its deadly consequences.[3] And ongoing events in Pakistan further underline the significance of community allegiances. Loyalty and identity are complex forces; it becomes increasingly essential that we understand more of how they operate within communities. An important field for further exploration is to ask why and when people choose one aspect of belonging or loyalty over another and how the choice may be shaped by particular contexts. The study of how people change allegiance is salient in understanding both local situations and wider currents in the world today.

The ethnographic present is only ever a snapshot that reflects the time of ethnographic engagement, in the constant movement of people's lives and sociocultural change.[4] Its temporary nature has been sharply delineated in this study by the civil war that has since overtaken the mosque program and the women who attended it—their lives caught up in the violent turbulence of inter-communal conflict which has left no family untouched. Choices of communal loyalty have taken on life-and-death significance. This snapshot, taken at a more peaceful time, may still contribute to understanding the competing allegiances to local and wider communities, and how these allegiances are lived out in ways which shape people's lives and decisions in times of both peace and of war.

---

3. The official toll from the government assault on the Red Mosque was eighty-nine deaths; however, none of the 1,000 burial wraps handed out by police to the military troops were returned (Bano, *Conclusion*, 513).

4. Heath and Street (*Ethnography*, 7) propose culture as a verb, rather than a noun, to reflect its dynamic nature.

Appendix 1

Grid and Group

GRID–GROUP THEORY WAS ORIGINALLY developed by Mary Douglas in her book *Natural Symbols*. Since then it has been taken up and further developed in a range of contexts.[1]

Douglas proposes that societies can be analyzed along two dimensions. The vertical axis assesses the extent of shared classification or understanding in worldview and values in a society, and Douglas names this axis "Grid." A strong grid society has more extensive rules and potential roles for people; a person's identity is more defined by the position they have in society. However, not all roles are available to everyone—only a few people can become a doctor or a president. Conversely, a weak grid society only has a few roles that are accessible to all—mother, father, herdsman, farmer. This axis is characterized by the question, "Who am I?"[2]

The horizontal line measures the impact of group demands on a person's behavior and so this axis is labeled "Group." A strong group society (beginning from the right-hand side) exerts more pressure on its members, requiring a higher level of accordance with social conventions or group rules (e.g. Amish, Freemasons). A low group society offers more individual freedom in decision-making to its members. Group membership is voluntary rather than obligatory and does not define the individual (e.g., belonging

---

1. For some discussion of the theory and its application in different disciplines, see Caulkins, "Grid/Group"; Grendstad and Sundback, "Socio-Demographic," 289–306; Hendry, "Cultural," 557–59; Hood, "Control," 207–30; the whole issue of *Innovation*, 21:3; Jayne, "Many Voices," 959–81; Lockhart, "Cultural," 862; Lockhart, "Grid-Group" 51–82; Lockhart, "Political," 517–48; Lockhart, "Tax Regimes," 379–97; Mitleton-Kelly, "Information," 289–323; Tansey, "Risk," 17–32; Turner, "Grid/Group," 6–7; Vaughan, "Punishments," 411. An intriguing attempt to map gender and personality type onto Grid–Group is found in Franzwa et al., "Social," 185–208.

2. For further explanation of the development of the Grid axis, see Douglas, *Natural*, 171–176.

to a Sunday School class). The horizontal axis concerns the question, "How should I behave?"[3]

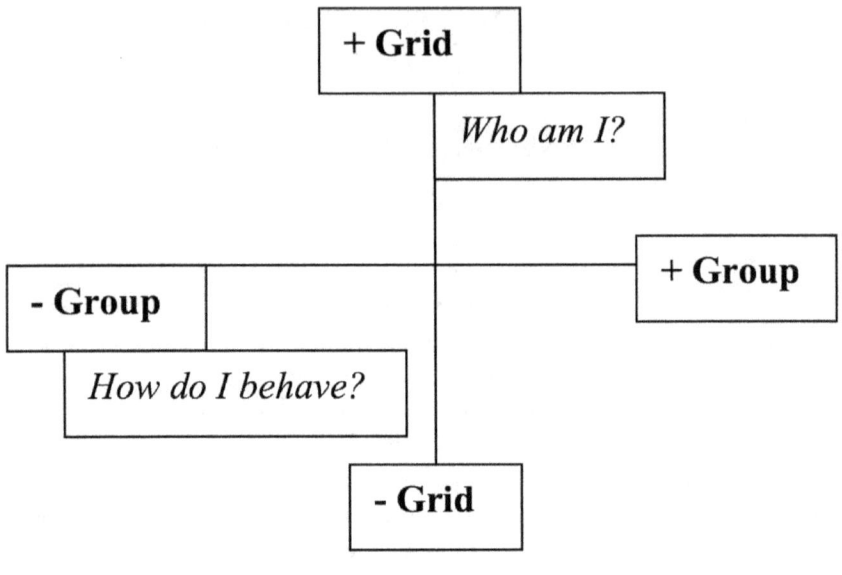

Figure 3

Social groups can then be positioned within four quadrants derived from the intersection of the two axes. These quadrants are as shown in figure 2 with their characterizations: High Grid and High Group, Low Grid and High Group, Low Grid and Low Group, and High Grid and Low Group.

Hierarchical—High Grid, High Group

The High Grid and High Group quadrant describes hierarchical societies, with strong boundaries. The group has priority over individual desires. There are set rituals and ways of relating to God and each other. Wrongdoing is against both God and the community. Controlling powers are modeled on human figures (ancestral figures or the creator God), activated by moral situations. Monastic and military communities and the Catholic Church hierarchy are examples of this social shape.

Pain and suffering are seen as either the proper punishments of individual misdeeds or accounted for by transcendental bookkeeping so that

---

3. Wildavsky, cited in Mamadouh (*Grid-Group*, 398) suggests these questions for the axes. I have found it useful to define the quadrants also by questions.

the effects of one man's virtue are chalked up for the common good and his faults are likewise charged to the community. The view of wrongdoing takes no account of the state of mind or purpose of the actor: wrongdoing in itself is bad, danger is automatically unleashed, and blame automatically ascribed. Misfortune is used to uphold the moral law. Failure is attributed to moral failure or bad luck.

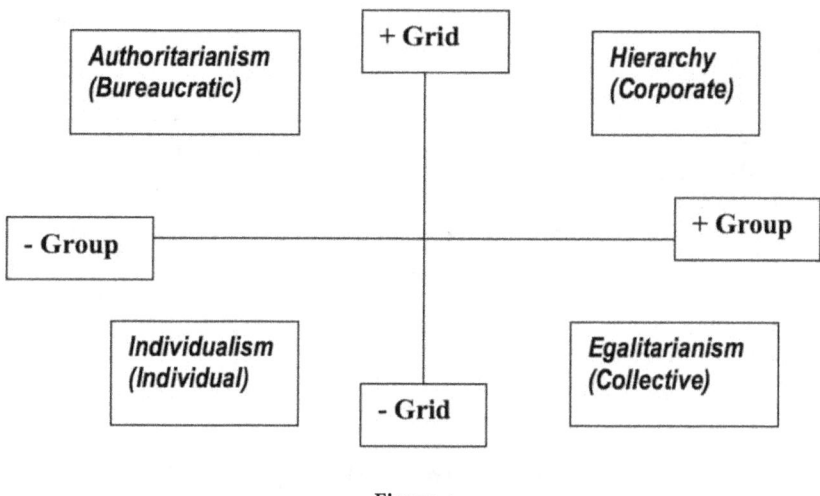

Figure 4

Intellectual categories tend to be taken as God-given, immutable truths. A firm distinction exists between the public and private parts of life, so any eruption of the organic into the social domain is abhorrent, requiring ritual purification, and there are strong boundaries between purity and impurity. Rituals celebrate the transcendence of the whole over the part, and rituals and symbols are accounted as potent. People are concerned with profit or loss of the whole community. Interpersonal relations are assumed to be subordinate to the public pattern of roles. High value is set on the control of consciousness.

Nature is seen as both perverse and tolerant. Nature is robust so long as we remain in the safe zone. If we go too far, things go wrong and we need experts to evaluate the safety of the situation. Humans are born sinful but can be redeemed by good institutions. The environment is robust within limits.

The question asked in this quadrant is, "Who is allowed to do what?"

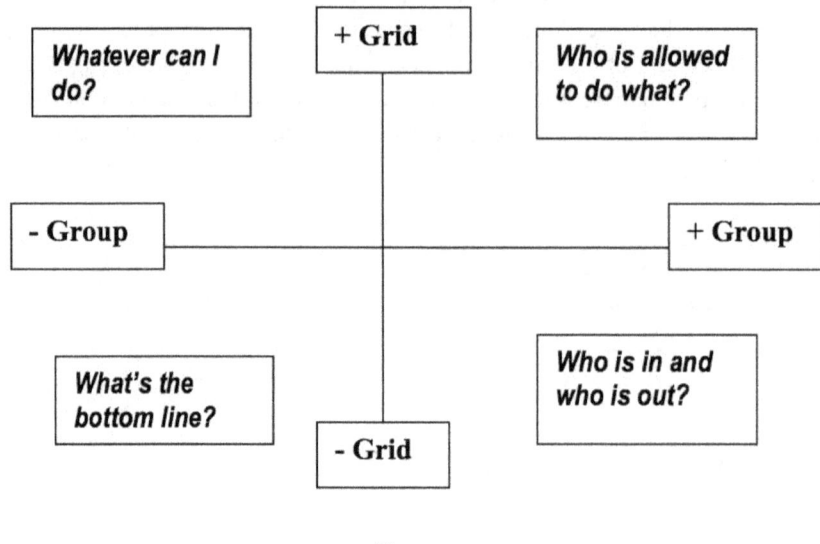

Figure 5

Egalitarian—Low Grid, High Group

On the lower right-hand side of the figure, Low Grid and High Group, are small-scale social units characterized by clear boundaries and flat internal relations. The group boundary is the main definer of rights: people are classed as members or strangers. The boundary is associated with danger and evil is seen as a foreign threat introduced by foreign agents in disguise. Group members accuse deviants of allowing evil to penetrate, leading to fission of the group. It is a society with strong group boundaries and group control but little hierarchy and mostly flat relationships within the group, which are bonded together by opposition against the outside world. Groups such as the Brethren, the Mormons in their early days, are examples of this quadrant.

In this cosmology, the universe is divided between warring forces of good and evil in a contest of demons and competing powers. God doesn't always protect his faithful.

Leadership is precarious, roles ambiguous and undefined. Members are intolerant of imperfection, focusing on impossible standards of good. There is minimum classification, and one strong outer boundary. With weak hierarchy and leadership, control is exerted through what Douglas describes as the "witch" doctrine, characterized as follows: The bad is outside, the good inside. The inside is under attack, and needs protection. Human wickedness is perceived on a cosmic scale. And the above doctrines are used in political manipulation.

Members are preoccupied with rituals of cleansing, expulsion of enemy agents, and redrawing of boundaries. Failure is ascribed to hostile, occult power of a neighbor, and the cosmos is endangered by vile, irrational behavior of human agents of evil.

Nature is basically ephemeral, fragile. Humans are essentially good, but our nature is highly susceptible to institutional influences. The environment is under duress.

In this quadrant the question asked is, "Who is in, and who is out?"

Individualistic—Low Grid, Low Group

The Low Grid and Low Group society is characterized by individualism. It is opposite to the hierarchical quadrant, and these two social shapes on the one diagonal occur most frequently. In the individualistic quadrant the desires of the individual have priority over the group. Rituals and symbols are seen as expressive rather than effectual. Religion is private, meaning and motivation are internally determined, rather than regulated by external rewards and punishment. Discussion of wrongdoing is concerned entirely with the wishes and intentions of the actor, which are more significant than the consequences of the act.

The individualist (the entrepreneur) is the one who relates freely to others, promoting open competition and the right of individuals to choose their own rules and way of life. So (in contrast with the hierarchy) any person only has limited influence over anyone else. There is affirmation of spiritual joys and asceticism. People live for inner experience, contemplation, the internal evolution of the self.

This is the domain of the stock market, of pop culture, and open competition. American Vineyard churches also demonstrate an individualistic social structure, which has little formal organization and structured leadership, and where the individual attender is as likely to receive a prophetic message as a staff member.[4]

Nature is both robust and benign, and can take plenty of experimentation. Human nature is stable and basically self-seeking. Rather than worrying about the niceties of status and who should do what, the individualist is ultimately pragmatic, wanting only to know, "What's the bottom line?"

---

4. See also Lingenfelter, *Transforming*.

APPENDIX 1

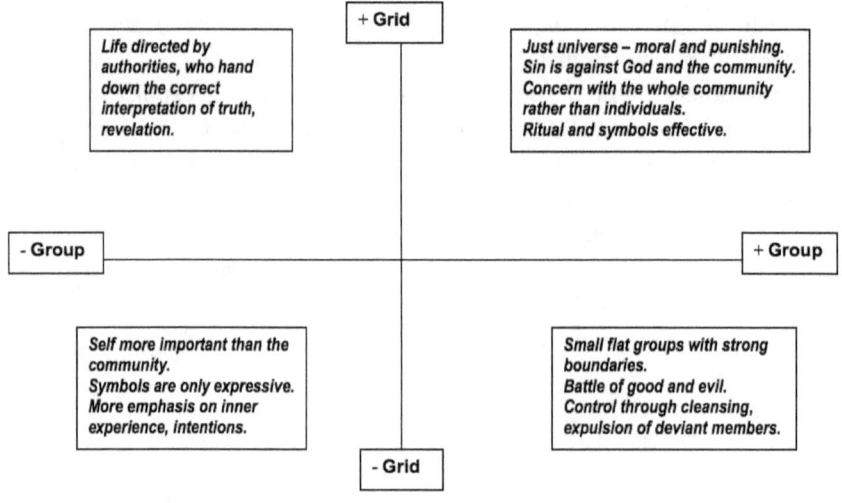

Figure 6

Authoritarian—High Grid, Low Group

The final quadrant, High Grid and Low Group, includes people who exist in strong hierarchies and are excluded from decision-making or power. They have little say in what happens to them—life is beyond their control. They are fatalists. Revelation comes from the authoritative sources (tradition, sacred writings) and is explained and interpreted by authorized leaders who pass down the truth. Supernatural forces are seen more in terms of impersonal powers or principles. People are focused upwards on the received traditions and rulings and sources of authority, rather than being connected or committed to each other. This category includes feudal societies, slaves, and prison inmates.

Nature is capricious and human nature unpredictable.

The question they ask, helplessly, is, "Whatever can I do?"

All these groups are present in any society in a dynamic tension. A change in society signifies a change in the balance of the groups, so a different group will become more dominant.

Cultural Theory Implications

Mamadouh suggests three important implications of the Grid–Group analysis as a cultural theory:

1. Culture matters. All our human preferences and relations are culturally-shaped.

2. There are a limited number of cultural types (or we could call them social orders, ways of life, or rationalities). This means that rationality is plural: there are a number of self-confirming ways for people to behave rationally. These viable combinations of rational choice can be determined by analyzing societies along the two main dimensions discussed.

3. This typology can be applied to understand and even predict the choices people will make, their perceptions and values, according to their preferred position along these two axes.[5]

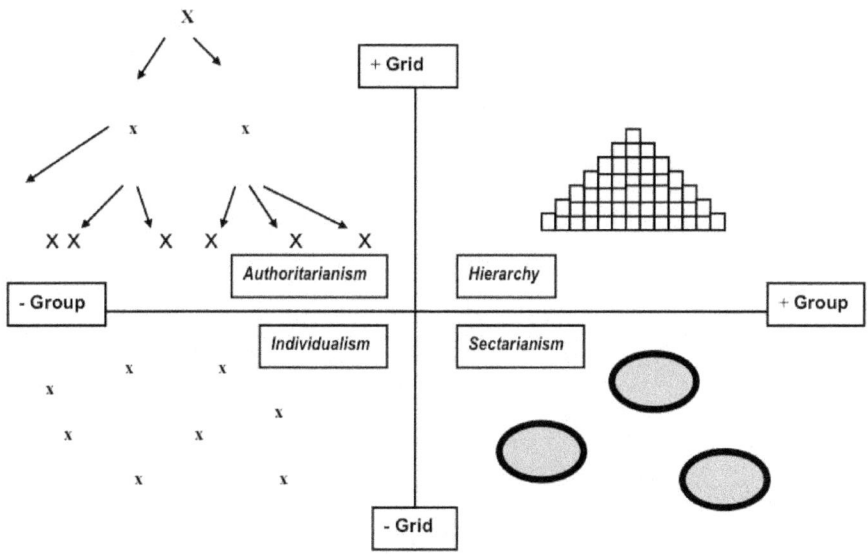

Figure 7

---

5. Mamadouh, ibid., 396–97.

Appendix 2

Tajwid—Instruction and Practice Observed

THE LESSONS ARE GIVEN to small groups of women, allowing a high level of engagement with the opportunities to practice. The teacher explains the rules and sometimes gives her hearers opportunities to practice and be affirmed or corrected in their pronunciation. She ties the rules to Qur'anic examples, quoting the *surah* they are from and giving the phrasal context. Sometimes she asks questions to test her hearers' understanding of a rule or asks them to find examples from a section of the Qur'an related to the rule that they're discussing. At another point all the learners take up a Qur'an and the teacher recites it phrase by phrase with the learners reciting it after her. At one point the teacher corrected the recitation of a learner and the other women listening disagreed with her correction. The teacher accepted their position: the classes require the women to go beyond imitation to understand and justify their pronunciation. The lessons provide the framework for the key place of learning—individual hearings for each learner/reciter. These can involve mostly listening, or extensive feedback, depending on the learner's needs. Sometimes the examples are drawn from everyday life: "Lengthen the 'Ya,' as when you're calling someone, 'Yaa,[6] so-and-so.'" They are encouraged to focus on accuracy rather than on extensive memorization, while they are learning the rules, repeating the section until they get it right. One teacher told the woman she was hearing recite: "I don't care if it's ten pages—it's better to do two well. Just learn three or four pages, not ten, we want the foundation without mistakes. Repeat these pages." She commented to me, "If there's a thousand mistakes, each time, another time, it gets better and better." Here are excerpts from my notes on a *tajwid* class.

---

6. Arabic vocative.

In the main area there is a small group seated in front of a young woman with dark scarf and skirt, white top, standing explaining. In front of her are two lines of mattresses on the floor, each line two mattresses end-to-end, and four chairs behind, about ten women sitting facing her on mattresses, chairs, carpeted floor, all ages, listening intently. The teacher explains a point, than asks for volunteers to say it. About three or four volunteer and she listens and commends or corrects them.

She is describing the sounds according to a number of different categories. She describes some of the letters as *fakham* (emphasized, given weight) and mentions *kh*, *gh*, *q*, as a group. She distinguishes before their pronunciation according to whether they precede an *u* or *i* sound.

She describes seven special characteristics. One of them is *al-qita' al-qalqalah* (agitated segments) which are made by lips or tip of tongue (*takhruj min harf al-fam*). Another is *al-safir* (whistling—emphatic S, s, z); *takrir* (reiteration—flapped r and *al-taqalah* (heaviness—emphatic dh).

The teacher describes *al-qalqalah* (agitation) in more detail, as water boiling, moving, but not in the sense of moving from place to place, rather movement in one place. She describes still letters and moving ones. "Still" letters (*al-haruf al-sakanah*) are ones where the two parts of the mouth used close, as in (*ab*—father) (syllable-final). She gets the class to make the sounds of *m*, *s*, *q*, after her. "Moving" letters (*al-haruf al-muharak*) are those where there is an opening of the two points of articulation, where they are followed by *fatah*, *kasra* and *dumma* (short *a*, *i* and *u*). *Al-haruf al-maksurah* ("*kasra*"-ed letters) are those opening to the *i* sound (*kasra*).

She makes the sound of *yad'u*, showing how there is a continuity/connection between the *d* and *ain* rather than stopping one before beginning the other. . . . She has individuals practice saying *q*, *w*, *m*. People practice it—this is harder. She comes to us and sees my notes and realizes I'm a foreigner, so I introduce myself, and she gets me to say them and corrects me till I get it right. She continues revising the three mistakes:

i. to finish one letter and then begin the next, so separating them instead of having them connected.

ii. prolonging a sound too long.

iii. putting the short vowels on consonants that don't accept them (example of *b* in "Ibrahim").

And continues: After doubled letters, *al-haruf al-mashdid*, open for the second letter of the two to take a short vowel. A moving letter plus a still letter becomes a doubled letter. She finishes the lesson saying, *in sha'Allah yakun fadah min al-'adah* (God willing, there's benefit from our time sitting together).

She explains to me that she is listening to women do the *tajwid* now—that she is here from 9:00 a.m. each Saturday, hearing the women, teaching the theory, the *dhikr*, and hearing the women who are learning; and suggests that I would also benefit and understand more from hearing them and her as she corrects them.

So I sat in after another lesson while Amal heard the women recite.

I go with Amal and the other young woman into the office on the right of the entrance. There are curtained glass windows on two sides, a desk with a computer, salon chairs, boxes of equipment stacked. A bar heater on the wall warms us. Amal takes a seat: she is holding a Qur'an and pencil. She gives the woman a phrase; she closes her eyes and begins. Amal recites quietly with her, concentrating, correcting her occasionally. She tells her, "Don't start the word with a vowel before the letter." (She had an *i* sound before "*rabbina*.") Amal stops the woman, who sits silently, while Amal reviews the text and makes a couple of comments. She gives her another phrase and the woman begins again. It sounds very different from standard Arabic. The reciter repeats a word and continues—intonation, nasalization, pronunciation—Amal is listening to pick up any errors, as she sits cross-legged on the chair, the girl facing her in the neighboring chair, knee to knee.[7] When she has finished, another young woman asks the reciter, "Do you recite it in *salah*?" The reciter nods, and the girl says, "it shows."[8]

The other girl begins, facing Amal in the chair across from her, while the first reciter packs up, collects her things, and leaves. Amal picks this one up far more often on the vowel quality. She tells her, "Attention—shape your mouth like this, more open—bring the *u* through a tunnel," (demonstrating) "making it last." She holds her nose to show her how to end right. The woman tries, retries—Amal explains, demonstrates, smiles, and tells her, "Well done." Amal's mobile phone rings—she gets it out, silences it, and returns it to her pocket. She gives this reciter lots of explanation and revision. She focuses on the length of syllables, of the *n* and occasionally corrects a word. She talks about the position of the tongue for *n*: "I used to know, then I heard Dr . . . saying that the tongue should be at the tip of the teeth, not behind them." She gives me a quick explanation of *ghunnah* (nasality): "The

---

7. Thus repeating the traditional pattern of learning *hifz*, in which the student/candidate repeats the passages he has mastered or learned by ear, sitting on the floor knee-to-knee with the teacher (Kahteran, *Hafiz*, 232).

8. This indicates that *tajwid* goes beyond a mechanical auditory rendering, but can become part of the reciter's effective performance of *salah*.

m and *n* are blocked in the mouth, so the air comes through the nose—this is *ghunnah*."

The first woman spent about 10 minutes; this woman has been 25 minutes already. She yawns, and sits up—Amal's bright black eyes are fixed on her. When the reciter forgets, Amal asks her, "What did Sayyidna Musa say to the people?" to prompt her. When the reciter says, "*tuub*" (repent), Amal tells her, "*fakhkham al-ta*" (emphasize the *ta*). The reciter finishes, says, "*sadaq Allah al-'adhim*" (faithful is God the Great—a traditional phrase of completion) quickly, and goes.

Another girl arrives to have Amal hear her, with a tiny Qur'an—Amal says she'll have to do it from memory as the print is so small. She follows it with the reciter.

Bibliography

'Ali Qutb, Muhammad. *Women Around the Messenger*. Riyadh: International Islamic Publishing House, 2007.
Abdullah, Zulkarnaini. "Religious Practices: Ablution, Purification, Prayer, Fasting, and Piety. Southeast Asia." In *Encyclopedia of Women & Islamic Cultures*, edited by Suad Joseph, 5:276–79. Leiden: Brill, 2007.
Abu-Lughod, Lila. "The Debate about Gender, Religion, and Rights: Thoughts of a Middle East Anthropologist." *PMLA* 121, no. 5. The Humanities in Human Rights: Critique, Language, Politics (2006) 1621–30.
Abu-Odeh, Lama. "Honor Killings and the Construction of Gender in Arab Societies." *American Journal of Comparative Law* 58, no. 4 (2010) 911–52.
Abudi, Dalya. *Mothers and Daughters in Arab Women's Literature. The Family Frontier*. Women and Gender. The Middle East and the Islamic World 10. Leiden: Brill, 2011.
Abugideiri, Hibba. "Qur'an: Modern Interpretations. Arabic and Urdu." In *Encyclopedia of Women & Islamic Cultures*, edited by Suad Joseph, 5:249–52 Leiden: Brill, 2007.
———. "Qur'an: Modern Interpretations. Euro-American Languages." In *Encyclopedia of Women & Islamic Cultures*, edited by Suad Joseph, 5:252–55. Leiden: Brill, 2007.
———. "The Renewed Woman of American Islam: Shifting Lenses toward 'Gender Jihad?'" *Muslim World* 91, no. 1–2 (2001) 1–18.
Ackerly, Brooke, and Jacqui True. "Reflexivity in Practice: Power and Ethics in Feminist Research on International Relations." *International Studies Review* 10, no. 4 (2008) 693–707.
Adeney, Miriam. *Daughters of Islam. Building Bridges with Muslim Women*. Leicester: IVP, 2002.
Afshar, Haleh, Rob Aitken, and Myfanwy Franks. "Feminisms, Islamophobia and Identities." *Political Studies* 53 (2005) 262–83.
Agpeya: The Book of Hours. www.agpeya.org/Prime/prime.html#prayerofthanksgiving.
Ahmad, Sadaf. *Transforming Faith: The Story of Al-Huda and Islamic Revivalism Among Urban Pakistani Women*. Gender and Globalization. New York: Syracuse University Press, 2009.
Ahmed, Leila. *A Quiet Revolution: The Veil's Resurgence, from the Middle East to America*. New Haven: Yale University Press, 2011.
———. "Early Feminist Movements in the Middle East." In *Muslim Women*, 111–123. Beckenham, UK: CroomHelm Ltd, 1984.
———. *Women and Gender in Islam*. New Haven: Yale University Press, 1992.

Akhtar, Sayyid Wahid. "The Islamic Concept of Knowledge." *Al-Tawhid: A Quarterly Journal of Islamic Thought and Culture* 12, no. 3. http://www.al-islam.org/al-tawhid/islam-know-conc.htm.

Al-Banna, Imam Shaheed Hasan. *Al-Ma'thurat* المأثورات. Swansea, UK: Awakening, 2001.

Alcalde, M. Cristina. "Going Home. A Feminist Anthropologist's Reflections on Dilemmas of Power and Positionality in the Field." *Meridians: Feminism, Race, Transnationalism* 7, no. 2 (2007) 143–62.

Al-Faisal, Toujan. "They Insult Us ... and We Elect Them!!" In *Faith and Freedom: Women's Human Rights in the Muslim World*, 232–37. London: Tauris, 1995.

Al-Ghazali, Muhammad. *A Thematic Commentary on the Qur'an*. 2nd ed. Selangor, Malaysia: Islamic Book Trust, 2001.

Al-Habash, Muhammad. كيف تقرأ القرآن؟ كيف تحفظ القرآن؟ كيف وصل إلينا القرآن؟ *How do we read the Qur'an? How do we memorize the Qur'an? How did the Qur'an come to us?* Beirut: 2001, دار الخير.

Al-Hashimi, Muhammad Ali. *The Ideal Muslimah*. Translated by Nasiruddin al-Khattab. 5th ed. Riyadh: International Islamic, 2005.

Al-Hilali, Dr Muhammad Taqi-ud-Din, and Dr Muhammad Muhsin Khan. *Translation of the Meanings of The Noble Qur'an in the English Language*. Madinah, K.S.A.: King Fahd Complex for the Printing of the Holy Qur'an, 1404.

Al-Husaynaan, Shaykh Khaalid. *More than 1,000 Sunan (Sayings and Acts of the Prophet) Every Day and Night*. 2nd ed. Riyadh: Darussalam, 2006.

Ali, Abdullah Yusuf. *The Holy Qur'an. Text, Translation and Commentary*. Lahore: Sh. Muhammad Ashraf, 1938.

Ali, Kecia. "Religious Practices: Obedience and Disobedience in Islamic Discourses." In *Encyclopedia of Women & Islamic Cultures*, edited by Suad Joseph, 5:309–13. Leiden: Brill, 2007.

Alison, James. "Girard's Breakthrough." *James Alison. Theology*, 1996. http://www.jamesalison.co.uk/texts/eng05.html.

Al-Islam. "Some Traditions that Appear to Conflict with Hadith al-Thaqalyn." http://www.al-islam.org/thaqalayn/nontl/Traditions.htm.

Al- Munajjid, Shaykh Muhammad Saalih, "Do Her Children From Breastfeeding Have Any Relationship With Her Second Husband." *Fiqh of the Family*. http://islamqa.info/en/45620.

———. "Ruling on a woman leading men in prayer," *Principles of Fiqh*, http://islamqa.info/en/39188.

———. "Women Leading Prayers," *Principles of Fiqh*, http://islamqa.info/en/14247.

———. "Women's 'awrah in front of other women and mahrams," *Principles of Fiqh*, http://islamqa.info/en/82994.

———. "What is the ruling on drinking one's wife's milk?" *Fiqh of the Family*. http://islamqa.info/en/2864.

Al-Musnad, Muhammad bin Abdul-Aziz, and Jamaal Al-DinM. Translated by Zarabozo. *Islamic Fatawa Regarding Women*. Riyadh: Darussalam, 1996.

Al-Qaradawi, Dr Yusuf. *Islamopedia online. Translation, News and Analysis of Contemporary Islamic Thought*. http://www.islamopediaonline.org/fatwa/dr-yusuf-al-qaradawi-comments-females-leading-co-gender-friday-prayers-and-women-leading-other.

Al-Qahtani, Sa'id bin Ali bin Wahf. ورد الصباح والمساء من الكتاب والسنة. *Private Devotions For Morning and Evening From the Qur'an and the Sunnah.* Riyadh: Darussalam, 1996.

Al-Qahtani, Sa'id bin Wahf. حصن المسلم. *Fortress of the Muslim. Invocations from the Qur'an and Sunnah.* 5th ed. Riyadh: Darussalam, 2006.

Al-Shibeeb, Dina. "New Islamic ruling on singing stirs debate." http://www.alarabiya.net/articles/2010/09/18/119639.html.

Al-Sistani, Al-Sayyid Ali Al-Husseini. "Moon Sighting." http://www.sistani.org/english/qa/01266/#14987.

Alter, Robert. *The Book of Psalms. A Translation with Commentary.* New York: W.W.Norton, 2007.

Altorki, Soraya. "At Home in the Field." In *Arab Women in the Field. Studying Your Own Society*, 49–68. Modern Arab Studies. Syracuse, NY: Syracuse University Press, 1988.

Altorki, Soraya, and Camillia Fawzi El-Solh. *Arab Women in the Field. Studying Your Own Society.* Modern Arab Studies. New York: Syracuse University Press, 1988.

Al-Turayri, Sheikh 'Abd al-Wahhab. "Islam Today." En.islamtoday.net/quesshow-12-814.htm.

Aluwihare-Samaranayake, Dilmi. "Ethics in Qualitative Research: A View of the Participants' and Researchers' World from a Critical Standpoint." *International Journal of Qualitative Methods* 11, no. 2 (2012) 64–81.

Ammar, Nawal H. "Wife Battery in Islam: A Comprehensive Understanding of Interpretations." *Violence Against Women* 13 (2007) 516.

Anderson, Benedict. *Imagined Communities: Reflections on the Origin and Spread of Nationalism.* 2nd ed. London: Verso, 1991.

Andrade, Gabriele. "Rene Girard." *Internet Encyclopedia of Philosophy.* http://www.iep.utm.edu/girard/.

Anwar, Etin. "Bodily Waste." In *Encyclopedia of Women & Islamic Cultures*, edited by Suad Joseph, 3:27–33. Leiden: Brill, 2006.

Arthur, Linda B. "Deviance, Agency, and the Social Control of Women's Bodies in a Mennonite Community." *NWSA Journal* 10, no. 2 (1998) 75–99.

Asad, Talal. *Formations of the Secular. Christianity, Islam, Modernity.* Stanford, California: Stanford University Press, 2003.

———. *Genealogies of Religion. Discipline and Reasons of Power in Christianity and Islam.* Baltimore: John Hopkins University Press, 1993.

———. "Remarks on the Anthropology of the Body." In *Religion and the Body*, 42–52. Cambridge Studies in Religious Traditions 8. Cambridge: Cambridge University Press, 1997.

As-Sunnah Foundation of America. "Questions on Dhikr." http://sunnah.org/ibadaat/dhikrtable.htm.

Aziz, Jean. "Islamic Clerics Oppose Lebanese Law Protecting Abused Women," *Lebanon Pulse, Al Monitor.* http://www.al-monitor.com/pulse/originals/2013/07/womens-rights-activists-lebanon-domestic-violence-law.html#

Auda, Jasser. "Reflection: A Marvelous Form of Worship." www.onislam.net/english/shariah/refine-your-heart/advice/452676-isolation-and-reflection.html.

Austin, Jane. *Pride and Prejudice.* Public Domain, 1813.

Aydinli, Osman. "Ascetic and Devotional Elements in the Mu'tazile Tradition: The Sufi Mu'tazilites." *The Muslim World* 97 (2007) 174–89.

Badran, Margot. *Feminism in Islam. Secular and Religious Convergences.* Oxford: Oneworld, 2009.

Baig, Khalid. "Home, Sweet Home." www.albalagh.net/women/home.shtml.

Bano, Masooda. "Conclusion: Female Leadership in Mosques: An Evolving Narrative." In *Women, Leadership, and Mosques. Changes in Contemporary Islamic Authority*, 507-33. Women and Gender. The Middle East and the Islamic World 11. Leiden: Brill, 2012.

Bano, Masooda, and Hilary Kalmbach, eds. *Women, Leadership, and Mosques. Changes in Contemporary Islamic Authority* 11. Women and Gender. The Middle East and the Islamic World 11. Leiden: Brill, 2012.

Barakaati, Sayyid Shah Aal-e-Rasool Nazmi, "A Woman's Duties towards her Husband." www.ahlesunnat.net/media-library/downloads/regularupdates/wifeduties.htm

Barlas, Asma. *"Believing Women" in Islam. Unreading Patriarchal Interpretations of the Qur'an.* Austin: University of Texas Press, 2002.

Baron, Beth Ann. *The Women's Awakening in Egypt: Culture, Society, and the Press.* New Haven: Yale University Press, 1994.

Baron, Beth Ann. "The Rise of a New Literary Culture: The Women's Press of Egypt, 1882-1919." PhD diss., University of California, 1988.

Bayat, Asef, and Linda Herrera. "Introduction: Being Young and Muslim in Neoliberal Times." In *Being Young and Muslim. New Cultural Politics in the Global South and North*, 3-24. Religion and Global Politics Series. Oxford: Oxford University Press, 2010.

Bell, R, and W. Mongomery Watt. *Bell's Introduction to the Qur'an. Revised and Enlarged by W.M. Watt.* Edinburgh: Edinburgh University Press, 1970.

Borg, Walter R., and Meredith D. Gall. *Educational Research.* New York: Longman, 1989.

Bourdieu, Pierre. *Outline of a Theory of Practice.* Cambridge: Cambridge University Press, 1977.

Bowie, Fiona. "Belief or Experience? The Anthropologists' Dilemma." *2nd Series Occasional Paper* 33 (2002). Religious Experience Research Centre, Dept of Theology and Religious Studies, University of Wales.

———. *The Anthropology of Religion.* Oxford: Blackwell, 2000.

Brockwell, Joshua. "Paradise Is At the Feet of Mothers." *About Religion.* Islam.about.com/od/elderly/a/mothers.htm.

Bruner, Jerome. "Life as Narrative." *Language Arts* 65, no. 6 (1988) 574-83.

Bucaille, Maurice. *The Bible, The Qur'an and Science.* 4th ed. Indianapolis: North American Trust, 1978.

Buergener, Elisabeth. "Becoming What I Am: Syrian Muslim Women's Journey to Devoutness." PhD diss., Birmingham University, 2013.

Buitelaar, Marjo. "Space: Hammam—Overview." In *Encyclopedia of Women & Islamic Cultures*, edited by Suad Joseph, 4:541-43. Leiden: Brill, 2007.

Bunton, Martin. "The Arab Middle East." In *The Islamic World*, 11-23. The Routledge Worlds. London: Routledge, 2008.

Burnett, David. *Unearthly Powers. A Christian Perspective on Primal and Folk Religion.* Eastbourne, UK: MARC, 1988.

Burns, N., and S. Groves. *The Practice of Nursing Research: Conduct, Critique and Utilization.* 4th ed. Pennsylvania: W. B. Saunders, 2001.

Canard, M. "Da'wa." *Encylopaedia of Islam.* Leiden: Brill, 1965.

Carter, Michael. "Foreign Vocabulary." In *The Blackwell Companion to the Qur'an*, 120–139. Chichester, UK: Wiley-Blackwell, 2009.

Caulkins, D. Douglas. "Is Mary Douglas's Grid/Group Analysis Useful for Cross-Cultural Research?" *Cross-Cultural Research* 33 (1999).

Caulley, Darrel N. "Document Analysis in Program Evaluation." *Evaluation and Program Planning* 6 (1983) 19–29.

Christian, Jr, William A. "Folk Religion." *The Encyclopedia of Religion*. New York: MacMillan, 1987.

Christopher, Colin. "Female Imam Leads Eid Prayer." *Inside Islam: Dialogues and Debates*. http://insideislam.wisc.edu/2010/11/female-imam-leads-eid-prayer/.

Churchill, Mary C. "The Oppositional Paradigm of Purity versus Pollution in Charles Hudson's the Southeastern Indians." *American Indian Quarterly* 20, no. 3/4 (1996) 563–94.

Clarke, Morgan. "Integrity and Commitment in the Anthropology of Islam." In *Articulating Islam: Anthropological Approaches to Muslim Worlds*, 209–27. Muslims in Global Societies Series 6. Springer: Springer, 2013.

Coakley, Sarah. *Religion and the Body*. Cambridge Studies in Religious Traditions 8. Cambridge: Cambridge University Press, 1997.

Cohen, Louis, Lawrence Manion, and Keith Morrison. *Research Methods in Education*. 7th ed. Oxon, New York: Routledge, 2011.

Coleman, Isobel. *Paradise Beneath Her Feet. How Women Are Transforming The Middle East*. New York: Random House, 2010.

Cooke, Miriam. "Religion, Gender and the Muslimwoman." *Journal of Feminist Studies in Religion* 24, no. 1 (2008) 91–119.

Cragg, Kenneth. *Alive to God: Muslim and Christian Prayer Compiled with An Introductory Essay*. London: Oxford University Press, 1970.

———. *Muhammad and the Christian: A Question of Response*. London: Darton, Longman and Todd, and Orbis, 1984.

———. *The Call of the Minaret*. 2nd ed. London: Collins, 1985.

———. *The Event of the Qur'an*. London: George Allen and Unwin, 1971.

———. *The Mind of the Qur'an*. London: George Allen and Unwin, 1973.

Cragg, Kenneth, and Marston Speight. *Islam from Within: Anthology of a Religion*. Belmont, California: Wadsworth, 1980.

Creswell, John W. *Qualitative Inquiry and Research Design. Choosing Among Five Approaches*. 3rd ed. Thousand Oaks, London: Sage, 2013.

———. *Research Design. Qualitative, Quantitative and Mixed Methods Approaches*. 3rd ed. Los Angeles: Sage, 2009.

Crumbley, Deidre Helen. "Partriarchies, Prophets, and Procreation: Sources of Gender Practices in Three African Churches." *Africa* 73, no. 4 (2003) 584–606.

Dale, Moyra. "Domains of Responsibility and Authority in Islam: Qualifications, Purity and Pollution." Southlands College, University of Roehampton, London, 2012.

———. "Rote Learning in a Performance-Based Pedagogy." *Australian Journal of Adult Learning* 41, no. 3 (2001).

———. *Women In Egypt: Lives and Literacies. Purposes and Practices of Literacy, From Selected Classes in Egypt*. Saarbrucken, Germany: Lambert Academic, 2012.

Davidson, Mary. "Women's Gatherings and Leadership." In *Longing For Community*, 193–204. Pasadena: William Carey Library, 2013.

Dawood, N.J. *The Koran*. 4th ed. The Penguin Classics. Harmondsworth, England and Baltimore, USA: Penguin, 1974.
De Troyer, Kristin, Judith A. Herbert, Judith Ann Johnson, and Anne-Marie Korte. *Wholly Woman, Holy Blood: A Feminist Critique of Purity and Impurity*. Harrisburg, PA: Trinity, 2003.
Deeb, Lara. "Piety Politics and the Role of a Transnational Feminist Analysis." *Journal of the Royal Anthropological Institute* 15 (2009) 112–126.
———. "Religious Practices: Preaching and Women Preachers. Arab States (excepting North Africa and the Gulf." In *Encyclopedia of Women & Islamic Cultures*, edited by Suad Joseph, 5:335–336. Leiden: Brill, 2007.
Dehlvi, Sadia. "Women Sufis," http://www.aulia-e-hind.com/dargah/womensufis.htm.
Demircan, Adnan, and Atay Rifat. "Tafsir in Early Islam." *The Qur'an: An Encyclopedia*, edited by Oliver Leaman, 624–31. London: Routledge, 2006.
Denzin, Norman K. *Interpretive Ethnography. Ethnographic Practices for the 21st Century*. London: Sage, 1997.
deSilva, David A. *Honor, Patronage, Kinship and Purity. Unlocking the New Testament Culture*. Illinois: IVP Academic, 2000.
Diamant, Anita. *The Red Tent*. Crows Nest, Australia: Allen and Unwin, 1998.
Digges, Dianne. "Double Vision; On Gender and Nationalism in the Palestinian Women's Movement." *Cairo Times*. 2–15 September 1999.
Douglas, Mary. *Natural Symbols: Explorations in Cosmology*. 2nd ed. London and New York: Routledge Classics, 1996.
———. *Purity and Danger. An Analysis of the Concepts of Pollution and Taboo*. London and New York: Routledge, 1966.
———. "The Background of the Grid Dimension: A Comment." *Sociological Analysis* 50, no. 2 (1989) 171–76.
———. *Thinking In Circles. An Essay on Ring Composition*. New Haven: Yale University Press, 2007.
Douglas, Mary, and Gerald Mars. "Terrorism: A Positive Feedback Game." *Human Relations* 56, no. 7 (2003) 763.
Doumato, Eleanor Abdella. *Getting God's Ear: Women, Islam, and Healing in Saudi Arabia and the Gulf*. New York: Columbia University Press, 2000.
Duderija, Adis. "A Case Study of Patriarchy and Slavery: The Hermeneutical Importance of Qur'anic Assumptions in the Development of a Values-Based and Purposive Oriented Qur'an-Sunna Hermeneutic." *Journal of Women of the Middle East and the Islamic World* 11 (2013) 1–30.
———. *Constructing a Religiously Ideal "Believer" and "Woman" in Islam. Neo-Traditional Salafi and Progressive Muslims' Methods of Interpretation*. Palgrave Series in Islamic Theology, Law, and History. New York: Palgrave Macmillan, 2011.
Dunn, Shannon, and Rosemary B Kellison. "At The Intersection of Scripture and Law. Qur'an 4:34 and Violence against Women." *Journal of Feminist Studies in Religion* 26, no. 2 (2010) 11–36.
Edge, J., and K. Richards. "May I See Your Warrant Please? Justifying Outcomes in Qualitative Research." *Applied Linguistics* 19, no. 3 (1998) 334–56.
El Fadl, Khaled Abou. "Foreword." In *Inside the Gender Jihad. Women's Reform in Islam*, vii–xiv. Oxford: Oneworld, 2006.

———. *Speaking in God's Name. Islamic Law, Authority and Women*. Oxford: Oneworld, 2001.
El Guindi, Fadwa. *By Noon Prayer. The Rhythm of Islam*. Oxon, New York: Berg, 2008.
El Saadawi, Nawal. *A Daughter Of Isis. The Autobiography of Nawal El Saadawi*. London: Zed, 1999.
———. *Memoirs From The Women's Prison*. Translated by Marilyn Booth. London: The Women's Press Limited, 1986.
———. *Memoirs of a Woman Doctor*. Translated by Catherine Cobham. London: Saqi, 1988.
———. *The Hidden Face of Eve. Women in the Arab World*. London: Zed Press, 1980.
———. *Two Women in One*. Translated by Osman Nusairi and Jana Gough. London: Al Saqi, 1985.
Emerick, Yaya. *What Islam Is All About*. Kuala Lumpur, Malaysia: A.S.Noordeen, 2002.
Engineer, Asghar Ali. *The Rights of Women In Islam*. London: C. Hurst and Company, 1992.
EsinHome. "Can the Testimony of a Woman Be Accepted With Regard To Sighting The New Moon Of Ramadan?" *EsinIslam Ramadan*. http://www.esinislam.com/Ramadan/Ramadan_TestimonyOfAWomanSightingTheNewMoon.
Esposito, John L. "Women in Islam and Muslim Societies." In *Islam, Gender and Social Change*, Ed. Yvonne Yazbeck Haddad and John L. Esposito. Oxford: Oxford University Press, 1998.
Fathi, Muhammad. "Introduction to Tajwid and Rules of Reading Qur'an," *on islam*. http://www.onislam.net/english/shariah/quran/introduction-to-the-quran/455828-an-introduction-to-tajwid.html.
Feminijtihad, *Strategic Advocacy for Human Rights*. http://feminijtihad.com/womens-rights-in-courts/.
Fernea, Elizabeth. "Women In Muslim History." http://www.historytoday.com/elizabeth-fernea/women-muslim-history/.
Finlay, Linda. "'Outing' the Researcher: The Provenance, Process and Practice of Reflexivity." *Qualitative Health Research* 12 (2002) 531–45.
Fitzgerald, Daniel W., Cecile Marotte, Rose Irene Verdier, Warren D. Johnson Jr., and Jean William Pape. "Comprehension during Informed Consent in a Less-Developed Country." *Lancet* 360, no. 9342 (2002) 1301–2.
Flint, Chris. "Church and Mosque. A Comparison of a Christian View of EKKLESIA and a Muslim View of the Mosque as Part of the UMMAH and an Analysis of the Missiological Implications of These Views." *St. Francis Magazine* 8, no. 5 (2012) 599–695.
Fluehr-Lobban, Carolyn. "Ethics." In *Handbook of Methods in Cultural Anthropology*, 173–202. Walnut Creek: AltaMira, Sage, 1998.
Foucault, Michel. *Ethics, Subjectivity and Truth*. Vol. 1. No. 3. Essential Words of Foucault 1954–84 1. New York: The New Press, 1997.
Franzwa, Gregg, and Charles Lockhart. "The Social Origins and Maintenance of Gender: Communication Styles, Personality Types and Grid-Group Theory." *Sociological Perspectives* 41, no. 1 (1998) 185–208.
Frazer, James. *The Golden Bough*. 3rd ed. Hertfordshire: Wordsworth, 1993.
Gaffney, Patrick D. *The Prophet's Pulpit: Islamic Preaching in Contemporary Egypt*. Comparative Studies in Muslim Societies, Vol. 20. Berkley: University of California Press, 1994.

Ganiel, Gladys, and Claire Mitchell. "Turning the Categories Inside-Out: Complex Identifications and Multiple Interactions in Religious Ethnography." *Sociology of Religion* 67, no. 1 (2006) 3–21.

Gauvain, Richard. "Ritual Rewards: A Consideration of Three Recent Approaches to Sunni Purity Law." *Islamic Law and Society* 12, no. 3 (2005) 333–93.

Gee, James Paul. "Literacy and Social Minds." In *The Literacy Lexicon*, 5–14. Sydney: Prentice Hall, 1996.

Geels, Antoon. "A Note on the Psychology of Dhikr: The Halveti-Jerrahi Order of Dervishes in Istanbul." *International Journal for the Psychology of Religion* 6, no. 4 (n.d.) 229–30.

Geertz, Clifford. *The Interpretation of Culture: Selected Essays*. 2nd ed. New York: Basic, 2000.

Gelling, L. "A Feminist Approach to Research." *Nurse Researcher* 21, no. 1 (2013) 6–7.

Ghadanfar, Mahmood Ahmad. Revised by Sheikh Safium-Rahman Al-Mubarapuri. *Great Women of Islam Who Were given the Good News of Paradise*. 1st ed. Riyadh: Darussalam, 2001.

Ghadially, Rehana. "A Hajari (Meal Tray) for Abbas Alam Dar: Women's Household Ritual in a South Asian Muslim Sect." *The Muslim World* 92, no. 2 (2003) 309–22.

Gibb, H. A. R., and J. H. Kramers. *Shorter Encyclopaedia of Islam*. Leiden: E.J.Brill, 1974.

Gilbert, Marvin, and Johan Mostert. "Obtaining Informed Consent in Missiologically Sensitive Contexts." *International Bulletin of Missionary Research* 37, no. 1 (2013) 3–8.

Girard, Rene. *The Girard Reader*. New York: Crossroad Publishing Company, 1996.

Glassé, Cyril. *The Concise Encycylopaedia of Islam*. 3rd ed. London: Stacey International, 2008.

Glesne, C., and A. Peshkin. *Becoming Qualitative Researchers: An Introduction*. White Plains, New York: Longman, 1992.

Graham, William A., and Navid Kermani. "Recitation and Aesthetic Reception." In *The Cambridge Companion to the Qur'an*, 115–41. Cambridge: Cambridge University Press, 2006.

Grant, Audrey N., and Moyra Buntine Dale. "A Multistoried Approach to Studying Women's Lives and Literacies in Egypt." In *Refereed Conference Proceedings and Keynotes*. Hamilton, New Zealand, 2003.

Grendstad, Gunnar, and Susan Sundback. "Socio-Demographic Effects on Cultural Biases: A Nordic Study of Grid-Group Theory." *Acta Sociologica* 46, no. 4 (2003) 289–306.

Guessoum, Nidhal. "Religious Literalism and Science-Related Issues in Contemporary Islam." *Zygon: Journal of Religion and Science* 45, no. 4 (2010) 817–40.

———. "The Qur'an, Science, and the (Related) Contemporary Muslim Discourse." *Zygon: Journal of Religion and Science* 43, no. 2 (2008) 411–31.

Haddad, Sh.G.F. "On Dhikr Remembrance of God," *Living Islam*. http://www.livingislam.org/n/dhkr_e.html.

Haddad, Yvonne Yazbeck. "Islam and Gender: Dilemmas in the Changing Arab World." In *Islam, Gender and Social Change*,. Yvonne Yazbeck Haddad and John L. Esposito, eds. 3–29. Oxford: Oxford University Press, 1998.

Haddad, Yvonne Yazbeck, and John L Esposito, eds. *Islam, Gender, and Social Change*. Oxford: Oxford University Press, 1998.

Hafez, Sherine. *An Islam of Her Own. Reconsidering Religion and Secularism in Women's Islamic Movements*. New York: New York University Press, 2011.

Hamdy, Sherine. "Science and Modern Islamic Discourses." In *Encyclopedia of Women & Islamic Cultures*, edited by Suad Joseph, 3:360–65. Leiden: Brill, 2006.

Hammer, Julianne. "Activism as Embodied Tafsir: Negotiating Women's Authority, Leadership and Space in North America." In *Women, Leadership, and Mosques. Changes in Contemporary Islamic Authority*, 457–80. Women and Gender. The Middle East and the Islamic World 11. Leiden: Brill, 2012.

Haneef, Suzanne. *What Everyone Should Know About Islam and Muslims*. Chicago: Kazi, 1979.

Harding, Susan F. "Invited by the Holy Spirit: The Rhetoric of Fundamental Baptist Conversion." *American Ethnologist* 14, no. 1 (1987) 167–81.

Hasan, Abu Nimah. "Realizing the Danger and Reconsidering." *The Washington Report on Middle East Affairs* 25, no. 3 (2006) 36–7.

Hashmi, Taj. *Women and Islam in Bangladesh: Beyond Subjection and Tyranny*. London: Palgrave Macmilland and St. Martin's, 2000.

Hassan, Mona. "Reshaping Religious Authority in Contemporary Turkey: State-Sponsored Female Preachers." In *Women, Leadership, and Mosques. Changes in Contemporary Islamic Authority*, 85–103. Women and Gender. The Middle East and the Islamic World 11. Leiden: Brill, 2012.

Haye, Sevald, and Elisabeth Severinsson. "Methodological Aspects of Rigor in Qualitative Nursing Research on Families Involved in Intensive Care Units: Literature Review." *Nursing and Health Sciences* 9, no. 1 (2007) 61–68.

Heath, Shirley Brice, and Brian V. Street. *Ethnography. Approaches to Language and Literacy Research*. Language and Literacy Series. New York: Teachers College Press, 2008.

Hegland, Mary Elaine. "Shi'a Women's Rituals in Northwest Pakistan: The Shortcomings and Significance of Resistance." *Anthropological Quarterly* 76, no. 3 (2003).

Helminski, Camille Adams. *Women of Sufism. A Hidden Treasure. Writings and Stories of Mystic Poets, Scholars and Saints*. Boston: Shambhala Publications, 2003.

Hendry, John. "Cultural Theory and Contemporary Management Organization." *Human Relations* 52, no. 5 (1999) 557–59.

Hesse-Biber, Sharlene Nagy, and Patricia Leavy. *The Practice of Qualitative Research*. 2nd ed. Los Angeles: Sage, 2011.

Hibbert, Richard Y. "Defilement and Cleansing." *Missiology: An International Review* 36, no. 3 (2008) 343–55.

Hitchcock, G., and D. Hughes. *Research and the Teacher*. 2nd ed. London: Routledge, 1995.

Hofstede, Geert, and Gert Jan Hofstede. *Cultures and Organizations. Software of the Mind. Intercultural Cooperation and Its Importance for Survival*. 2nd ed. New York: McGraw-Hill, 2005.

Hood, Christopher. "Control over Bureaucracy: Cultural Theory and Institutional Variety." *Journal Of Public Policy* 15, no. 3 (1995) 207–30.

Hooker, Virginia Matheson. "History: East, South, and Southeast Asia." In *Encyclopedia of Women & Islamic Cultures*, edited by Suad Joseph, 1:350–57. Leiden: Brill, 2003.

Hoskins, Janet. "The Menstrual Hut and the Witch's Lair in Two Eastern Indonesian Societies." *Ethnology* 41, no. 4 (2002) 317–34.

Houghton, Catherine, Dympna Casey, David Shaw, and Kathy Murphy. "Rigor in Qualitative Case-Study Research." *Nurse Researcher* 20, no. 4 (2013) 12–17.
Hussain, Jamila. "Some Subversive Thoughts on Gender Relations within the Australian Muslim Community." In *Challenges to Social Inclusion in Australia: The Muslim Experience*. Melbourne, 2008.
Ibn Adam, Muhammad. "The Female Voice and Singing," *Hanafi Fiqh*, http://islamqa.org/hanafi/daruliftaa/7914.
Ibn Kathir. "Az-Sumar." *Quran Tafsir Ibn Kathir*. http://www.qtafsir.com/index.php?option=com_content and task=category and sectionid=43 and id=88 and Itemid=95.
Ibn Sa'd, Muhammad. *The Women of Madina*. Translated by Aisha Bewley. London: Ta-Ha, 1995.
Ibn Warraq. *Which Koran? Variants, Manuscripts, Linguistics*. New York: Prometheus, 2011.
Ibrahim, Hamidi. "The Qubaysi Ladies Take up Preaching in Syria with Government Approval." *Al-Hayat*. May 3, 2006. https://lists.ou.edu/cgi-bin/wa?A3=ind0605 and L=SYRIACOMMENT-L and E=quoted-printable and P=33426 and B=—and T=text%2Fhtml;%20charset=UTF-818/03/09.
Ibrahim, I.A. *A Brief Illustrated Guide To Understanding Islam*. 2nd ed. Houston: Darussalam, 1997.
Idilbi, Ulfat. *Grandfather's Tale*. Translated by Peter Clarke. London: Quartet Books, 1998.
———. *Sabriya. Damascus Bitter Sweet*. 3rd ed. Northhampton, Massachusetts: Interlink, 1995.
Ingersoll, Julie. "Against Univocality: Re-Reading Ethnographies of Conservative Protestant Women." In *Personal Knowledge and Beyond. Reshaping the Ethnography of Religion*, 162–174. New York: New York University Press, 2002.
Islam, Sarah. "The Qubaysiyyat: The Growth of an International Muslim Women's Revivalist Movement from Syria (1960–2008)." In *Women, Leadership, and Mosques. Changes in Contemporary Islamic Authority*, 161–83. Women and Gender. The Middle East and the Islamic World 11. Leiden: Brill, 2012.
Islam's Women. Jewels of Islam. "Marriage." http://www.islamswomen.com/marriage/fiqh_of_marriage_6.php.
Islamweb: A Ladies' Inclusive Site, "The rights of the husband upon the wife." www.islamweb.net/emainpage/index.php?page=articles and id=151196.
Ismail, Salwa. "Islamism and the Fashioning of Muslim Selves." 1–12. Galway, Ireland: The National University of Ireland, 2005.
———. "Islamism, Re-Islamization and the Fashioning of Muslim Selves: Refiguring the Public Sphere." *Muslim World Journal of Human Rights* 4, no. 1 (2007) Article 3.
Jamal, Amina. "Just between Us: Identity and Representation among Muslim Women." *Inter-Asia Cultural Studies* 12, no. 2 (2011) 202–12.
Jansen, Willy. "Religious Practices: Ablution, Purification, Prayer, Fasting, and Piety. North Africa." In *Encyclopedia of Women & Islamic Cultures*, edited by Suad Joseph, 5:373–374. Leiden: Brill, 2007.
Jaschok, Maria. "Sources of Authority: Female Ahong and Qingzhen Nusi (Women's Mosques) in China." In *Women, Leadership, and Mosques. Changes in*

Contemporary Islamic Authority, 37–58. Women and Gender. The Middle East and the Islamic World 11. Leiden: Brill, 2012.

Jaschok, Maria, and Shui, Jingjun. *The History of Women's Mosques in Chinese Islam*. Richmond, UK: Curzon, 2000.

Jawad, Haifaa A. *The Rights of Women in Islam*. Hampshire and New York: Macmillan and St. Martin's, 1998.

Jayne, Mark. "Too Many Voices, 'Too Problematic to Be Plausible': Representing Multiple Responses to Local Economic Development Strategies?" *Environment and Planning* 35 (2003) 959–81.

Jeffrey, Patricia, Roger Jeffrey, and Craig Jeffrey. "Leading by Example? Women Madrasah Teachers in Rural North India." In *Women, Leadership, and Mosques. Changes in Contemporary Islamic Authority*. Women and Gender: The Middle East and the Islamic World 11, 195–216. Leiden: Brill, 2012.

Jootun, Dev, Gerry McGhee, and Glenn R. Marland. "Reflexivity: Promoting Rigor in Qualitative Research." *Nursing Standard* 23, no. 23 (2009) 42–46.

Joseph, Suad. "Brother-Sister Relationships. Connectivity, Love, and Power in the Reproduction of Patriarchy in Lebanon." In *Intimate Selving in Arab Families. Gender, Self, and Identity*, 113–40. Syracuse, NY: Syracuse University Press, 1999.

———. "Feminization, Familism, Self, and Politics. Research as a Mughtaribi." In *Arab Women in the Field. Studying Your Own Society*, 25–47. Modern Arab Studies. Syracuse, NY: Syracuse University Press, 1988.

———. "Learning Desire: Relational Pedagogies and the Desiring Female Subject in Lebanon." *Journal of Middle East Women's Studies* 1, no. 1 (2005) 79–109.

———. "Preface." In *Encyclopedia of Women & Islamic Cultures*, edited by Suad Joseph, 1:i–xlix. Leiden: Brill, 2005.

Joseph, Suad, ed. *Gender and Citizenship in the Middle East*. Contemporary Issues in the Middle East. New York: Syracuse University Press, 2000.

———. *Intimate Selving in Arab Families. Gender, Self and Identity*. Gender, Culture, and Politics in the Middle East. Syracuse, NY: Syracuse University Press, 1999.

Jouili, Jeanette S. "Religious Practices: Ablution, Purification, Prayer, Fasting, and Piety. Western Europe." In *Encyclopedia of Women & Islamic Cultures*, edited by Suad Joseph, 5:281–84. Leiden: Brill, 2007.

Kahteran, Nevad. "Hafiz/Tahfiz/Hifz/Muhaffiz." In *The Qur'an: An Encyclopedia*, edited by Oliver Leaman, 231–34. London: Routledge, 2006.

———. "Tajwid." In *The Qur'an: An Encyclopedia*, edited by Oliver Leaman, 635–638. London: Routledge, 2006.

Kalmbach, Hilary. "Introduction: Islamic Authority and the Study of Female Religious Leaders." In *Women, Leadership, and Mosques. Changes in Contemporary Islamic Authority*, 1–27. Women and Gender. The Middle East and the Islamic World 11. Leiden: Brill, 2012.

———. "Social and Religious Change in Damascus: One Case of Female Islamic Religious Authority." *British Journal of Middle Eastern Studies* 35, no. 1 (2008) 37–57.

Kanno, Y., and B. Norton. "Imagined Communities and Educational Possibilities: Introduction." *Journal of Language, Identity, and Education* 2, no. 4 (2003) 241–49.

Kazuhiro, Arai. "Combining Innovation and Emotion in the Modernization of Sufi Orders in Contemporary Egypt." *Critique: Critical Middle Eastern Studies* 16, no. 2 (2007) 155–69.

Khalifa, Rashad. "The Writing of the Quran and the timing of the mathematical miracle." http://submission.org/verify_writing_of_Quran_and_the_timing_of_the_mathematical_miracle.html.

———. "Appendix 28 of the Authorized English translation of Quran." http://submission.org/App28.html.

Khan, Muhammad Zafrulla. *The Qur'an, Arabic Text, English Translation*. London: Curzon, 1981.

Khattab, Huda. *The Muslim Woman's Handbook*. 2nd ed. London: Ta-Ha, 1994.

Kirwan, Michael. *Girard and Theology*. Philosophy and Theology. London: T and T Clark, 2009.

Koch, Tina. "Establishing Rigor in Qualitative Research: The Decision Trail." *Journal of Advanced Nursing* 53, no. 1 (2006) 91–100.

Kramer, Martin. "Syria's Alawis and Shi'ism. How Syria's Ruling Sect Found Islamic Legitimacy." In *Shi'ism, Resistance, and Revolution*, 237–54. Boulder, Colorado: Westview, 1987.

Krause, Wanda. *Women in Civil Society. The State, Islamism, and Networks in the UAE*. New York: Palgrave Macmillan, 2008.

Kressel, G.M. "Shame and Gender." *Anthropological Quarterly* 65, no. 1 (1992) 34–46.

Künkler, Miriam, and Roja Fazaeli. "The Life of Two Mujtahidahs: Female Religious Authority in Twentieth-Century Iran." In *Women, Leadership, and Mosques. Changes in Contemporary Islamic Authority*, 127–60. Women and Gender. The Middle East and the Islamic World 11. Leiden: Brill, 2012.

Landres, J. Shawn. "Being (in) the Field: Defining Ethnography in Southern California and Central Slovakia." In *Personal Knowledge and Beyond. Reshaping the Ethnography of Religion*, 100–112. New York: New York University Press, 2002.

Lane, E.W. *Manners and Customs of the Modern Egyptians*. 3rd ed. London: Everyman's Library, 1860.

Lassiter, Luke Eric. "Collaborative Ethnography and Public Anthropology." *Current Anthropology* 46, no. 1 (2005) 83–106.

Le Renard, Amelie. "From Qur'anic Circles to the Internet: Gender Segregation and the Rise of Female Preachers in Saudi Arabia." In *Women, Leadership, and Mosques. Changes in Contemporary Islamic Authority*, 105–26. Women and Gender. The Middle East and the Islamic World 11. Leiden: Brill, 2012.

Leemhuis, Fred. "From Palm Leaves to the Internet." In *The Cambridge Companion to the Qur'an*, 145–161. Cambridge: Cambridge University Press, 2006.

Lehmann, Uta Christina. "Women's Rights To Mosque Space: Access And Participation In Cape Town Mosques." In *Women, Leadership, and Mosques. Changes in Contemporary Islamic Authority*, 481–506. Women and Gender. The Middle East and the Islamic World 11. Leiden: Brill, 2012.

Lenning, Larry G. *Blessing in Mosque and Mission*. Pasadena: William Carey Library, 1980.

Lincoln, Yvonna S., and Egon G. Guba. *Naturalistic Inquiry*. Beverley Hills, California: Sage, 1986.

Lindgren, Tomas. "The Narrative Construction of Muslim Prayer Experiences." *International Journal for the Psychology of Religion* 15, no. 2 (2005) 159–76.

Lingenfelter, Sherwood G. *Transforming Culture*. Michigan: Baker, 1998.

Lockhart, Charles. "American and Swedish Tax Regimes: Cultural and Structural Roots." *Comparative Politics* 35, no. 4 (2003) 379–97.

---. "Cultural Contributions to Explaining Institutional Form, Political Change, and Rational Decisions." *Comparative Political Studies* 32 (1999) 862-93.
---. "Political Culture, Patterns of American Political Development, and Distinctive Rationalities." *The Review of Politics* (2007) 517-48.
---. "Using Grid-Group Theory to Explain Distinctive Japanese Political Institutions." *East Asia* (2007) 51-82.
Loftsdottir, Kristin. "Feminist Theory and That Critical Edge." *Nordic Journal of Feminist and Gender Research* 19, no. 3 (2011) 198-204.
Maalouf, Amin.. *On Identity*. Translated by Barbara Bray. London: The Harvill Press, 2000.
Maghen, Ze'ev. "Close Encounters: Some Preliminary Observations on the Transmission of Impurity in Early Sunni Jurisprudence." *Islamic Law and Society* 6, no. 3 (1999) 348-92.
Maher, Bridget. *Veiled Voices*. DVD, Documentary. Typecast Releasing, 2010.
Mahmood, Saba. "Feminist Theory, Embodiment, and the Docile Agent: Some Reflections on the Egyptian Islamic Revival." *Cultural Anthropology* 16, no. 2 (2001a) 202-37.
---. *Politics of Piety. The Islamic Revival and the Feminist Subject*. Princeton: Princeton University Press, 2005.
---. "Rehearsed Spontaneity and the Conventionality of Ritual: Disciplines of Salat." *American Ethnologist* 28, no. 4 (2001b) 827-53.
Mahmoud, Mohamed. "To Beat or Not to Beat: On the Exegetical Dilemmas over Qur'an, 4:34." *Journal of the American Oriental Society* 126, no. 4 (2006) 537-50.
Makol-Abdul, Pute Rahimah, and Saodah Abdul Rahman. "Religious Associations. Malaysia and Indonesia." In *Encyclopedia of Women & Islamic Cultures*, edited by Suad Joseph, 2:708-711. Leiden: Brill, 2005.
Malas, Nour. "Opposition Meeting in Syria Shows Split Among Activists," *The Wall Street Journal*, June 28, 2011. http://www.wsj.com/articles/SB10001424052702303627104576411823852036718.
Malik, Muhammad Farooq-i-Azam. *The Meaning of Al-Qur'an. The Guidance for Mankind*. 2nd ed. Malaysia: A.S.Noordeen, 1998.
Malina, Bruce J. *The New Testament World. Insights from Cultural Anthropology*. 3rd ed. Louisville: Westminster John Knox, 2001.
Mallouhi, Christine A. *Miniskirts, Mothers and Muslims. A Christian Woman in a Muslim Land*. 2nd ed. Oxford: Monarch, 2004.
Malti-Douglas, Fedwa. *Woman's Body, Woman's Word. Gender and Discourse in Arabo-Islamic Writing*. Princeton: Princeton University Press, 1991.
Mamadouh, Virginie. "Grid-Group Cultural Theory: An Introduction." *GeoJournal* 47, no. 3 (1999).
Marlette, Doug. "The Muslim Cartoon Controversy Exposed an Absence of Courage." *Nieman Reports* 60, no. 2 (2006) 84-87.
Matthew the Poor. *Orthodox Prayer Life. The Interior Way*. New York: St Vladimir's Seminary Press, 2003.
Maududi, Abul A'la. *Purdah and the Status of Woman in Islam*. Translated by Al-Ash'ari, ed. 2nd ed. Delhi: Markazi Maktabi Islami, 1981.
Mauss, Marcel. "Techniques of the Body." *Economy and Society* 2, no. 1 (1973) 70-88.
McDonald, Brian. "Violence and the Lamb Slain." *Touchstone* 16, no. 10 (December 2003). http://www.touchstonemag.com/archives/issue.php?id=66.

Mellor, Philip A., and Chris Shilling. "The Religious Habitus. Embodiment, Relgion, and Sociological Theory." In *The New Blackwell Companion to the Sociology of Religion*, 201–20. Blackwell Companions to Sociology. Chichester, UK: Wiley-Blackwell, 2010.

Meltzer, Julia, and Laura Nix. *The Light In Her Eyes*. DVD, Documentary. Clockshop and Felt Films, 2012. www.TheLightInHerEyesMovie.com.

Mernissi, Fatima. "A Feminist Interpretation of Women's Rights in Islam." In *Liberal Islam: A Sourcebook*, 112–126. Oxford: Oxford University Press, 1998.

———. *Beyond the Veil. Male-Female Dynamics in a Modern Muslim Society*. Cambridge, Massachusetts: Schenkman, 1975.

———. *The Forgotten Queens of Islam*. Translated by Mary Jo Lakeland. Cambridge: Polity Press, 1990.

———. *The Harem Within. Tales of a Moroccan Girlhood*. London: Bantam, 1994.

———. *Women's Rebellion and Islamic Memory*. London: Zed, 1996.

Mernissi, Fatima (trans. Mary Jo Lakeland). *Islam and Democracy. Fear of the Modern World*. Lakeland, Massachusetts: Addison-Wesley, 1992.

Miller, Edward. "The Respect of a Cousin." *The Washington Report on Middle East Affairs* 25, no. 3 (2006) 37.

Minesaki, Hiroko. "Gender Strategy And Authority In Islamic Discourses: Female Preachers in Contemporary Egypt." In *Women, Leadership, and Mosques. Changes in Contemporary Islamic Authority*, 393–412. Women and Gender. The Middle East and the Islamic World 11. Leiden: Brill, 2012.

Minganti, Pia Karlsson. "Challenging From Within: Youth Associations And Female Leadership In Swedish Mosques." In *Women, Leadership, and Mosques. Changes in Contemporary Islamic Authority*, 371–391. Women and Gender. The Middle East and the Islamic World 11. Leiden: Brill, 2012.

Mir, Mustansir. "Scientific Exegesis of the Qur'an-A Viable Project?" *Islam and Science* 2, no. 1 (2004). 33–42.

Mitleton-Kelly, Eve. "The Information Systems Professional as a Hermit." *Innovation: The European Journal of Social Science Research* 17, no. 4 (2004) 289–323.

Moghadam, Valentine M. *Gender and National Identity. Women and Politics in Muslim Societies*. London: Zed, 1994.

———. "Islamic Feminism and Its Discontents: Toward a Resolution of the Debate." In *Gender, Politics, and Islam*, 15–51. Chicago: University of Chicago Press, 2002.

Motzki, Harald. "Alternative Accounts of the Qur'an's Formation." In *The Cambridge Companion to the Qur'an*, 59–75. Cambridge: Cambridge University Press, 2006.

Moucarry, Chawkat. *The Search For Forgiveness. Pardon and Punishment in Islam and Christianity*. Leicester, England: IVP, 2004.

Mujahid, Abdul Malik (ed.) *Prayer for Beginners*. Riyadh: Darussalam, 2000.

Muller, Markus. "Interview With Rene Girard." *Anthropoetics—The Electronic Journal of Generative Anthropology* II, no. 1 (1996).

Musk, Bill. *The Unseen Face of Islam*. Speldhurst, Kent, UK: MARC (Monarch), 1989.

———. *Touching The Soul of Islam*. 2nd ed. Oxford: Monarch, 2004.

Muslim. "Awrah: body parts which must be covered from others," *Islamic Terminology*, http://islamic-dictionary.tumblr.com/post/5658467793/awrah-arabic-%D8%B9%D9%88%D8%B1%D8%A9-is-a-term-used#description

Myers, Michael D, ed. "Qualitative Research in Information Systems." *MISQ Discovery* (1997). http://www.researchgate.net/publication/220260372_Qualitative_Research_in_Information_Systems/file/60b7d51803a28485c3.pdf.

Nadwi, Mohammad Akram. *Al-Muhaddithat: The Women Scholars in Islam*. Oxford: Interface, 2007.

Nahim, Hassan A. *The Division After Prophet Muhammad*. USA: Xlibris, 2012.

Naik, Zakir. *The Qur'an and Modern Science, Compatible or Incompatible*. Houston: Darussalam, 2008.

Naqshbandi. "Dhikr—Remembrance of God," *Naqshbandi Sufi Way*. http://www.naqshbandi.org/teachings/topics/dhikr-remembrance-of-god/.

Nelson, Kristina. *The Art of Reciting the Qur'an*. Cairo: The American University in Cairo Press, 2001.

Neuwirth, Angelika. "Structural, Linguistic and Literary Features." In *The Cambridge Companion to the Qur'an*, 97–113. Cambridge: Cambridge University Press, 2006.

Norton, Bonny. "IATEFL Plenary Video." 2009. http://lerc.educ.ubc.ca/fac/norton/.

———. *Identity and Language Learning: Gender, Ethnicity and Educational Change*. Harlow, UK: Pearson Education Limited, 2000.

Norton, Bonny, and Farah Kamal. "The Imagined Communities of English Language Learners in a Pakistani School." *Journal of Language, Identity, and Education* 2, no. 4 (2003) 301–17.

Norton, Bonny, and Kelleen Toohey. "Identity, Language Learning, and Social Change." *Language Teacher* 44, no. 4. State-of-the-Art-Article (2011) 412–46.

Nurbakhsh, Javad. *Sufi Women*. 3rd ed. London: Khaniqahi Nimatullahi, 2004.

Padwick, Constance E. *Muslim Devotions: A Study of Prayer-Manuals in Common Use*. Oxford: Oneworld, 1961.

Pemberton, Kelly. "Religious Practices: Ablution, Purification, Prayer, Fasting, and Piety. South Asia." In *Encyclopedia of Women & Islamic Cultures*, edited by Suad Joseph, 5:274–276. Leiden: Brill, 2007.

Philips, Abu Ameenah Bilal. *Islamic Rules on Menstruation and Post-Natal Bleeding*. Kuala Lumpur, Malaysia: A.S. Noordeen, 1995.

Pickthall, Mohammed Marmaduke. *The Meaning of the Glorious Koran. An Explanatory Translation*. Lahore: Accurate Printers, n.d.

Pierce, Matthew. "Remembering Fatimah: New Means of Legitimizing Female Authority in Contemporary Shi'i Discourse." In *Women, Leadership, and Mosques. Changes in Contemporary Islamic Authority*, 345–62. Women and Gender. The Middle East and the Islamic World 11. Leiden: Brill, 2012.

Plankey-Videla, Nancy. "Informed Consent as Process: Problematizing Informed Consent in Organizational Ethnographies." *Qualitative Sociology* 35, no. 1 (2012) 1–21.

Pressenza. "Non violence has strong odds in Syria," *International Press Agency*. 02.12.2011. http://www.pressenza.com/2011/12/non-violence-has-strong-odds-in-syria/

Rahman, Fazlur. *Islam*. 2nd ed. Chicago: University of Chicago Press, 1979.

———. *Major Themes of the Qur'an*. Chicago and Minneapolis: Bibliotheca Islamica, 1980.

Rasmussen, Anne. *Women, the Recited Qur'an, and Islamic Music in Indonesia*. Berkley: University of California Press, 2010.

Rausch, Margaret J. "Religious Practices: Preaching and Women Preachers. Egypt and North Africa." In *Encyclopedia of Women & Islamic Cultures*, edited by Suad Joseph, 5:335–354. Leiden: Brill, 2007.

———. "Women Mosque Preachers and Spiritual Guides: Publicizing and Negotiating Women's Religious Authority in Morocco." In *Women, Leadership, and Mosques. Changes in Contemporary Islamic Authority*, 59–83. Women and Gender. The Middle East and the Islamic World 11. Leiden: Brill, 2012.

Reinharz, Shulamit. *Feminist Methods in Social Research*. Oxford: Oxford University Press, 1992.

Rippin, Andew. *Muslims. Their Religious Beliefs and Practices*. 3rd ed. London: Routledge, 2005.

———. *The Islamic World*. The Routledge Worlds. London: Routledge, 2008.

Rippin, Andrew. "Qur'an: Qur'an and Early Tafsir." In *Encyclopedia of Women & Islamic Cultures*, edited by Suad Joseph, 5:266–68. Leiden: Brill, 2007.

Rizvi, Sayyid Muhammad. "I. Najasat and Taharat." *The Ritual and Spiritual Purity*. http://www.al-islam.org/ritual-and-spiritual-purity-sayyid-muhammad-rizvi/i-najasat-taharat.

Roded, Ruth, ed. *Women in Islam and the Middle East. A Reader*. 2nd ed. New York: I.B.Tauris, 2008.

Rugh, Andrea B. *Family in Contemporary Egypt*. Cairo: The American University in Cairo Press, 1985.

Sabra, Adam. "Poverty." In *Encyclopedia of Women & Islamic Cultures*, edited by Suad Joseph, 4:490–92. Leiden: Brill, 2007.

Saeed, Abdullah. *Interpreting the Qur'an. Towards a Contemporary Approach*. Oxon, New York: Routledge, 2006.

Safi, Omid. "Shattering the Idol of Spiritual Patriarchy: Towards a Gender-Fair Notion of Prayer in Islam." *Tikkun* 20, no. 4 (2005).

Safran, Janina M. "Rules of Purity and Confessional Boundaries: Maliki Debates about the Pollution of the Christian." *History of Religions* 42, no. 3 (2003) 197–213.

Saqib, Muhammad Abdul Karim. *A Guide to Salat (Prayer)*. Riyadh: Darussalam, 1997.

Schimmel, Annemarie. Tran. Susan H.Ray. *My Soul Is a Woman. The Feminine in Islam*. New York and London: Continuum, 2003.

Schleifer, Aliah. *Motherhood in Islam*. Islamic Monograph Series. Cambridge: The Islamic Academy, 1986.

Schrag, Brian. "Piercing the Veil: Ethical Issues in Ethnographic Research." *Science and Engineering Ethics* 15, no. 2 (2009) 135–60.

Scott, Rachel M. "A Contextual Approach to Women's Rights in the Qur'an: Readings of 4:34." *The Muslim World* 99, (2009) 60–85.

Seale, Patrick. *Asad. The Struggle for the Middle East*. Berkley: University of California Press, 1988.

Semerdjian, Elyse. "Naked Anxiety: Bathhouses, Nudity, and the DHIMMI Woman in 18th-Century Aleppo." *International Journal of Middle East Studies* 45 (2013) 651–76.

Shaaban, Bouthaina. "Persisting Contradictions: Muslim Women in Syria." In *Women in Muslim Societies: Diversity Within Unity*, 101–117. Boulder, London: Lynne Rienner, 1998.

———. "The Muted Voices of Women Interpreters," In *Faith and Freedom. Women's Rights in the Muslim World*. Ed. Mahnaz Afkhami, 1995.

Shakir, Imam Zaid. "Female Prayer Leadership (Revisited)," *New Islamic Directions*. http://www.newislamicdirections.com/nid/articles/female_prayer_leadership_revisited.

Shakry, Omnia. "Schooled Mothers and Structured Play: Child Rearing in Turn-of-the Century Egypt." In *Remaking Women, Feminism and Modernity in the Middle East*, 126–170. Cairo: The American University in Cairo Press, 1998.

Shannon, Jonathon H. "The Aesthetics of Spiritual Practice and the Creation of Moral and Musical Subjectivities in Aleppo, Syria." *Ethnology* 43, no. 4 (2004).

Shehadeh, Lamia Rustum. *The Idea of Women in Fundamentalist Islam*. Gainesville: University Press of Florida, 2003.

Shoup, John A. *Culture and Customs of Syria*. Culture and Customs of the Middle East. Wesport, Connecticut. London: Greenwood, 2008.

Silvers, Laury. "Representations: Sufi Women, Early Period, Seventh-Tenth Centuries." *Encyclopaedia of Islam*. Leiden: Brill, 2007.

Smith, Dorothy E. *Institutional Ethnography. A Sociology For People*. The Gender Lens. Lanham, New York: AltaMira, 2005.

———. *Writing the Social: Critique, Theory and Investigations*. Toronto: University of Toronto Press, 1999.

Smith, Margaret. *Rabi-a The Mystic And Her Fellow Saints in Islam*. Cambridge: Cambridge University Press, 1928.

Smith, Susan E. *Women in Mission From the New Testament to Today*. American Society of Missiology Series 40. Maryknoll, New York: Orbis, 2007.

Spickard, James V., J. Shawn Landres, and Meredith B. McGuire, eds. *Personal Knowledge and Beyond. Reshaping the Ethnography of Religion*. New York: New York University Press, 2002.

Spielhaus, Riem. "Making Islam Relevant: Female Authority and Representation of Islam in Germany." In *Women, Leadership, and Mosques. Changes in Contemporary Islamic Authority*, 437–455. Women and Gender. The Middle East and the Islamic World 11. Leiden: Brill, 2012.

Stake, Robert E. *The Art of Case Study Research*. Thousand Oaks: Sage, 1995.

Stewart, Pamela J, and Andrew Strathem. "Power and Placement in Blood Practices." *Ethnology* 41, no. 4 (2002) 349–364.

Stoller, Paul. "The Presence of the Ethnographic Present: Some Brief Comments on Loïc Wacquant's 'Body and Soul.'" *Qualitative Sociology* 28, no. 2 (2005) 197–99.

Stowasser, Barbara Freyer. "Gender Issues and Contemporary Qu'ran Interpretation." In *Islam, Gender and Social Change*, edited by Yvonne Yazbeck Haddad and John L. Esposito, 30–44. Oxford: Oxford University Press, 1998.

———. "The Status of Women in Early Islam." In *Muslim Women*, 11–43. Beckenham, UK: CroomHelm, 1984.

———. *Women in the Qurán, Traditions, and Interpretation*. Oxford: Oxford University Press, 1994.

Sullivan, Zohreh, T. "Eluding the Feminist, Overthrowing the Modern? Transformations in Twentieth-Century Iran." In *Remaking Women, Feminism and Modernity in the Middle East*, 215–42. Cairo: The American University in Cairo Press, 1998.

Sunni Forum, "Criteria of a Sufi Naqshbandi Sheikh." http://www.sunniforum.com/forum/showthread.php?76292-Criteria-of-a-Sufi-Naqshbandi-Sheikh.

Syed, Ibrahim B. "52 Weak Ahadith," www.irfi.org/articles/articles_251_300/52_weak_ahadith.htm.

Syria Constitution. http://www.law.yale.edu/rcw/rcw/jurisdictions/asw/syrianarabrep/syria_constitution.htm.

Tansey, James. "Risk as Politics, Culture as Power." *Journal Of Risk Research* 7, no. 1 (2004) 17–32.

Taussig, Michael. *Mimesis and Alterity: A Particular History of the Senses*. New York: Routledge, 1993.

Taylor, Jerome. "First woman to lead Friday prayers in UK," *The Independent*, http://www.independent.co.uk/news/uk/home-news/first-woman-to-lead-friday-prayers-in-uk-1996228.html.

Thompson, Elizabeth. "Public and Private in Middle Eastern Women's History." *Journal of Women's History* 15, no. 1 (2003) 52–69.

Tobin, Gerard A., and Cecily M. Begley. "Methodological Rigour within a Qualitative Framework." *Journal of Advanced Nursing* 48, no. 4 (2004) 388–96.

Turner, Bryan S. "Mapping the Sociology of Religion." In *The New Blackwell Companion to the Sociology of Religion*, 1–29. Blackwell Companions to Sociology. Chichester, UK: Wiley-Blackwell, 2010.

———. "The Body in Western Society: Social Theory and Its Perspectives." In *Religion and the Body.*. Cambridge Studies in Religious Traditions 8. Cambridge: Cambridge University Press, 1997.

Turner, Bryan S. (ed). *The New Blackwell Companion to the Sociology of Religion*. Blackwell Companions to Sociology. Chichester, UK: Wiley-Blackwell, 2010.

Turner, Robert. "Grid/Group Analysis." *RAIN* no. 53 (1982) 6–7.

Tweed, Thomas A. "Between the Living and the Dead: Fieldwork, History, and the Interpreter's Position." In *Personal Knowledge and Beyond. Reshaping the Ethnography of Religion*, 63–74. New York: New York University Press, 2002.

Uthaymeen, Shaykh, "Islamic Knowledge—Islam, Sunnah, Salafiyyah," http://salaf-us-saalih.com/2009/08/22/feed-a-fasting-person-for-the-sake-of-allaah/.

Van Wolputte, Steven. "Hang On To Your Self: Of Bodies, Embodiment, and Selves." *Annual Review of Anthropology* 33 (2004) 251–70.

Vanderwaeren, Els. "Muslimahs' Impact On And Acquisition Of Islamic Religious Authority In Flanders." In *Women, Leadership, and Mosques. Changes in Contemporary Islamic Authority*, 301–22. Women and Gender. The Middle East and the Islamic World 11. Leiden: Brill, 2012.

Vaughan, Barry. "Cultured Punishments: The Promise of Grid-Group Theory." *Theoretical Criminology* 6 (2002) 411.

Vom Bruck, Gabriele. "Elusive Bodies: The Politics of Aesthetics among Yemeni Elite Women." In *Gender, Politics, and Islam*, 161–200. Chicago: University of Chicago Press, 2002.

Von Grunebaum, Gustave E. *Muhammadan Festivals*. Maryland, USA: Rowman and Littlefield, 1951.

Vygotsky, Lev S. "Interaction between Learning and Development." In *Readings on the Development of Children*, 29–36. 2nd ed. New York: W.H.Freeman and Company, 1997.

Wadud, Amina. *Inside the Gender Jihad. Women's Reform in Islam*. Oxford: Oneworld, 2006.

———. "Qur'an and Woman." In *Liberal Islam: A Sourcebook*, 127–38. New York and Oxford: Oxford University Press, 1998.

———. *Qur'an and Woman. Rereading the Sacred Text from a Woman's Perspective.* Oxford: Oxford University Press, 1999.

Walker, Carol M. "Not Just Decoration: Rhetoric and Women Characters in Selected Biblical and Qur'anic Texts." PhD diss., Middlesex University, 2011.

Wansbrough, John. *Quranic Studies. Sources and Methods of Scriptural Interpretation.* New York: Prometheus, 2004.

Waugh, Earle H. "Ritual Leadership in the Dhikr: The Role of the Munshidin in Egypt." *Journal of Ritual Studies* 5, no. 1 (1991) 93–108.

Wehr, Hans. *A Dictionary of Modern Written Arabic.* 4th ed. Beirut and London: Librairie Du Liban, and Macdonald and Evans, 1974.

Weismann, Itzchak. "Sufi Brotherhoods in Syria and Israel: A Contemporary Overview." http://www.ou.edu/mideast/Additional%20pages%20-%20non-catagory/Sufism%20in%20Syriawebpage.htm.

Welch, A.T. "Al-Kuran." In *Encylopaedia of Islam*, 400–29. Leiden: Brill, 1986.

Wilcox, Melissa M. "Dancing on the Fence: Researching Lesbian, Gay, Bisexual and Transgender Christians." In *Personal Knowledge and Beyond. Reshaping the Ethnography of Religion*, 47–62. New York: New York University Press, 2002.

Wild, Stefan. "Reading." *The Qur'an: An Encyclopedia*, edited by Oliver Leaman, 532–535. London: Routledge, 2006.

Williams, James G. *The Bible, Violence, and the Sacred. Liberation from the Myth of Sanctioned Violence.* Valley Forge, PA: Trinity, 1991.

———. *The Girard Reader.* New York: Crossroad, 1996.

Winchester, Daniel. "Embodying the Faith: Religious Practice and the Making of a Muslim Moral Habitus." *Social Forces* 86, no. 4 (2008) 1753–80.

Wynn, Lisa. "Religious Practices: Ablution, Purification, Prayer, Fasting, and Piety. The Gulf." In *Encyclopedia of Women & Islamic Cultures*, edited by Suad Joseph, 5:270–71. Leiden: Brill, 2007.

Yahya, Ali. "What did the Prophet do? An Evaluation of the 'Islamic Basis' for Female-Led Prayers." www.bakkah.net/articles/muslim-women-leading-prayers4.htm.

Yin, Robert K. *Case Study Research. Design and Methods.* 4th ed. Applied Social Research Methods Series 5. Thousand Oaks: Sage, 2009.

Yusuf, Abu Muhammad. "Motherhood: Much more than a job." Muslimvillage.com/2015/05/06/81317/mother-hood-much-job/.

Zadeh, Travis. "Touching and Ingesting: Early Debates over the Material Qur'an." *Journal of the American Oriental Society* 129, no. 3 (2009) 443–66.

Zeidan, Joseph T. *Arab Women Novelists. The Formative Years and Beyond.* Albany: State University of New York Press, 1995.

Zoepf, Katherine. "In Syria, a Quiet Islamic Revolution." *International Herald Tribune*, August 28, 2006. http://www.nytimes.com/2006/08/28/world/africa/28iht-syria3.2620838.html?pagewanted=2 and _r=1.

www.ingramcontent.com/pod-product-compliance
Lightning Source LLC
Chambersburg PA
CBHW050345230426
43663CB00010B/1999